The First Liberian Civil War

Society and Politics in Africa

Yakubu Saaka
General Editor

Vol. 17

PETER LANG
New York • Washington, D.C./Baltimore • Bern
Frankfurt am Main • Berlin • Brussels • Vienna • Oxford

George Klay Kieh, Jr.

The First Liberian Civil War

The Crises of Underdevelopment

PETER LANG
New York • Washington, D.C./Baltimore • Bern
Frankfurt am Main • Berlin • Brussels • Vienna • Oxford

Library of Congress Cataloging-in-Publication Data

Kieh, George Klay.
 The first Liberian civil war: the crises of underdevelopment / George Klay Kieh, Jr.
   p. cm. — (Society and politics in Africa; vol. 17)
 Includes bibliographical references and index.
 1. Liberia—History—Civil War, 1989– —Causes. I. Title.
 DT636.5.K54 966.6203'3—dc22   2007000758
          ISBN 978-0-8204-8839-4
          ISSN 1083-3323

Bibliographic information published by **Die Deutsche Bibliothek**.
Die Deutsche Bibliothek lists this publication in the "Deutsche
Nationalbibliografie"; detailed bibliographic data is available
on the Internet at http://dnb.ddb.de/.

**Library
University of Texas
at San Antonio**

The paper in this book meets the guidelines for permanence and durability
of the Committee on Production Guidelines for Book Longevity
of the Council of Library Resources.

© 2008 Peter Lang Publishing, Inc., New York
29 Broadway, 18th floor, New York, NY 10006
www.peterlang.com

All rights reserved.
Reprint or reproduction, even partially, in all forms such as microfilm,
xerography, microfiche, microcard, and offset strictly prohibited.

Printed in the United States of America

For my role models, my late parents George and Madea Kieh.

TABLE OF CONTENTS

List of Tables		ix
Preface		xi

PART I: BACKGROUND

1	Introduction: Shattering the Illusion of Stability and Prosperity in Liberia	3
2	Explaining the First Liberian Civil War: Theoretical Frameworks	17

PART II: THE FUNDAMENTAL

3	Setting the Stage: The Travails of the Liberian State	33

PART III: THE CRISES OF UNDERDEVELOPMENT

4	The Crisis of Political Underdevelopment	65
5	The Crisis of Economic Underdevelopment	87
6	The Crisis of Social Underdevelopment	107
7	The Crisis of Cultural Underdevelopment	123
8	From the Crises of Underdevelopment to Civil War	143

PART IV: THE INSIGHTS

9	Summary, Lessons, Prescriptions, and Conclusion	165
Bibliography		183
Index		199

LIST OF TABLES

3.1	The Colonial Agents of the American Colonization Society, 1820–1838	39
3.2	The Governors of the Commonwealth of Liberia, 1838–1847	43
3.3	The Roster of Delegates to the 1847 Constitutional Convention of Liberia	47
4.1	Liberia's Human Rights Index, 1972–1989	84
5.1	Liberia's External Debts, 1950–1985	95
5.2	Foreign Private Investments in Liberia, 1950–1985	98
5.3	The Rate of Unemployment in Liberia, 1950–1988	103
5.4	Liberia: The Distribution of Income, 1960–1985	104
6.1	Liberia's Illiteracy Rates, 1950–1985	111
6.2	Liberia: Life Expectancy and Infant Mortality Rates, 1960–1985	116
7.1	Liberia's Ethno-Cultural Composition	126
7.2	Liberia's Indigenous Ethnic Clusters	127

PREFACE

Since the 1980s, there has been a phenomenal increase in the incidence of civil wars on the African continent. At the beginning of the decade, civil wars were raging in Angola and Mozambique. In addition, the long-standing wars in the Sudan and Senegal continued as well. By the end of the decade, Somalia was embroiled in an inferno that ultimately led to the total state disintegration. Then came Liberia, and the list goes on and on. As a consequence of this development, there have been increased scholarly interests in conflict studies. This is evidenced by, among other things, the publication of books, monographs, book chapters, and journal articles on the various aspects of these conflicts. One of the dimensions of the civil conflict problematic, which has, and continues to receive scholarly attention revolves around the causes of civil conflicts—including wars. In other words, scholars have, and continue to show profound interests in deciphering the root causes or taproots of these civil wars.

In the case of the first Liberian civil war, various books, monographs, book chapters, and journal articles began to adorn the academic and policy landscape, beginning in 1989. Importantly, all of these publications share one major commonality: They all devote some space to discussions of the causes of the first Liberian civil war. As I explore in some detail in Chapter 2, the various studies on the causes of the first Liberian civil war can be grouped into four schools of thought: the ethnic, elite pathology, institutional pathology, and spiritual anarchy perspectives. My basic problem with the four frameworks is that they discuss some of the manifestations rather than the root causes of the first Liberian civil war. For example, I argue that ethnic antagonisms in Liberia were outcomes of the basic complexion of the settler then the neo-colonial Liberian state. In other words, the nature, mission, character, policies, and other attributes of the Liberian state are intrinsically antithetical to, inter alia, the promotion of peaceful coexistence between and among the country's various ethnic groups. Hence, one has to undertake a much deeper analysis of the state architecture to comprehend the source of ethnic antagonisms and the sundry other dimensions of the multifaceted crises of underdevelopment that have engulfed Liberia, since the country gained independence in the mid-nineteenth century.

Accordingly, it is my dissatisfaction with the state of the academic literature on the causes of civil wars in Africa in general and Liberia in particular that inspired me to write this book. The thrust of my effort is to contribute an alternative analytical mode for examining the causes of the first Liberian civil war.

This book would not have been possible without the kind assistance of several persons. I am grateful to my longtime friend, colleague, and brother Professor Pita Ogaba Agbese of the Department of Political Science at the University of Northern Iowa for his immense contributions to the development of my intellectual interest in the state, especially the peripheral capitalist African formation. At Morehouse College, where the idea of the book was conceived during my tenure on the institution's faculty, I would like to thank my longtime colleague and friend Professor Hamid Taqi of the Department of Political Science for his very useful critique and advice as I wrestled with the development of the theoretical framework for this book. At Grand Valley State University, I am grateful to my colleague and friend Professor Richard Yidana of the Department of Sociology, who provided invaluable assistance to me in the identification of the relevant sociological literature on the peripheral state. Also, he made useful suggestions that helped me in the development of the theoretical framework for this study. Professor John Mukum Mbaku of the Department of Economics at Weber State University, Utah, a longtime friend, colleague and brother, provided me assistance in the preparation of the camera-ready copy and some of the editorial chores for the book. I am grateful to him for his usual willingness to bring his great editorial and publication skills to bear on several of my book projects. As usual, my wife, Doris, provided support on many fronts. Two of the most important were bringing her knowledge of social stratification to bear on the formulation of my arguments about classes and ethnic groups in Liberia, and allowing me to spend countless hours on researching and writing this book. For these and others, I am thankful to her. Finally, at Peter Lang Publishing, I would like to express my appreciation to Phyllis Korper, the Senior Acquisition Editor, Professor Yakubu Saaka (Oberlin College), the African Series Editor, and Sophie Appel and the staff of the Production Department. I alone assume full responsibility for the final contents of this book.

George Klay Kieh, Jr.
Grand Rapids, Michigan, USA

PART I: BACKGROUND

CHAPTER 1

Introduction: Shattering the Illusion of Stability and Prosperity in Liberia

Introduction

For more than a century, Liberia was portrayed and acclaimed as an island of stability and prosperity in both the African region and the West African sub-region that were plagued by military *coups d'état* and civil wars. The high hopes and expectations that greeted the post-independence era on the continent quickly dissipated to disappointment, anguish, and what Ramsay (1993: 3) refers to as the "desperate struggle for survival." Significantly, Africa's degeneration into putsches and civil wars was evidence that the neocolonial state fashioned by the forces of colonialism and imperialism and bequeathed to Africa during the wave of political independence was incapable of shepherding the process of democratic development.

Against this backdrop, the "men on horseback" used the multifaceted crises of underdevelopment generated by the neocolonial African state as pretext to intervene in politics and arrogate the role of governors. Beginning with the military coup in Egypt in 1952, the incipient "coup virus" infected various African states across the continent. As Gupta (1996: 18) observes "Coup by far account[ed] for the greatest number of government changes in post-colonial Africa." West Africa was the most coup-prone sub-region on the African Continent with the region having suffered more than 22 coups by the end of 1970s (Kieh, 2004: 45).

Correspondingly, by the mid-1950s, the crises of underdevelopment and the attendant contradictions generated by the neocolonial African state set the stage for the civil war and its associated cataclysmic consequences. Beginning with Sudan, a wave of civil wars then rocked Senegal and Nigeria. By the mid-1970s, Angola and Mozambique became part of the "caudillo of civil wars" on the continent as various domestic forces and their international supporters became locked in deadly civil wars in the epic struggles to deposit their competing visions into the vessel of the state (Mutua, 2001).

In the midst of the inferno of putsches and civil wars that had engulfed Africa, Liberia remained stable, and continued to be the darling of international finance capital as evidenced by the influx of foreign capital in the form of private investment. As the British Foreign and Commonwealth Office (2005: 1) notes "Liberia was renowned for its stability, its functioning economy and the large amount of foreign investment it attracted largely in the rubber plantations and the iron ore mines." For example, by the late 1960s, "the massive dosage of foreign investment" that had flowed to Liberia from the metropolis for more than two and a half decades stood at $300 million (Lowenkopf, 1972: 98).

Importantly, I argue the appearance of stability and prosperity in Liberia concealed the deep and penetrating fissures that had been developing on the core of the polity, since the country gained "flag independence" in 1847. Hence, the outward manifestations of peace and prosperity created illusions and a false sense of security for the Liberian ruling class and its metropolitan based patrons, the politically unconscious Liberians, and others. Accordingly, various epochal events in Liberia during the late 1970s and the early and late 1980s—the "April 14, 1979, mass demonstration" against the failure of the neocolonial Liberian state to cater to and address the basic human needs of the masses; the April 12, 1980, military coup; and finally the first civil war, which began on December 24, 1989—which shattered the illusions of stability, came as surprises. In essence, Liberia appeared stable, despite the fact that its base structure was being eaten away by the termites of political repression, economic inequities, and mass social malaise, because of a confluence of what I term "conflict inhibitors"—political repression, a massive patronage network, mythology, a military that was a cesspool of "nokos." So, although the various African states that experienced coups and civil wars from the 1950s to the 1970s were similar to Liberia in that they all were (and still are) neocolonial constructs, Liberia's conflict inhibitors were pivotal to delaying the country's affliction with the twin diseases of state decay and disintegration. These issues are revisited later on in this chapter.

This chapter focuses on five interrelated issues. First, the issue of the facade of stability and prosperity in Liberia by discussing the nature and dynamics of the phenomenon. Second, the conflict inhibitors developed by the Liberian state and its ruling class as bulwarks against coups and civil wars. Third, the epochal events, which shattered the illusion of stability and prosperity in Liberia. Fourth, the central argument of the book is articulated.

This will serve as the compass for navigating the various chapters of the book. Fifth, the structure of the book will be discussed.

The Nature of the Facade of Stability and Prosperity

The facade of stability and prosperity in Liberia, which was quite dominant before the April 14, 1979 mass uprising, was based on the illusion of "Liberian exceptionalism," the idea that Liberia and Liberians were quite different in Africa and among African states. Operationally, Liberians were portrayed as inherently peaceful, hospitable, and magnanimous. Accordingly, these sterling qualities made it possible for Liberians from divergent class, ethnic, regional, religious, and professional backgrounds to live together harmoniously, devoid of any violent conflicts.

Another aspect of the nature of the facade was based on the false notion that "Liberians were God-fearing people." And this attribute was brought to bear on the way in which Liberians related to one another. This self-righteous tenor was used to trumpet the professed "godliness" of Liberians.

The prosperity dimension of the facade was based on two major premises. First, the influx of foreign multinational corporations and the creation of jobs in the extractive and agricultural sectors of the economy created the mass illusion that "life was good," and that the majority of Liberians were doing well economically. Second, the little crumbs from the tables of the members of the ruling class, which trickled down to the members of the subaltern classes, created a sense of contentment in the lower classes.

The Maintenance of the Facade: The Conflict Inhibitors

The facade of stability and prosperity in Liberia was maintained through a complex of interlocking mechanisms. At the vortex was mass socialization. The Liberian ruling class employed a battery of socialization agents—the schools, the media, and the traditional church—to condition Liberians to believe that their country was peaceful, stable, and prosperous. For their part, the educational institutions—both public and private—taught students to be docile and to uncritically accept the illusion that Liberia was peaceful and prosperous. Moreover, students were taught the "virtues" of the Liberian system, including its peripheral capitalist political economy, and to reject ideas that questioned the system. Also, students were taught to be obedient to authority by accepting edicts without raising questions. As Sarup (1978: 149) correctly notes "[Because] other premises [were] not accepted, it [was] difficult to change the givens."

Similarly, the media—both print and electronic—bestowed praises on the custodians of state power and, more important, avoided critically analyzing the political economy and the performance of the ruling class. Concomitantly, they functioned as what Nordenstreng (1982: 4) calls "hegemonic filters." They screened and deleted news items that were antithetical to the interests of the ruling class. Mattlehart's (1980: xxv) general analysis of the subservient role of the media in peripheral capitalist formations vividly captures the role played by the media in Liberia in the maintenance of the façade

> The bourgeoisie and imperialism have imposed on us the forms of communication which corresponds to a particular mode of producing life. It is this intimate integration of communications into the totality of relations of production and social relations which must be grasped if we are to understand its function in reproducing the everyday legitimacy of bourgeois relations of domination.

In the case of the traditional church, it socialized Liberians to believe that the state of their country was "divinely ordained." For example, it peddled the idea that the custodians of state power were "ordained by God" to rule Liberia. Accordingly, Liberians were required to obey their leaders' decisions, because to challenge these leaders would have been an "act of disobedience to God."

Cumulatively, the agents of socialization succeeded in developing a compliant and complacent mindset among Liberians. This mindset was epicentral to the reproduction and maintenance of the facade. As Marx (1984: 1) aptly observes, ". . . every child knows that a social formation which did not reproduce the conditions of production at the same time as it is produced would not last a year."

Another mechanism was the development and propagation of the myth that the ruling class was invincible. Anyone who wanted to challenge the supremacy of the ruling class and to consequently untie the proverbial "Gordian Knot" that it had around the neck of the Liberian polity would be engaging in a futile exercise. This was because the ruling class had the capacity to detect plots, even as they were being conceived. In the case that the plot of destabilization transitioned from conception to reality, the ruling class had a vast arsenal of weapons that it would use to quickly crush such a plot. Accordingly, Liberians became complacent and accepted the status quo as the natural state.

Also, a bastardized division of labor between the ruling and the subaltern classes was essential to the maintenance of the illusion. Under this arrangement, which was contrived by the ruling class, the members of Liberian subaltern classes were influenced to accept the idea that control of the political sphere was the exclusive preserve of the ruling class. That is, in the natural state of things, which was providentially determined, only the members of the ruling class and their relatives could control the country's political system through, among other things, the occupation of the presidency. For their part, the members of the subaltern classes were to find occupations in the technical and vocational fields such as accountancy, agriculture, chemistry, engineering, carpentry, and plumbing.

The operation of a vast state-based patronage system was also central to the maintenance of the facade. The patronage system operated in three major ways. One way was through the dispensing of government positions. The public bureaucracy was routinely expanded to provide jobs. For example, during the Tubman era, vast numbers of Liberians throughout the country were employed as public relations officers of the state. Interestingly, the major function of these so-called public relations officers was to spy on the population. Specifically, they were required to collect information on any person or group that was fomenting dissent, especially if the person or group was making critical comments about the president and the government. Cooptation was one of the major instruments that was used by the ruling class to silence anyone who was determined to be critical of the system. This was done through the payment of hush money and appointments to government positions. Another form was the routine practice of the president of Liberia making financial contributions to various public and private projects. These contributions, which were taken from the public coffers, provided opportunities for the leaders of the various projects to privately accumulate wealth.

The institutionalization of corruption was one of the mechanisms used to maintain the facade. The official state rhetoric notwithstanding, public servants—both high-level government officials and low-level civil servants, military, police, and security personnel—were allowed to use their respective positions as vehicles for rent-seeking. They could seek rent either by directly plundering and pillaging the public's coffers and/or through extracting bribes from citizens and others who sought the provision of governmental services. The late President Tubman, the principal designer of the system, called this phenomenon "live and let's live." Importantly, public servants used the ill-gotten money to undertake various personal projects—the construction of homes, the establishment of businesses, and the provision of assistance to relatives and friends.

Another mechanism to maintain the façade was the use of the vast network of security agencies with overlapping functions to deter would-be troublemakers by instilling in the mass public the fear of swift and massive punishment, if apprehended. Beginning with the Tubman regime, a large and complex security system was established. Each security organization had a vast network of agents and informants based throughout the country. Particularly, the security organizations established bridgeheads on the campuses of the University of Liberia, the country's flagship university, and Cuttington University, a private institution. Students were hired as both full-time agents and informants and stationed at the two campuses. The rationale was that any opposition to the system would emanate from either one or both universities.

Repression was a major weapon in the arsenal of the ruling class. With its monopoly over instruments of coercion, the ruling class never hesitated to use overwhelming force when it felt that its stranglehold overpower in Liberia was threatened by an individual or group. For example, in the 1960s, the rubber tappers at the Firestone Plantation Company, then an American multinational corporation, went on strike on three occasions. Essentially, the strikes were ostensibly designed to protest the paltry salaries and the horrendous working and living conditions on the plantation. Characteristically, on each occasion, the state marshaled its coercive instruments and cowed the workers into submission. Specifically, this was done by meting out brutal beatings, and through torture, arrest, and imprisonment. Importantly, the state's action in all three cases was to clearly demonstrate to the workers at Firestone and elsewhere and to the totality of the Liberian citizenry that the government would not hesitate to use violence if the interests of the ruling class are threatened.

Also, the nature and functions of the military were important to the maintenance of the facade. By its nature, the Liberian military has historically been an unprofessional force, whose membership was primarily drawn from the ranks of the illiterate and the hoi polloi. The officer corps consisted of malleable individuals carefully screened and selected by the ruling class. So, essentially, the military was an instrument of the ruling class. Functionally, the military was initially created to help expand the territorial ambit of the Liberian state, especially in the hinterland where some ethnic groups were resistant to the imposition of state control over their autonomous polities. Subsequently, the military was assigned the function of collecting hut tax in the rural areas. As the state developed its bureaucracy, the military then assumed the customary role of defending the state. Significantly, the military's notoriety for brutality created an adversarial role between it and the larger society. Hence, the larger society did not trust and respect the military.

Collectively, the various mechanisms served as conflict inhibitors. That is, they militated against the occurrence of any violent conflict that would

Introduction: Shattering the Illusion of Stability and Prosperity in Liberia 9

have threatened the suzerainty of the ruling class. Thus, the facade of stability and prosperity was maintained, amid percolating conflict.

The Shattering of the Façade

By the early 1970s, there were three major developments that had profound implications for the maintenance of the facade of stability and prosperity in Liberia. First, there was an emergent mass fatigue with the excesses of the ruling class, especially during the 27-year rule of William V. S. Tubman. Despite the overall success of the confluence of mechanisms or conflict inhibitors in maintaining the facade, there were emerging pockets of resistance to the ruling class. Sensing the challenge, President William R. Tolbert, who succeeded President Tubman in 1971, openly took some steps to arrest the rising tide of disaffection with the ruling class. One major measure was the restructuring of the vast security network that was a major hallmark of the Tubman presidency. The goal was to convince the growing corpus of politically conscious Liberians that the new regime was committed to political liberalization and its associated freedoms of speech, thought, association, assembly, and the press. However, this measure had an unintended impact on the maintenance of the facade: It reduced the ruling class's ability to effectively police the population, a factor that was critical to the maintenance of the facade of stability. Correspondingly, the public relations officers system was dissolved. Again, little did the Tolbert regime realize that this action was detrimental to the maintenance of the facade in that it helped undermine the patronage system. Another major step taken by the regime was allowing Liberians to exercise their constitutional rights. This was of significance because beginning in 1955 and for the remainder of its tenure, the Tubman regime suppressed constitutionally guaranteed political rights and civil liberties. This step emboldened the various pockets of resistance that were forming in various quarters to transition from covert to overt actions and activities. Ultimately, this helped unravel the facade of stability and prosperity.

Second, various pro-reform groups began to emerge on the Liberian political landscape. In 1970, at the University of Liberia, the state's flagship tertiary institution, the Student Unification Party emerged as the vehicle for championing the cause of reform-minded students, who were opposed to the excesses of the ruling class. Two years later, the Movement for Justice in Africa (MOJA) was organized by a corps of reform-minded Liberian intellectuals (most of them studied in the United States and began returning to Liberia in the early 1970s) as the umbrella unit for helping to mobilize moral, financial, and material support for the various liberation struggles against colonialism and imperialism in Angola, Cape Verde, Guinea-Bissau, Mozambique, South Africa, and Zimbabwe. However, as the contradictions generated by the failure of the neocolonial Liberian state began to sharpen, MOJA was transformed into a national social movement. With the growing dissatisfaction with the condition of the country, despite the so-called political liberalization program of the Tolbert regime, MOJA's ranks grew as Liberians from divergent ethnic, regional, religious, gender, age, and professional backgrounds joined the organization. Couched in populist language, MOJA advocated a reform agenda that essentially called for political liberalization and the improvement of the lives of ordinary Liberians. Importantly, MOJA's message of change resonated with reform-minded intellectuals—professionals and students—and the members of the subaltern classes.

Programmatically, MOJA, among other things, undertook a well-organized national campaign designed to build the political consciousness of the Liberian people. MOJA was able to build constituencies among technocrats, the students, and laborers. Significantly, with MOJA as the national umbrella movement for change, the various constituencies in the student and labor movement embarked on their own programs of political conscientization. By the mid-1970s, the reform movement emerged as the de facto "opposition party" to the True Whig Party-led one-party based ruling class. Realizing that its "political liberalization program" had produced a major unintended resultant effect, the Tolbert regime reverted to the authoritarian approach of its predecessor. Unfortunately, with a significant portion of the Liberian population politically conscious, it was very difficult for the regime to cow people into submission once again. Then by 1974, the All People's Freedom Alliance (APFA) emerged as the second national social movement. The size of APFA's membership base and its scope of operations were comparatively smaller than those of MOJA. APFA drew its members from among the student movement groups and semiprofessionals. Also, the scope of its operations was confined to the urban centers. Ideologically, APFA was different from MOJA in that it advocated Marxism-Leninism. In terms of its agenda, APFA advocated a radical transformation of Liberia's peripheral capitalist economy and its associated relations of production. The organization, among its various activities, published a magazine that served as a medium for articulating its radical brand of systemic transformation in Liberia. Four years later, the situation worsened for the ruling class and its regime when the Progressive Alliance of Liberia (PAL) emerged as the second national social reform movement (the third national social movement). PAL was organized in the United States by Liberians, some of whom were studying at various universities and colleges. Among its various activities, the movement published a newspaper. Ideologically, PAL vacillated from one end of the spectrum to another—liberal democracy to African socialism. But, in reality, PAL, like MOJA, had a populist ideology. However, there were three major differences. Unlike MOJA, PAL did not hesitate to use violent confrontation with the government as a deus ex machina. Also, PAL was interested in transforming itself into an opposition political party to challenge the ruling True Whig Party for state power. In terms of its constituency, PAL drew the bulk of its membership from among the lumpen proletariat—there were few members from the corps of technocrats and the student movement groups.

Third, the price of iron ore, one of the mainstays of the country's peripheral capitalist economy, began to experience precipitous decline. As a consequence, the country's revenue base dwindled. In turn, this adversely affected the capacity of the ruling class to dispense prebends and to fund the expansive patronage system that was critical to the maintenance of the facade of stability and prosperity. To make matters worse, the Liberian Mining Company (LMC), based in the western part of the country, and the Liberian American Swedish Mining Company (LAMCO), situated in the northwest portion, closed down their respective operations. The rationale was that the decline in the price of iron ore had adversely affected the companies' profit margins to the extent that they were experiencing losses. Therefore, the most viable option for the companies was to close their operations. The actions by the two corporations sent shock waves throughout the ruling class and the general population. In the case of the state, the closure of the two firms meant the loss of revenues. For the members of the ruling class, the closure meant the loss of corporate largesse. As for the workers of the two corporations, it meant the loss of jobs, income, and the ability to provide financial and material support for their legion of relatives. Cumulatively, these two episodes dealt fatal blows to the prosperity dimension of the facade that had enveloped Liberia for almost three decades. Characteristically, the reform movements, especially MOJA, used the country's precarious economic situation to espouse the argument that the ruling class was insensitive to the plight of ordinary Liberians. As the Liberian economy was in a doldrums, the message resonated well with the members of the country's subaltern classes, and, more important, helped lay bare the facade of stability and prosperity.

Against this background, on April 14, 1979, the facade of stability and prosperity was shattered, when a massive demonstration was held to protest decades of the ruling class's excesses. The demonstration, which was organized by a broad national coalition consisting of MOJA, ALFA, PAL, the University of Liberia Student Union, and the ruling Student Unification

Party of the University of Liberia, was triggered by the decision of the Tolbert government to increase the price of rice, the country's staple food. The coalition argued that such an increase would have benefited President Tolbert and the other members of the ruling class, who were "absentee farmers" and imposed additional economic hardship on the subaltern classes. Strategically, the coalition saw the "rice issue" as a glorious opportunity to challenge the decades of political repression and socioeconomic malaise that was concealed by the facade of stability and prosperity. After various meetings between the Tolbert regime and the coalition, there was an impasse: On the one hand, the government was insistent that the increase would take place, and that any resultant protest and demonstration would be crushed through the use of massive force. However, on the other hand, the coalition was adamant that it would resist the increase and would demonstrate this through the holding of massive protests throughout the country. Ultimately the talks collapsed and the proverbial "battle lines" were drawn. The coalition went ahead with the planned nationwide demonstrations, and the government kept its words by unleashing state security forces to crush the demonstrations. In the end, scores of people were killed and wounded by the state security forces. Interestingly, the rank and file of the military adopted a passive attitude to the implementation of the "shoot to kill orders" given by the Tolbert regime. Sensing the emergence of disloyalty in the ranks of the military establishment, the president sought and received military assistance from his friend Guinean President Ahmed Sékou Touré. President Toure dispatched a contingent of Guinea troops to take over Liberia's security during the tense aftermath of the "April 14 episode." This action by the Tolbert regime further infuriated the rank and file of the Liberian military and increased the alienation between the military and the government. Ultimately, the episode exposed the tenuous basis of the ruling class's power base and energized the reform movement.

With the crisis of legitimacy of the state having reached its crescendo, the military staged a coup d'état on April 12, 1980. Seventeen noncommissioned officers—from the rank of private to master sergeant—stormed the presidential palace and killed President Tolbert, with very little resistance. The coup dealt the final blow to the maintenance of the facade of stability and prosperity. This issue of the coup is discussed in Chapter 4.

Finally, Liberia's first civil war aptly demonstrated that the fabric of the neocolonial Liberian state was tattered by more than a century of failure compounded by the dismal performance of the Doe military and military-cum-civilian regimes. Importantly, the coup, that was expected to set into motion the process of the democratic reconstitution of the state, instead maintained the totality of the repressive political economy that it inherited.

Introduction: Shattering the Illusion of Stability and Prosperity in Liberia 13

To make matters worse, the Doe regime became the most oppressive in the political history of the country. And this was reflected in its excessive reliance on the use of violence as the kernel of state-society relations.

The Focus of the Book

The growing corpus of scholarly literature on the causes of civil war in Africa and the rest of the third world tend to lay the responsibility for the scourge primarily on two major pillars: ethnicity and elite pathologies. Similarly, the literature on the first Liberian civil war attributes the causes of the conflict to the aforementioned factors. In addition, other theories such as institutional pathology, spiritual deprivation, and political culture have been offered as explanatory frameworks for analyzing the causes of the first Liberian civil war. In Chapter 2, I undertake a more detailed examination and analysis of these various factors and the larger theoretical crucibles in which they are lodged.

Importantly, this book proposes and takes a different approach to the understanding of the causal factors that occasioned the first Liberian civil war. Essentially, the central argument is that the first Liberian civil war was caused by the multifaceted crises of underdevelopment—political, economic, social, and cultural—engendered by the failure of the country's neocolonial state. Specifically, I argue that the nature, mission, character, values, structures, rules, processes, and policies of Liberia's settler and neocolonial formations created contradictions and crises that provided a fertile ground for the sowing, nurturing, and germination of the seeds of conflict and eventually civil war. The gathering clouds that eventually unleashed the "storm of civil war" formed, to use Braudelian parlance, during a "longue durée" (a long period of time). I contend further that instrumental ethnicity, elite pathologies, and other pantomimes were reflections and manifestations of the deeper multifaceted crises generated by the settler and subsequently neocolonial Liberian state. Hence, an understanding of the taproots of the first Liberian civil war would require a comprehension of the features and travails of the country's settler and neocolonial formations.

The Organization of the Book

The book is divided into nine chapters. Chapter 1 provides the context of the book. It begins with a general survey of the African political landscape during the first 30 years of political independence. Specifically, the chapter examines the phenomena of coups and civil wars as consequences of the failure of the neocolonial state in Africa to promote democratic development based, among other things, on the respect for individual and group political rights and civil liberties, the promotion of social justice, addressing the basic needs of the citizens, and promoting a "culture of peaceful coexistence" between and among the various ethnicities, regions, and religions. The chapter also initially introduces the thesis of the book by exposing the venal underbelly of Liberia's acclaimed stability and prosperity from the 1950s to 1970s. Subsequently, the chapter discusses the nature and dynamics of the illusion of stability and prosperity in Liberia, the mechanisms that were used to maintain the facade (what I term the "conflict inhibitors"), and the epochal events that ultimately revealed that the "emperor"—the neocolonial Liberian state—was indeed "naked." This is followed by an elaboration of the central argument of the book, against the background of the dominant Weltanschauungs that are used to explain the causes of civil wars in Africa and the rest of the third world. Finally, the chapter concludes with the organization of the book.

In Chapter 2, the theoretical framework that the book uses is articulated. First, the chapter commences with an examination of the major theoretical models—ethnic, elite pathology, institutional pathology, spiritual deprivation, and political culture—that are used as the analytical animus for explaining the causes of the first Liberian civil war. Specifically, the various arguments of each model are summarized followed by a critique of the various theories. Second, the peripheral capitalist state theory is proffered as the theoretical architecture of the book.

Chapter 3 is the epicenter of the book. It focuses on the pedigree of the settler and later the neocolonial Liberian state. Specifically, the chapter examines the evolution of the Liberian state from the early 1800s to 1989. Basically, the discussion seeks to identify and analyze critical junctures in the formation of the Liberian state that were pivotal to fashioning the construct's peripheral capitalist and neocolonial orientation. This is then followed by an examination of the features—nature, mission, character, values, institutions, rules, processes, and policies—of the neocolonial formation. Significantly, it is argued that the confluence of the characteristics of the neocolonial Liberian state led to the failure of the construct as a viable instrument of democratic development. In turn, the failure of the neocolonial Liberian state generated multifaceted crises of underdevelopment—political, economic, social, and cultural. These crises led to the first civil war.

In Chapter 4, the locus is on the political crisis generated by the failure of the neocolonial Liberian state. Specifically, the chapter examines the issues of the constitution, the operations of the three branches of government,

Introduction: Shattering the Illusion of Stability and Prosperity in Liberia 15

the state of political human rights, the rule of law, elections, and civil society.

Chapter 5 examines the nature and dynamics of the economic crisis. It addresses issues such as the mode of production, classes and class relations, disparities in income and wealth, foreign investments, corruption, mismanagement, unemployment, and the standard of living.

In Chapter 6, the scope and dimensions of the social crisis are discussed. This includes education, health, sanitation, access to safe drinking water, mortality rates, life expectancy, and housing.

Chapter 7 focuses on the cultural crisis generated as a consequence of the failure of the settler and later the neocolonial Liberian state to develop a culture on the basis of ethnic pluralism, mutual respect, and peaceful coexistence. Specifically, the chapter explores the relationship between the African Americans who were repatriated to Liberia (the "Americo-Liberians" or the "settlers" as they are called) and the indigenous ethnic groups or the "indigenes," and the Krahn ethnic group, on the one hand, and other ethnic groups—especially the Gio and the Mano—on the other.

In Chapter 8, the linkages between the crises of underdevelopment generated by the failure of the settler and neocolonial Liberian state and the degeneration into war are discussed. In other words, why and how did the crises of the neocolonial state plunge the country into civil war in 1989?

Chapter 9 summarizes the major issues addressed by the book, draws the various lessons from the study, and offers an alternative state construct as the best path to building holistic democracy in Liberia. This is then followed by the resummation of the major issues addressed in the book.

CHAPTER 2

Explaining the First Liberian Civil War: The Theoretical Frameworks

Introduction

Since the 1980s, there has been a phenomenal increase in scholarly interests in the study of civil wars in Africa. Given the multidimensionality of civil wars and their concomitant basic conflicts, scholars have examined issues such as the root causes; the protagonists involved; and the peacemaking, peacekeeping, and post-conflict peacebuilding efforts. Similarly, in the case of Liberia, there is an emerging corpus of scholarly literature on the aforementioned issues in the context of the country's first civil war. The dimension of the root causes of Liberia's first civil war has received the greatest attention in the scholarly literature. This is evidenced by the fact that all of the studies, irrespective of their foci, devote the initial section to exploring the taproots of the civil war. In essence, each of the studies begins by posing the fundamental question embodied in the title of Ted Gurr's (1970) seminal study: *Why Men Rebel* (in the Liberian case). Characteristically, there have been divergent responses to the question. These responses can be grouped into five theoretical frameworks: The ethnic framework (Daniels, 1992; Ero,1995; Lowenkopf, 1995; Catholic Justice and Peace Commission, 1995; Ellis, 1995; Huband, 1998; Ellis, 1999; Levitt, 2005); elite pathology (Lowenkopf, 1976; Sawyer, 1992; Lowenkopf, 1995; Sawyer, 2005a); institutional pathology (Dolo, 1996); spiritual anarchy (Ellis, 1995; Ellis, 1999); and political culture (Yoder, 2003).

Against this background, this chapter summarizes the major arguments of the five major theoretical frameworks that have been proffered for explaining the causes of the first Liberian civil war. Next, each theory is critiqued. This is followed by my suggestion of the settler state and peripheral capitalist state theories as alternative frameworks for explaining the root causes of the first Liberian civil war.

The Theoretical Frameworks

Five major theories have been used as the overarching tapestries for explaining the *causa movens* of the first Liberian civil war: ethnic, elite pathology, institutional pathology, spiritual anarchy, and political culture. In this section of the chapter, the focus is on the summation of the basic contours of each theory.

The Ethnic Theory

The ethnic theory has been the dominant framework used for explaining the occurrence of the first Liberian civil war. The theory is based on several postulates. First, the major actors in Liberian politics were ethnic stocks and groups—the "Americo-Liberian" or "settler stock" and the 16 indigenous ethnic groups. Each group has its own set of institutions, practices, and values. In other words, as Levitt (2005: 246) asserts "Settler and indigenous societies were established on diametrically opposed principles."

Second, each ethnic stock or group had its own set of distinctive interests and agendas. That is, there were competing sets of ethnic interests spanning the broad gamut—from political to economic. For example, the main agenda of the Americo-Liberian stock was the control of the Liberian state.

Third, the Liberian state was dominated by the Americo-Liberian stock from 1847 to 1980, and by the Krahn ethnic group from 1980 to 1999. According to the Catholic Justice and Peace Commission, the Americo-Liberians established two societies: One was the Western society that was patterned after the United States and based on Christianity and the other was the indigenous society that was based on traditional values. Furthermore, the Commission (1995: 6) posits that during the Tubman regime (1944–1971), attempts were made to integrate the two societies. However, overall, the Americo-Liberian ethnic group continued to wield all political, social, and economic powers. Similarly, Ero (1995: 2) argues that despite the fact that they constituted only 5% of the total population, the Americo-Liberians were able to dominate Liberia's political, social, and economic life for more than 130 years. Ero (1995) argues further that the 1980 military coup d'état terminated the hegemony of the Americo-Liberian ethnic group and presented the opportunity for the regime of Samuel Doe to construct a democratic society. However, the postcoup order (1980–1989) was dominated by and benefited only the Krahn ethnic group.

Fourth, the incompatible agendas of the various ethnic stocks and groups was exacerbated by what Ero (1995: 2) calls the "hegemonic practices" of the two ethnic groups—Americo-Liberians and the Krahns—that have dominated Liberia since its origin. That is, each hegemonic ethnic group monopolized power and marginalized the other ethnic groups. For example, Lowenkopf (1995: 99) argues that "Doe's tribe, the Krahn . . . quickly grabbed the rewards and symbols of high office."

Fifth and related, the cumulative effects of the ethnic-based "tugs and pulls" eventually degenerated into violence and the first Liberian civil war. In other words, over the years, the differences between Liberia's dominant and subordinate ethnic groups became irreconcilable; hence, civil war became the by-product.

The Elite Pathology Theory

The elite pathology theory is anchored on several caveats. The major actors in the Liberian polity are the ruling elites, consisting of government officials and leaders of the ruling True Whig Party before the 1980 military coup, and subsequently the ruling National Democratic Party of Liberia from 1986 to 1990.

Given their dominance, the ruling elites imposed ground rules on the rest of the citizens. The norms that governed the society were not designed through the process of national discussions among the citizens of Liberia. Instead, the ruling elites designed the rules without the input of the masses of the citizens, and imposed them on the body politic.

Another tenet is that the elites used their respective positions to accrue personal benefits. As Lowenkopf (1976: 47) notes, "[The elites] enjoyed the greater parts of the economic fruits, either directly from the nation's treasury, or from opportunities concomitant with handling the nation's business." In other words, the ruling elites monopolized the levers of politics and economics, and marginalized the majority of the citizens.

Also, a major pathology of the ruling elites was that they repeatedly demonstrated immoral behavior: They engaged in corruption and the mismanagement of societal resources. In turn, this precipitated grave economic crises during several periods. The resultant economic crises occasioned increased hardship for ordinary Liberians.

Similarly, the ruling elites abused power and desecrated the rules of the democratic game. In other words, the elites contravened the provisions of the constitution, and governed Liberia on the basis of their caprices. Thus, there was a constitution but without constitutionalism.

Finally, the various pathologies of the elites undermined their legitimacy and alienated them from ordinary Liberians. Exasperated by the failure of the elites to provide democratic leadership in addressing the country's problems, the majority of ordinary Liberians were desirous of regime change.

The Institutional Pathology Theory

The institutional pathology theory is premised on the assertion that the causes of the first Liberian civil war were the defects in the country's structures or institutions (Dolo, 1996: 4). The defects included the failure of the various institutions, especially the public ones, to perform their assigned functions effectively. For example, the legislature failure to provide effective oversight in its relationship with the executive. Similarly, the judiciary failed to render justice in an impartial way. Ultimately, the executive branch, particularly the presidency, became very dominant by subordinating the other two coequal branches to its dictates.

Another element is that the elites were conditioned by the dynamics of the institutional defects and came to accept them as normal. As Dolo (1996: 4) argues "The elites are products of a dysfunctional institutional arrangement which provides fertile ground for the growth and development of their pathological behaviors." In essence, the "culture of institutional atrophy" was promoted and protected by elites who were captives of the phenomenon.

Finally, the structural pathologies made the government incapable of addressing the various challenges that confronted Liberia. This generated mass resentment and hostility toward the elites, the managers of the various defective public institutions. The resultant conflict provided fertile ground for the first civil war.

The Spiritual Anarchy Theory

The spiritual anarchy theory emerged as an integral part of what Hacket (2003: 61) calls the "discourses on demonism and satanism." In the context of explaining civil wars in Africa, the theory presents the continent as a barbarous culture of political violence undergirded by religious cosmologies that rationalize anarchy. Applied to the Liberian case, the theory is based on several assumptions. In traditional Liberian religious beliefs, there is an intrinsic connection between the invisible spiritual world and the physical one. For example, any case of disorder in the spiritual world occasions a similar situation in the physical one. So, the roots of the first Liberian civil war can be traced to various cycles of disorder and anarchy in the spiritual world. In short, religion shaped the roots of the civil war.

The related point is that since spiritual forces condition political behavior, the cycles of disorder in the traditional Liberian religious cosmos were the sources of the rebellious behavior first developed by the National Patriotic Front of Liberia (NPFL) and subsequently by the other militias. In other words, the effects of the cycles of anarchy in the spiritual realm conditioned the NPFL to begin the insurgency that culminated in the first Liberian civil war. Central to the spiritual world–physical world nexus is the role of what Ellis (1999: 24) terms "spiritual imagination." This entails a mental process of legitimizing the linkages among political, physical, and spiritual powers. In other words, using the mind of an individual as the religious crucible, war-making is rationalized as a by-product of the interplay between the forces of the spiritual and the physical worlds.

Another tenet is that the spiritual power is accessed through the engagement in ritualistic killings, including acts of cannibalism. Acts of unmitigated violence are rationalized by combatants as integral to the maintenance of the connections with the spiritual forces that serve as the sources of the war. In other words, since the war was caused by rumblings in the invisible world, the making of human sacrifices during the act of warfare is pivotal to the maintenance of the causal chain.

The Political Culture Theory

The political culture theory attributes the causes of the first Liberian civil war to the country's illiberal and undemocratic values (Yoder, 2003). From this base argument, there are several derivatives. There is the argument that both the settlers or the Americo-Liberians and the indigenous ethnic groups did not have democratic political cultures. In other words, before the expansion of the Liberian state, there were two distinct political systems: the settler political system and the indigenous ones. In their respective political systems, the settlers and the indigenes had authoritarian political orientations.

Another tenet is that after the expansion of the settler state and the subsequent establishment of a Liberian polity that embodies both settlers and indigenes, a national political culture was crystallized. The incipient national political culture was the by-product of decades of interactions between the settlers and the various indigenous ethnic groups. During these interactions, both clusters exchanged values and each cluster was ultimately influenced by the values of the other. That is, as a result of physical, social, and intellectual proximity, the newly arrived settlers and indigenous Africans developed a political culture charter that played a powerful role in the way political relationships and affairs unfolded in the nineteenth and twentieth-centuries (Yoder, 2003: 4). As Liberians interacted with people from various countries, especially the United States, that have democratic systems, they were introduced to liberal democratic values—the emphasis on political rights and civil liberties, including tolerance and pluralism. However, because Liberians had been socialized in the values of their illiberal political culture, they were thus unaffected by the exposure to democratic values.

The related argument is that the emergent national political culture is based on several dominant features: hierarchy, control, deference, stability, and patronage. As Yoder (2003: 4) asserts "Liberian political culture places an excessively high emphasis on order and stability while tolerance, accountability, and innovation are afforded too little importance." In essence, the Liberian political culture is an authoritarian one that requires conformity rather than diversity.

A Critique of the Theoretical Frameworks

This study disagrees with the arguments of the five theories that have been offered to explain the root causes of the first Liberian civil war. In the case of the ethnic model, it treats cultural groups as monoliths. On the contrary, evidence shows that there were sharp divisions in the so-called hegemonic ethnic stocks and groups that governed Liberia from 1847 to 1980 (the Americo-Liberian stock), and from 1980 to 1989 (the Krahn ethnic group). As the other ethnic groups, the members of the so-called hegemonic ethnic groups had divergent positions on the various issues that confronted the country. For example, the late Albert Porte, the veteran advocate of democracy in Liberia, who hailed from the Americo-Liberian stock, criticized the governments that were led by his kin as well as the Doe regime for their virulent violation of human rights. Another shortcoming of the theory is its failure to recognize the fact that ethnicity was instrumentally used by various politicians for the advancement of their personal agendas; hence, the issues at hand usually had nothing to do with the general interests of the various ethnic groups.

As for the elite pathology model, it fails to identify the systemic roots of the various pathologies—corruption, greed, graft, and mismanagement of state resources, among others. In other words, how did the elites acquire these pathologies? More important, the theory does not explain why and how these elites were able to engage in these immoral behaviors for such protracted period of time.

The institutional pathology theory has two basic weaknesses. First, it does not explain the forces and factors that shaped the development of Liberia's public institutions. In other words, how did these institutions come into existence? Second and related, the theory fails to explain the rationales for the creation of these institutions. Accordingly, the theory wrongly assumes that these public institutions were designed to function in ways that would benefit the masses of the Liberian people. The fact is that state institutions were designed to serve the interests of the dominant class. This is the reason why the ruling class did not have problems with the ways these institutions functioned. In other words, as the institutions served their interests, the members of the ruling class did not see the need to reform or change them.

The basic weakness of the spiritual anarchy theory is that it ignores the centrality of concrete political, economic, cultural, and social phenomena embodied in the state construct in creating the conditions for civil conflict, including war and violence. Irrespective of their divergent religious cosmologies, the Liberian masses were collectively affected by cultural, economic, social, and political vagaries of the settler and later the neocolonial state. In other words, the various state-induced crises created the conditions for civil conflict and eventually war in Liberia.

The political culture theory has several weaknesses. First, it incorrectly postulates that both the settlers and the indigenous ethnic groups had similar undemocratic political values. Evidence clearly shows that Liberia's various indigenous ethnic groups, despite the variations and differences in their respective state systems, were based on democratic principles such as consultation, mass participation, and checks and balances. Moreover, their political economies were based on an egalitarian value anchored on the collective ownership of the major means of production. The egalitarian ethos militated against, among other things, the exploitation and inequities that are the hallmarks of liberal democracy and its capitalist mode of production. In the case of the settlers, the theory fails to recognize the fact that they brought to Liberia the values they had learned during slavery in the United States—racism, discrimination, segregation, exploitation, inequalities, and the sacrosanctity of private property. In addition, like the United States (till the passage of the Civil Rights Act in 1964), the settler Liberian state was based on liberal democratic principles in the context of an apartheid-like system. The settler political culture was a reflection of the particular stage of development of the settler state. During that stage, the political economy was dominated by an indigenous embryonic capitalist class; thus, the state had relative autonomy. Accordingly, liberal democratic values such as the freedoms of speech, thought, assembly, association, press, religion, a multiparty political system, the holding of regular elections, the rule of law, and checks and balances were practiced within the crucible of the exclusion of the indigenes (similar to how blacks were excluded from the American political system until 1964). In short, the settler political culture was dictated by the imperatives of the complexion of the settler state at that time.

Second, when the settler state lost its relative autonomy in the late 1860s, particularly as a consequence of the collapse of the indigenous embryonic capitalist class, the emergent political culture began to replace the liberal political values with authoritarian ones. That is, when state power became coterminous with economic power, liberal democratic values became anachronistic and irrelevant to the altered complexion of the state and its political economy.

Third, the theory conveys the wrong impression that what became the national political culture of Liberia was developed through a sort of mutual agreement between the settlers and the indigenes. On the contrary, when the indigenous ethnic groups were incorporated into the settler state, they were forced to adopt the political culture of the state. This was part of the resultant tugs and pulls between the two stocks.

Collectively, all of the five theories have some shared weaknesses. The base weakness is that they all ignore the centrality of the state as the overarching architecture that sets the parameters within which ethnic groups, elites, institutions, spiritual sects and groups and political cultures operate. Essentially, the state decides what is permissible and what is not. Moreover, the state conditions all of the aforementioned elements and makes them conform to its imperatives and dictates. Hence, as the overarching framework, the settler then the peripheral capitalist Liberian state shaped and dictated the relationships between and among ethnic groups, elites, and others. A related problem is that the theories failed to recognize that groups—ethnic, and so on—operate in a mode of production that shapes their orientation and activities. In the Liberian case, the country's peripheral capitalist mode of production and political economy conditioned the nature of the activities of ethnic, elitist, and spiritual groups. In addition, its values were embodied in the political culture. Another shortcoming of the theories is that they accord no attention to the critical importance of classes in Liberia. The fact of the matter is that the Liberian polity was dominated by classes—ruling and subaltern—not ethnic groups, elites, institutions, and spiritual sects. This is because in every society classes and class relations are the roots of the political economy; other groups are secondary. In essence, Liberia had two broad clusters of classes: ruling and subaltern—petit bourgeois, working and peasantry, and the lumpen proletariat. The antagonisms between the ruling class, on the one hand, and the subaltern classes, on the other, were the pivotal struggle that took place embedded in the neocolonial Liberian state. Finally, the theories failed to recognize the importance of the international capitalist system in fostering the "development of underdevelopment" in Liberia (Frank, 1969).

Alternative Theoretical Frameworks: The Settler State and Peripheral Capitalist State Theories

Background

This book argues that the settler and the peripheral capitalist state theories are the best frameworks for explaining the root causes of the first Liberian civil war. Accordingly, both frameworks are used as the crucibles for examining the development of the settler and the neocolonial Liberian state. The settler state theory is useful for explaining the travails of the Liberian state from 1847 to 1926. The peripheral capitalist theory is appropriate for explaining the pedigree of the Liberian state from 1926 to 1989 (from the formalization of Liberia's incorporation into the global capitalist system to the outbreak of the first civil war).

The Settler State Theory

The settler state theory is based on several assumptions. The major actors within the settler state are two major cultural clusters: a settler and an indigenous one. Both clusters may be based on racial or ethno-communal characteristics. The settler group immigrates from abroad and seeks to establish its domination and rule over the indigenous one (Mitchell, 1993: 715). The resultant effect is conflict between the two groups, as one tries to impose domination and the other attempts to resist it.

Another element is the nature of the relationship between the settler and the indigenous groups. Generally, the relationship is driven by two major currents. There is an ideology based on segregation and discrimination grounded in a "superior-inferior myth." The settler group tries to convey and convince the indigenous group and its associated constituents to accept the notion that the former is superior to the latter. Thus, it is imperative for the latter to submit to the former as the precondition for the undertaking of the "civilizing mission." In short, the settler group promotes the idea of being interested in civilizing the indigenes, since the latter's cultures are barbaric. Also, the relationship between the two groups is driven by mutual distrust, suspicion, and insecurity. Each group believes that the other poses a grave danger to its security and well-being, including its survival. In turn, this fuels the antagonisms between the two groups and their determination to pursue their respective courses of action. However, over time, the settler group tries to assimilate the indigenous one through a variety of means—intermarriages, child rearing, the cooptation of pliant indigenes, and so on.

Since the settler group does not have land, it formulates and undertakes a policy of territorial expansion that is based on conquest and questionable purchases. In some cases, the settlers employ force as the instrument for seizing land from the indigenes. In other instances, the settlers would buy land from the indigenes under highly dubious terms. Generally, the colonial processes of territorial acquisition and state formation contribute to a continuous assault on the political and cultural autonomy of indigenous peoples (Hibbard, 2005: 172).

Another element is the settler group's initial reliance on its "mother country," the metropolitan power, for military, economic, political, and moral support as it tries to establish its foothold and eventual control over an indigenous territory. In some cases, the mother country may even send personnel to directly help the settlers in the imposition of the control and rule over an indigenous area.

Ultimately, the success of the settler imperial project is dependent on three major factors. First, the settler group needs to maintain intragroup solidarity and cohesion (Weitzer, 1990: 28). That is, irrespective of their differences, the settler group needs to be united in its dealings with the indigenous group. Second, the settler group needs to consolidate control over the indigenous population (Weitzer, 1990: 27). Third, the settler group needs to achieve autonomy from the mother country in the exercise of political authority and coercive power (Weitzer, 1990: 26). Overall, in the long term, the settler group needs to cease to identify with its metropolitan state and assume an identity that is distinct from the indigenous group and the state it left (the mother country) (The Imperial Archive, 2006: 1).

Finally, the state construct that emerges under the control of the settler group embodies its vision, interests, and values. The nature, mission, character, institutions, rules, processes, and policies of the state are geared toward the promotion of the general agenda of the settler group. Accordingly, the settler state becomes an instrument for serving the interests of settlers. In the performance of this overall function, the state routinely subjected the indigenous population to violent actions.

The Peripheral Capitalist State Theory

The peripheral capitalist state theory is rooted in several interlocking tenets. Generally, a peripheral capitalist state is constructed as a reflection of class interests. As Ziemann and Lanzenderfer (1977: 151) argue, "The necessity for the existence, form and function and the inner structure of the state in capitalist society is determined as an essential, integral element of society by the economic and social reproduction of the society. As an organic product and a necessary structural element in the society, it is the expression of the dominant contradictory social relations." However, there are differences in terms of the specific origins of various peripheral capitalist formations. For example, during the colonial period, the state was organized because of the need to subordinate precapitalist, generally nonfeudal formations to the imperative of colonial capitalism (Saul, 1974: 353). During the postcolonial era, the core of the state was redesigned to reflect the new political and economic realities.

Second, like all other capitalist constructs, the peripheral state has a capitalist-materialist base. This base is reflected in, among other things, the private ownership of the major means of production, the sacrosanctity of private property, the centrality of the profit motive, and the suzerainty of the market. In short, the materialist base shapes and conditions the forces and dynamics that are germane to the reproduction of capitalism.

Third, the features of the state—nature, mission, character, institutions, rules, processes, and policies—reflect the imperatives of the peripheral capitalist mode of production. For example, the nature of the state is determined by the forces and factors that shaped its formation—the dominant class and its attendant vision. The character of the peripheral capitalist is multidimensional. It has variously been described as exploitative, violent, predatory, criminalized, prebendal, neopatrimonial, negligent, and vampirish, among others. Depending on the particular historical circumstance, a particular aspect or aspects of the state's character may be dominant.

Fourth, the structure of the state's political economy has two interlinked dimensions: the state's structure and the economic structure. Basically, the former consists of various institutions—the public bureaucracy, the legislature, and the courts and laws. The various state institutions and rules are administered by state managers or what Prado (1966) calls the "bureaucratic bourgeoisie." Importantly, the bureaucratic bourgeoisie performs its functions in accordance with the state's relationships with the various social classes. Also, depending on the specific nature of the peripheral capitalist formation, the bureaucratic bourgeoisie can either be independent of the ruling class (relatively autonomous) or dependent on it, when the relationship is an economic one. Essentially, the economic structure of the global capitalist system determines that of the peripheral capitalist state (Ziemann and Lanzendorfer, 1977: 145). The two are interwoven by the economic conditions (Ziemann and Lanzendorfer, 1977: 145). In other words, there is the impregnation of the satellite's domestic economy with the same capitalistic structures and their fundamental contradictions (Frank, 1978: 23). The economic structure is made up of classes and the production and allocation processes. Generally, there are two broad clusters of classes: the dominant or the ruling class that owns the means of production and controls the levers of state power and the subordinate classes, consisting of the working, the peasant, and others. In some cases, the dominant class consists of internal/local and external wings. The internal wing usually comprises a non-hegemonic section, whereas the external wing consists of the foreign-based owners of the major means of production. The production process is a social activity involving workers, who perform various functions to create products. The capitalist class does not directly participate in the actual production of goods. On the other hand, the allocation process reflects a core contradiction of capitalism: The dividends from collectively produced goods are appropriated by the capitalists, who own and control the major means of production.

Fifth, the peripheral capitalist state performs several functions. At the core is the reproduction of the social, political, and economic structures of the ruling class's dominance (Fatton, 1988: 253). Also, the state performs what Graff (1994: 11) refers to as "law and order" functions. That is, the peripheral capitalist state uses its coercive instruments—either as threats or as actuality—to create and maintain an environment that is conducive to the capitalist reproduction. Also, the state performs various economic functions. It tries to create a climate that is propitious for the private accumulation of capital, especially by the members of the ruling class. Moreover, the state appropriates privately produced surplus through taxation. Furthermore, the state is a direct "producer and appropriator" of surplus produced by state enterprises (Canak, 1984).

Sixth, the state has various relationships both internal and external. At the internal level, the state relates to the dominant and the subaltern classes. Since the peripheral capitalist formations are created, by and large, as reflections of the interests and visions of the dominant classes, they therefore serve the general overall interests of the subaltern classes. So, in effect, the state is the business chief organizing the economy in the interests of the ruling class (Ziemann and Lanzenderfer, 1977: 148). Also, it is the job of the state to mediate conflicting interests among the various factions of the bourgeoisie, to be able to administrate in the common interest of the whole class (Miliband, 1973: 85). Significantly, in the context of the class struggle, the state is not a nonpartisan mediator; instead, it intervenes on behalf of the ruling class against the interests of the subordinate classes. At the external level, the peripheral capitalist formation is part of the international capitalist system. It was integrated through various modes—trade, foreign private investment, foreign aid, loans, and so on. The process of integration into the system varies from one peripheral formation to another. Also, the global capitalist system links the peripheral capitalist formations to the developed capitalist ones through arrangements such as the "international division of labor" and the "system of unequal exchange" (Emmanuel, 1972). Moreover, there is a dominant-subservient relationship between the peripheral capitalist and the advanced capitalist states that covers the various aspects of their relationships—economic, political, military, security, and so on. Importantly, the development of the advanced capitalist states and the corresponding underdevelopment of the peripheral capitalist formations are integral parts of the same dialectical process (Amin, 1970; Frank, 1969).

Seventh, the contradictions that are created by the performance of the peripheral capitalist state's various functions could lead to "crises of underdevelopment." In turn, these crises could engender conflicts between the ruling and the subordinate classes. Significantly, if the resultant conflicts are not managed well by the state, they could lead to rebellions, coups, revolutions, and civil wars.

Conclusion

The chapter has attempted to provide a theoretical foundation for the book. It began with a summary of the basic postulations of the five major theories that are used to explain the first Liberian civil war. This was followed by a critique of the theories individually and collectively. The basic general criticism is that all of the theories failed to take cognizance of the centrality of the state as the manufacturer of the crises that eventually lead to conflicts, including civil wars. Instead, each theory focused on various actors and processes without recognizing the fact that these constellations and their activities are shaped and conditioned by the state and its mode of production.

Alternatively, I offer the settler state and peripheral capitalist state theories as the best frameworks for explaining the taproots of Liberia's first civil war. The settler state theory is used to examine the pedigree of the Liberian state from 1847 to 1926, and the peripheral capitalist theory covers the period from 1926 to 1989. Specifically, the two theories examine, among other things, the origins of the Liberian state; the various forces that shaped the development of the state; and the features, functions, structures, relationships, and crises induced by the state.

PART II:THE FUNDAMENTAL

CHAPTER 3

Setting the Stage: The Travails of the Liberian State

Introduction

The Liberian state was the epicenter of the country's first civil war. The combination of its nature, mission, character, values, structures, rules, processes, and policies generated the multifaceted crises of underdevelopment that caused the war. Osaghae (1996: 84) puts the case thus:

> The significance of the civil war went beyond being a consequence of the militarism of the state. It was also an inevitable consequence of the larger crisis of the Liberian state which was bound to come to head sooner or later.

Hence, an analysis of the pedigree of the Liberian state—its formation, transformation, and features—is pivotal to the examination and understanding of the confluence of crises that caused the country's first civil war. In other words, the state-building project in Liberia has been shaped by the interplay between and among the various factors and forces. The resultant effects planted and nurtured the seeds that produced the country's first civil war.

Against this background, the purpose of this chapter is to map out the development of the Liberian state, including the various historical stages, the factors, forces, and the associated dynamics that shaped those eras and the consequent designing of the complexion of the state. Importantly, this chapter begins with a general assessment of the travails of the three major clusters of indigenous polities that presaged the formation of the settler and subsequently neocolonial Liberian state. This would be useful in providing comparative trajectories of the state-building enterprise. This would be followed by a discussion of the four major historical-political phases of the state-building project in Liberia—state formation (1847–1857), state expansion (1857–1904), state consolidation (1904–1950), and postconsolidation (1950–1989). On the basis of the dynamics of the various historical-political epochs, the chapter attempts to paint a portrait of the Liberian state—nature, mission, character, values, structures, rules, processes, and policies. In turn, the state provided the arena in which the country's various social struggles occurred.

Pre-Liberia: The Indigenous Polities

Before the arrival of the repatriated African Americans, beginning in 1822, Liberia was known as the Grain Coast. Portuguese explorers established contacts with Liberia as early as 1461 and named the area Grain Coast because of the abundance of grains of malegueta pepper (United States State Department, 2006: 2). The area was occupied by various indigenous ethnic groups, which can be classified into three major clusters: The Mel cluster consists of the Gola and Kissi ethnic groups; the Mande stock comprises the Gbandi, Gio, Kpelle, Lorma, Mandingo, Mano, Mende, and Vai ethnic groups, and the Kwa cluster embodies the Bassa, Belle, Dei, Grebo, Krahn, and Kru ethnic groups. The various constituents of these ethnic clusters had their own polities with their associated political economy and sociocultural systems. As Dunn and Tarr (1988: 21) observe, "For centuries before the 1822 arrival of the repatriates at Dozoa Island, the people of the Grain Coast existed under a variety of forms of indigenous political organizations." In his laudatory comments about the quality of these indigenous polities, Olfert Dapper, a Dutch observer of the seventeenth century noted, "The local population enjoyed high standard of political and social organization, with institutions similar to those of the ancient Western Sudanic empires" (Ranard et al., 2005: 6).

The sociopolitical systems of the Mel and Mande ethnic clusters had common features. Various patrilineages or lineage segments provided the *terra firma* of the polities (Sawyer, 1992). The system of governance was based on the hierarchical control through the lineage of the founding ancestor (Sawyer, 1992: 49). Importantly, for the purpose of "checks and balances," there was a council of elders that shared decision-making powers with the chief. Also, the poro (for boys and men) and sande institutions (for girls and women) served as countervailing forces.

As for the Kwa ethnic groups, their polities were acephalous. That is, political power was decentralized and disbursed through various structures. Each structure had autonomy over matters within its domain. At the various levels of the polities, there were checks and balances designed to militate against the emergence of dictatorial tendencies.

The three ethnic clusters had some common economic and political features. Economically, the dominant mode of production was communalism anchored on subsistence agriculture. The major means of production—the land—was collectively owned by the community. The members of the community were allowed to use various portions of land for agricultural production to support themselves and their families. Therefore production was for self-sustenance rather than profit-making. Interestingly, the surplus was usually used as a medium of exchange for obtaining goods from other communities and societies under the rubric of a barter system. This, for example, brought these polities in contact with European traders (Vander Kraaj, 1983). By the end of the 1500s, nevertheless, the Europeans were involved in trading such Grain Coast products as malaguetta pepper, ivory, camwood, wax, gold, and, later, slaves (Beyan, 1991: 29). However, the trade relations were conducted within the framework of a system of unequal exchange: The European traders exchanged their outdated, unmarketable, and cheap-quality goods for the high-value and quality products from the various indigenous polities. Significantly, the economic contact with the Europeans witnessed the introduction to Liberians of the values of the emerging capitalist system in Europe. For example, the various indigenous Liberian polities, especially the ones that were based along the coast, were introduced to values such as rugged individualism and the profit motive. Similarly, the foundation was laid for making the various Liberian ethnic polities' economies appendages of European imperialism. For example, in response to the economic imperatives of the various imperialist powers, the economies of the various Liberian ethnic polities began to produce commodities such as gold, ivory, and handwoven cloth. Characteristically, the emergence of this patron-client relationship fostered the development of a compradorial system in the various Liberian ethnic polities: Various individuals became intermediaries for the European imperialist powers. To perform their services to European merchant capital, the compradors learned European customs and capitalist-based business practices. Despite these developments, the various indigenous polities, in general retained the core of their respective political economies.

Politically, all of the indigenous polities had elements of checks and balances and other features of democratic decision making. The various institutions in each polity collectively constituted a semblance of a "balance of power system." Under the arrangement, each institution has functions with the concomitant authority. This arrangement helped to militate against the fostering of authoritarianism.

Constructing the Settler and Neocolonial Liberian State

The construction of the Liberian state spanned four major phases: The first phase commenced with the arrival of the repatriates from the United States in 1822, and their quest to establish their foothold and subsequently transform the Grain Coast and its various indigenous ethnic polities. Phase two (1823–1837) was characterized by the efforts of the American Colonization Society (ACS), the "colonial power," to establish a state architecture. The third phase (1837–1847) witnessed the granting of political autonomy to the settlers within the context of the suzerainty of the ACS. The final phase (1847–present) saw Liberia's emergence as a "sovereign and independent state." This phase has been characterized by various stages: state formation, state expansion, state consolidation, and post–state consolidation.

The "Clash of Civilizations:"[1] The Arrival of the Settlers

In the early 1800s, slavery and its plantation-based political economy began to experience various stresses. One of the major consequences was that several African-American slaves were freed. Consequently, the American ruling class and the majority white population were gripped by a grave sense of concern and fear. This was because, as Smith (1972: 3) notes, "the United States Government believed that the 'subsequent' emancipation and education of blacks coupled with their fast birth rate would in due course enable them to dominate the U.S." Importantly, a debate ensued regarding the formulation of the best approach to deal with the "black problem." The debate was informed by the proffering of various options by the stakeholders. For their part, the freed African Americans wanted to remain in the United States. Accordingly, they argued for the carving up of designated areas in the United States that they could occupy. Concomitantly, the freed African Americans were opposed to being repatriated to Africa. This was because according to the "Tarzan-like" stereotypical view of Africa that the freed African Americans had acquired, "[Africa] was a grim land cursed with a burning sun and torturing insects. [And] the [American government's] plan was [designed] to dump free Negroes into the savage wilds of Africa and a circuit route back to bondage" (Cassell, 1970:18). So, interestingly, having developed what Brown (1941:10) calls a "slave psychology," the African Americans became captivated with the very racist and exploitative system that had visited the vagaries of indignity and degradation on them.

Despite the opposition of the freed African Americans, the American ruling class and its government decided that it was in their best interests to repatriate the former group back to Africa, their ancestral homeland. Against this backdrop, the ACS was organized in 1816 as a colonial proxy for the U.S. government, in the implementation of the repatriation plan. The organization's membership consisted of some of the most prominent bourgeoisies in American society: Supreme Court Associate Justice Bushrod Washington, Treasury Secretary William Crawford, theologian Robert Finley, and General Andrew Jackson, a top military brass. The organization's constitution reflected the arrogance of American ethnocentrism and its attendant doctrine of "manifest destiny." For example, the major provision of the document bestowed on the ACS the right "to colonize, civilize and Christianize" people of color (Constitution of the American Colonization Society, Article II). Also, the organization served as an instrument for the establishment of American influence. Thus, the freed African-American slaves were to constitute the nucleus of this enterprise. The promotion of American national interest motif of the colonization plan was captured in Samuel Adams's pamphlet "A Plan for Training Freed Negroes in the American Colonies as Colonizers and Missionaries" (Wilson, 1947). In addition, various ancillary societies were organized to complement the ACS: Maryland, New York, Pennsylvania, and Mississippi Societies.

Against this background, the ACS commissioned an exploratory mission to Africa in search for a suitable settlement for the freed African-American slaves. The exploratory mission recommended that the western section of Africa was the ideal location for the resettlement of the freed African Americans. Both the U.S. government and the ACS accepted the recommendation; hence, the latter was authorized by the former to proceed with the implementation of the plan. In this vein, the U.S. government provided the ACS with the amount of $100,000 and military escort to repatriate the freed African-Americans slaves to Africa. Thus, in 1820, the ship, the Elizabeth, with 88 repatriates, set sail for Africa accompanied by the U.S. warship USS Cyane.

After several months of travel, the repatriates landed at Shebro Island in Sierra Leone. However, they encountered several major problems. The most critical challenge was the outbreak of malaria and other tropical diseases. Several of the repatriates fell ill and some of them eventually died. Another challenge was the inadequacy of the supplies for sustaining the repatriates in the short term. Finally, the lack of knowledge of the terrain hampered the repatriates' abilities to meet their pressing short-term challenges. Ultimately, the determination was made to move the settlement. Accordingly, another search for another land along the West African Coast was pursued. Eventually, the ACS and the settlers reached Dozoa Island on the Grain Coast (the name was later changed to Liberia). Significantly, the settlers' appetite for land brought them into conflicts with various indigenous polities they met in the area. However, backed by American military power, the settlers were able to secure a permanent settlement on Providence Island and subsequently Cape Mesurado. During the various negotiations for land with different indigenous polities, the threat of the use of force was employed as a "stick" for inducing the compliance. For example, during the negotiation for Cape Mesurado, American Navy Lieutenant Robert Stockton placed a loaded pistol on the ear of King Peter and forced him to sign the deed giving away Cape Mesurado to the settlers (Movement for Justice in Africa, 1980: 3). The "new" settlement was called Monrovia (named after President James Monroe of the United States). There were similar encounters between the settlers and the indigenes in other communities. Thus, the stage was set for the establishment of an enduring conflictual relationship between the settlers and various indigenous ethnic groups.

The "Colonial" Epoch (1820–1839)

Having acquired some territory through a mixture of dubious purchase and the use of force, the settlers were hopeful that they would have established a polity under their control. However, to their disappointment, the ACS established a colonial state (Liberia) replete with a political economy. Since the state was an authoritarian one, the ACS designed various repressive constitutional architectures as the *terra firma* of the governance system of the colony, including the Plan for Civil Government of 1824. Then, as the population of the settlement expanded, the ACS framed a new constitution for the Liberian colony (Beyan, 1991: 85). Under the arrangement, sovereignty resided in the Board of Directors of the ACS. Accordingly, the Board of Directors made all domestic and foreign decisions. The edicts of the Board were implemented by the colonial agent, who was akin to the European monarchs who ruled under the principle of "divine rule" (see Table 3.1). As the chief representative of the colonizer, the colonial agent was omnipotent with no checks on his or her powers by the citizens. Specifically, he exercised a broad range of powers. At the vortex of the agent's panoply of power was his fundamental role as the handmaid of the ACS. Accordingly, he conducted the affairs of the colony under the direction of the ACS's Board of Directors. Interestingly, the agent combined the powers of chief executive and chief justice of the colony under a system of the "fusion of powers." Also, the agent had broad and expansive appointive powers. For example, he appointed the vice agent from a list of three nominees submitted to him by the citizens; he also had the power to reject the citizens' nominations. Moreover, the agent appointed the various state committees—agriculture, public works, health, and defense—that had responsibilities for various functional areas within the colony. These appointments were made annually on the basis of the vote of the majority of the freeholders—those who were propertied. In addition, the colonial agent appointed all other officials of the colonial administration without the advice and consent of his or her rubber stamp: legislative council and the citizens.

Table 3.1
The Colonial Agents of the American Colonization Society, 1820–1838

Name	Tenure of Office
Samuel Bacon	1820
Samuel Crozer	1820–1822
Eli Ayers	1822–1823
Frederick James[a]	1823
Elijah Johnson	1823
Jehudi Ashmun	1823–1828
Lott Carey	1828
Richard Randall	1828–1829
Joseph Meclin	1829–1833
Joseph Pinney	1833–1834
Nathaniel Brander	1834
Anthony Williams	1834–1835
Ezekiel Skinner	1835–1836
Anthony D. Williams	1836–1838

Note: [a]Denotes acting colonial agent.
Source: Compiled by the author.

Also, there was a legal code that was designed to maintain the stranglehold of the repressive colonial state. Three major laws constituted the core of the statutes. The respect for authority law, which was deeply rooted in the feudal order and its system of chattel slavery, made it mandatory for citizens to unquestionably obey "authorities," whom they did not elect. Violators were charged with misdemeanor. The observance of the Sabbath law required the observance of "Sunday" in keeping with the Christian Doctrine. Infractions were classified as misdemeanor. The public nuisance law made it illegal for anyone to engage in profanity, and to organize and participate in demonstrations. This law had two major consequences. First, it restricted mass participation in the political process. Second, it curtailed the freedoms of association and assembly. Interestingly, there were several punishments for violating the public nuisance law (1) the imposition of fines, (2) imprisonment, (3) flogging, (4) the confiscation of property, and (5) banishment—a form of internal exile.

Like other colonial formations, the various compacts were designed without the participation of the settlers. Essentially, they were formulated by the ACS, the "colonial power" and imposed on the "colonized."

In the economic realm, the mode of production was based on feudal-embryonic capitalism with agriculture as the mainstay. In this vein, the focus was on the growing of food stuffs—(sugarcane, rice, vegetables, and fruits)—and cattle—(sheep and goats). In addition, industry and commerce were major economic activities. The domestic market consisted of various trading stations along the coast of Millsburg, Sesters, Cape Mount, and Monrovia (the major trading center). The major means of transportation were small boats that were owned and operated by the "merchant sector" of the light-skinned African-American stock. Trade took place at two levels: contagious indigenous polities and globally. In the case of the former, the settlers traded with the various indigenous polities that were outside the jurisdiction of the Liberian colonial state. The commodities included food stuffs and cattle. At the global level, the settlers traded with American merchants. The settlers sold their dye, woods, hides, ivory, and gold and in turn bought cotton cloth, tobacco, gun powder, and arms from the American traders. The colonial state was dependent upon the metropolis —the United States and Western European states—for the supply of equipment and manufactured goods. In turn, this occasioned the development of a system of unequal exchange: the settlers paid exorbitant prices for metropolitan products that were usually either damaged or antiquated.

The relations of production were anchored on a caste-cum-class system consisting of three strata. Under this arrangement, social groups were defined by two theoretically distinct but in reality overlapping characteristics (Burrowes, 1982: 27). Very often the obvious but static caste distinctions on the basis of skin color and ancestral origin coincided with class differences defined by the relationship of each group to the means of production and the state (Burrowes, 1982: 27). The upper caste-cum-class was occupied by the white colonial agent and the other functionaries of the ACS, who governed Liberia from 1820 to 1839 (Kieh, 1998a: 158). The class base of this group was essentially petit bourgeois: many were lawyers and doctors (Burrowes, 1982: 27).

The middle stratum was occupied by the mulattos or the light-skinned African Americans (Kieh, 1998a: 158). Class-wise, they were compradorial: With their relatively good educational background, they formed an alliance with the ACS (Kieh, 1998a: 158). In turn, they were rewarded with junior-level positions in the colonial bureaucracy.

The lowest tier had two sections. The upper one was occupied by the dark-skinned African Americans. In class terms, they were self-employed farmers and artisans. The bottom level comprised the Congos—those who were recaptured while en route to slavery—and those indigenes, who were under the jurisdiction of the colony. The members of this tier were principally free laborers and indentured servants (Kieh, 1989a: 38).

Characteristically, the caste-cum-class stratification engendered various conflicts between and among the various tiers. The conflicts revolved around an assortment of issues—ranging from the repressive effects of the state to various rivalries, including the light-skinned African Americans versus the dark-skinned ones.

The cultural system was dominated by Western values and English was the official language. Thus, the languages of the various ethnic groups were denigrated by being characterized as "dialects" that were only appropriate for intra- and intertribal communication. Also, dress and the mode of entertainment were patently American in character. For example, the tail coat and the top hat were dress codes; they were imposed on the indigenes as manifestations of civilization. The fact was that these Western dresses were not only alien culturally, but also unsuitable for the climatic conditions dominated by hot weather.

Similarly, the educational system was American in orientation. For example, the curriculum was designed based on the objective realities of the United States with very little relevance to local Liberian realities. Pupils were required to learn and master the operations of the American racist, feudal, and capitalist, cultural and political systems. Concomitantly, students were indoctrinated to view international events through an American-centric analytical animus.

Religion was based on the primacy of the American version of Christianity. The various indigenous religions were vilified and classified as paganistic. Given the dialectical tension between the two religious traditions, the various American Christian sects exported an army of missionaries to Liberia to "civilize the barbarians."

Constrained by the limitations of its geographic scope, the colonial Liberian state undertook various campaigns of territorial expansion. As expected, this fuelled conflicts between the colonial Liberian state and various adjacent indigenous polities. For example, in 1822, a coalition of Dei, Gola, and Bassa polities waged war against the colonial Liberian state. The war was caused by two major factors. First, these indigenous polities wanted to reclaim their lands, which were illegally annexed by the colonial

Liberian state. Second, they wanted to convey their deep sense of revulsion against the denigration of their cultures by the colonial Liberian state and its settler inhabitants. Similarly, in 1828, various indigenous polities around the St. Paul River forged an alliance against the colonial Liberian state in an effort to halt the campaign of territorial expansion and its attendant practice of the illegal annexation of lands. However, in both conflicts, the colonial Liberian state assisted by the American military might, prevailed.

The Commonwealth Epoch (1838–1847)

The impetus for the establishment of a commonwealth was provided by three major currents. The various autonomous colonies that were established by the ACS and its affiliates notably in Monrovia, Bassa, and Mississippi in Africa, or Sinoe, were experiencing financial difficulties; hence, it was decided that the formation of a union would help ease the situation. Another challenge was the jurisdictional problematic as reflected in the daunting problems of defining the various territories. Finally, the various colonies were experiencing sustained and increased resistance from the various indigenous polities. Against this background, it was decided to establish the "Commonwealth of Liberia" in 1839, merging the colonies of Monrovia, Bassa, and Sinoe. However, the new construct retained the essence of its colonial progenitor.

One of the major tasks that the emergent entity was charged with was the formulation of the constitutional architecture. This generated intense debate between the ACS, the suzerain, and its auxiliaries on the one hand, and the settlers or the Americo-Liberians, on the other. The crux of the controversy was the issue of power within the context of the new political order. For its part, the ACS wanted to continue its authoritarian rule. Whereas, the settlers, especially the light-skinned African Americans, wanted greater involvement in the administration of the state. The divergent positions were expressed in two draft constitutions. The settlers proposed the "Monrovia Draft" and the Board of Directors of the ACS proffered the "Greenleaf Draft."[2] After months of debate, the ACS imposed the "Greenleaf Constitution" on the settlers. Significantly, among other things, the constitution stated that sovereignty would continue to reside in the Board of Directors of the ACS. This meant that the organization would continue to enjoy the monopoly of power that was characteristic of the colonial epoch. Thus, the effort to stem the tide of authoritarianism was foiled.

Structurally, the government was divided into three branches: executive, legislative, and judicial. The executive branch was headed by the governor of the commonwealth, who served as the chief administrator (see Table 3.2). He or she was assisted by a council of the chief executive officers of the colonies of Bassa and Sinoe. The legislative powers were vested in a Congress. The membership was composed of the governor of the commonwealth, the chief executive officers of Bassa and Sinoe, and five delegates elected by the legislative councils of the three regions based on the following formula (1) three delegates from the colony of Monrovia and (2) one delegate each from the colonies of Bassa and Sinoe. Characteristically, the criterion for membership in the Congress was undemocratic: It was restricted to so-called civilized citizens. That is, by settler standards, the uncivilized and unchristianized indigenes, who were citizens of the Liberian commonwealth state, were ineligible to serve in the Congress. Similarly, the judiciary was controlled by the triumvirate of the governor of the Liberian state and his two lieutenants—the chief executive officers of Bassa and Sinoe. Clearly, the organizational structure epitomized the authoritarian and undemocratic character of the Liberian state. For example, the governor belonged to and dominated all three branches of the government.

Table 3.2
The Governors of the Commonwealth of Liberia, 1838–1847

Governor	Race	Tenure of Office
Thomas Buchanan	White	1838–1841
Joseph Jenkins Roberts	Black[a]	1841–1847

Note: [a]Joseph Jenkins Roberts belonged to the light-skinned or mulatto stratum of the Americo-Liberian or settler stock.
Source: Compiled by the author.

Significantly, two years after the inception of the commonwealth, the ACS decided to make a major concession to the settlers. It granted them authority to administer the day-to-day affairs of the state. However, the ACS retained the powers of judicial review, the authority to conduct foreign relations, and a veto power—the right to review and nullify the decisions of the government.

The economy experienced several major changes. First, the mainstay of the economy shifted from traditional agriculture to commerce. That is, the majority of the settlers became merchants and traders. The shift was occasioned by the fact that the trading sector was comparatively more lucrative than the agricultural one.

Second, there was a phenomenal expansion of foreign trade. This was precipitated by the commonwealth state's decision to diversify its trade relations. In this vein, England and France became major trading partners. The Liberian state exported products such as coffee, palm oil, and sugarcane to these imperialist powers and imported manufactured goods from them. It is important to note that Liberia's trade relations with these imperialist powers were conducted under the characteristic rubric of a system of unequal exchange and an inequitable division of labor. In the case of the system of unequal exchange, Liberia was required to pay more for the imports from these imperialist powers and forced to receive less for its exports. Similarly, in the case of division of labor, Liberia served as a plantation for the production of raw materials to feed the industrial-manufacturing complexes of the metropolis.

Third, the growth of external trade necessitated the formulation and implementation of laws dealing with customs and import duties and ports of entry for foreign vessels. The development of these legal codes was designed to establish the control of the commonwealth state over its territorial confines and to generate revenues. Interestingly, these actions by the Liberian state laid the basis for the development of conflictual relationships with both France and England. The two perennial imperialist powers saw the imposition of control mechanisms by the commonwealth state as an attempt to limit their economic activities, especially with the various indigenous polities that were outside the jurisdiction of the commonwealth state.

Fourth, the commonwealth state's strategy of having multiple trading partners was undermined by its continual overall dependence on the United States. For example, the dollar was the legal tender and the U.S. Congress established the standards of weight and measures that superintended economic activities and transactions in the Liberian commonwealth state.

Fifth, there were changes in the domestic relations of production. As a consequence of the ACS granting autonomy to the settlers, the light-skinned settlers or the mulatto graduated to the upper tier of the caste-cum-class structure. This was occasioned by the mulattos' dominant role in the emerging peripheral capitalist system. For example, the mulattos controlled internal commercial activities. The middle stratum was occupied by the dark-skinned settlers, whose class base remained rooted in the agricultural sector, despite the fact that some of them went into commerce. The lower tier had two sections: The upper one was occupied by the Congos, whereas the indigenes, who were under the jurisdiction of the commonwealth state, comprised the lower sector. Significantly, these shifts in the caste-cum-class structure resulted in various conflicts. For example, the upper and middle classes became locked in an epic battle for control of the state. On the other hand, the subaltern classes expressed their continuing dissatisfaction with the repressive and exploitative nature of the political economy, especially their

Setting the Stage: The Travails of the Liberian State 45

perpetual situation, which was based on destitution and servitude. A major consequence was a conflict between the mulatto-based ruling class and the indigenes-based lower tier of the subaltern class. The conflict revolved around several issues. The core one was the denial of citizenship and the attendant right of participation to the indigenes, who resided under the jurisdiction of the commonwealth state. Although the indigenes were not considered citizens, the commonwealth state coerced them to pay taxes and to perform sundry public works for the state. Moreover, the indigenes resented the recurrent actions by the commonwealth state to destroy their cultures. For example, the commonwealth state pursued a policy of subjecting indigenous cultures to ridicule by characterizing them as barbaric. Moreover, the state sought to alter some of the cultural fundaments of the indigenous cultures. A major case was the settlers' categorization of polygamy, the center of the family in indigenous cultures, as a sin and the subsequent imposition of monogamy as the new norm. Similarly, the indigenous peoples' right to the freedom of religion was curtailed by the commonwealth state's insistence that the former conform to the standards of American Christianity. Another dimension of the conflict spectrum pitted the agricultural wing, which had its base around the St. Paul River, against the Monrovia-based "commercial princes." The locus of the conflict was competition for control of the economy.

Importantly, the commonwealth state was entangled in various conflicts with an assortment of external forces. At one level, the Liberian state was locked in a series of conflicts with various indigenous polities over the issue of land. At the heart of these conflicts was the Liberian state's policy of territorial annexation, which involved encroachment on the sovereignty and territorial integrity of the various indigenous polities. Also, Britain and France, motivated by their desire for imperial expansion, refused to recognize the commonwealth state's jurisdiction over various portions of land notably in the western section. Similarly, the citizens of these imperialist powers, who were engaged in various economic activities within the confines of the commonwealth state, challenged the state's authority to impose taxes and regulate trade by refusing to pay taxes and adhere to regulations. Their rationale was that the commonwealth was not a sovereign state; hence, it was not clothed with the authority to undertake such activities.

Significantly, plagued by multiple internal and external conflicts and their associated challenges, a movement for independence emerged within the commonwealth state, especially among the light-skinned or mulatto settlers. The movement's principal argument was that the establishment of an independent and sovereign state would help provide the platform addressing the various challenges. However, the independence movement was vehemently opposed by the dark-skinned settlers who viewed it as a ploy by their light-skinned kin to consolidate their domination.

Independence Epoch (1847–Present)

State formation (1847–1857): In January 1846, amid the avalanche of pressure from the light-skinned settlers, the ACS acquiesced to their demand for the granting of independence. About a year later, the legislature of the commonwealth voted for the establishment of an independent and sovereign state. Accordingly, the various state-making processes were set into motion. The state formation process commenced with the formulation of a compact as the terra firma of the emergent Liberian state. This was done in a constitutional convention. The convention consisted of delegates from the three regions of the commonwealth: Monrovia, Bassa, and Sinoe. As Table 3.3 shows, seven of the delegates were from Monrovia, the primus inter pares, three delegates came from Bassa, and two came from Sinoe. Professionally, the majority of the delegates were theologians and educators. Class-wise, most of them were from the upper stratum—the province of the mulattos. Few of them were from the middle tier consisting of the dark-skinned section. Interestingly, there were no delegates from the subaltern classes comprising the indigene, who were resident in the state, and the Congos. So, in effect, all delegates came from the settler or Americo-Liberian stock. This is noteworthy because the composition of the delegates was critical to the designing of the essence of the state as a settler one. The constitutional convention met for a month in Monrovia, the capital city, to draft the constitution for the new Liberian state. Samuel Benedict and Hilary Teage served as chair and secretary of the Constitutional Convention respectively. During the process, the convention studied the constitutions of the Liberian colonial state, the Liberian commonwealth state, the constitutions of some of the states of the United States, and the American federal constitution. Interestingly, the convention did not consider the experiences of the various indigenous ethnic polities—Mel, Mande, and Kwa. These indigenous polities had established practices in, among other things, checks and balances and democratic decision making. Finally, the convention formulated a constitution that borrowed very heavily from the American Constitution and the constitutions of some of the states in the union (Burrowes, 1998). In effect, the compact that was designed reflected the realities of the United States rather than those of Liberia. Structurally, the constitution was based on the American presidential system of government with its attendant three separate but coequal branches of government—legislative, executive, and judicial. Also, the compact was based on the doctrines of the separation of powers, checks and balances, and judicial review. Economically, capitalism was maintained as the mode of production. Under this arrangement, there was a privileging of the propertied class in the conduct of the affairs of the state. In essence, the state that was fashioned was not designed to serve as a neutral mediator, but rather as a facilitator of the interests of the propertied class and the settlers. This was reflected in the fact that the constitutional architecture was anchored on the primacy of the settlers and the propertied. For example, the indigenes were not considered as citizens of Liberia. Only the settlers and the Congos were granted citizenship. Accordingly, the state was deliberately fashioned as an exclusionary and segregative construct reflecting the dynamics of the apartheid-like state order that was ascendant in the United States during this period. Also, even among the citizenships, the ownership of private property was the major determinant for the right to vote and to contest prominent political offices such as the presidency, vice presidency, and the legislature. Hence, the complexion of the state was settler based on preferential treatment for the propertied class.

Table 3.3
The Roster of Delegates to the 1847 Constitutional Convention of Liberia

Name of Delegate	*Region*
Samuel Benedict	Monrovia
Hilary Teage	Monrovia
Elijah Johnson	Monrovia
John N. Lewis	Monrovia
Beverly Wilson	Monrovia
John B. Gripon	Monrovia
John Day	Monrovia
Amos Herring	Bassa
Anthony W. Gardner	Bassa
Emphraim Titler	Bassa
R. E. Murray	Sinoe
Jacob W. Prout	Sinoe

Source: Compiled by the author.

Thus, with the adoption of the constitution, Liberia was declared an independent and sovereign state on July 26, 1847. As Liberty (2002: vi) poignantly notes "It may be accurately said that Liberia was conceived in controversy and developed in controversy." Accordingly, the resultant state-building project was bedeviled by conflicts and rancor as efforts were made to impose an alien social formation on the majority indigenous population that resided both within and outside of the jurisdiction of the incipient settler state.

State expansion (1857–1904): Several major challenges confronted the new state both at the domestic and global levels. In the case of the former, one of the major problems was the exigency of expanding its territorial base. Accordingly, the state commissioned various exploratory missions into the hinterland, which were then occupied by various independent indigenous polities. These indigenous polities were resistant to the expansionist agenda of the state. However, through the combination of purchase (some questionable) and the use of force, the settler Liberian state was able to gradually expand its territorial confines to the interior. Another lacuna was the continuing struggle between the light-skinned or mulatto and dark-skinned strata of the settler stock. Characteristically, the crux of the conflict was over the control of state power. Interestingly, both wings of the enduring caste-cum-class system shared a similar ideological commitment to capitalism, but were divided on the basis of skin pigmentation and the associated implications for their respective relationships to the major means of production and the state. In short, just as during the colonial and commonwealth eras, the intersection between skin pigmentation and class interests mediated the relationship between these two poles of the settler stock. The resultant differences found expressions in the formation of two rival political parties: The True Liberian Party and the Old Whigs Party (Kieh, 1988a: 204). The True Liberian Party, which in 1857 changed its name to the Republican Party, was the political vehicle for promoting the political, economic, and social interests of the light-skinned or mulatto-dominated ruling class. Its membership was predominantly drawn from the ranks of the "merchant and commercial princes," the intelligentsia, and the managers of the erstwhile commonwealth. The Old Whigs Party, which later changed its name to the True Black Man Party, was the political arm of the dark-skinned settlers. In the socioeconomic domain, there was a debate between advocates of the autonomous capitalist path to development and those of dependent capitalist development, who pressed for integration into the global capitalist system. In other words, although the autonomous capitalist perspective, like the dependent capitalist one, espoused the development of a relationship with the international capitalist order, the major difference was that the former wanted the Liberian economy to be controlled and dominated by indigenous capitalists. Importantly, the lack of an agreement between the adherents of the two models of development militated against the development of a comprehensive national development plan, especially the role of international finance capital.

At the global level, the settler Liberian state was faced with the enduring problem of French and British imperialism and the attendant impact on the issue of land and the conflictual relationship with the hinterland-based independent indigenous polities. The French and British were persistent in the pursuance of their respective policies of territorial expansion. In turn, as in the past, this meant the annexation of lands that were claimed by the settler state as part of its territory. Similarly, French and British citizens, who were engaged in various commercial activities in territories claimed by the settler state, refused to comply with the various commercial regulations—taxes, duties, fees, and entry—that were promulgated by the settler Liberian state. Again, their contention was that the settler Liberian state did not legally own these territories. To make matters worse, the French and British imperialists pursued strategies based on the exacerbation of the already antagonistic relationships between the settler state and the various independent indigenous polities. Clearly, these strategies were designed to achieve the goal of "divide and rule." That is, with the polarization between the settler state and the various indigenous polities, the French and British made the determination that they would then have carte blanche power to expand the territorial confines of their respective colonies in Cote d'Ivoire, Guinea, and Sierra Leone.

Significantly, the nature, mission, and character of the settler state hamstrung the ability of its custodians to design the appropriate modalities for addressing the incipient challenges of the state-building project. One of the resultant effects was the continual fostering of the fractionalization and factionalization of the body politic and an unending cycle of crises and conflicts. Interestingly, instead of rethinking and democratically reconstituting the settler state, the ruling class made the determination to stay the course. So, when the state experienced its first major economic shock in the late 1860s, the state managers relied preponderantly on the international capitalist system to help Liberia weather the storm (see Chapter 5 for a more comprehensive discussion of the crisis). In turn, this increased the Liberian state's vulnerability to the vicissitudes of the global capitalist system. Also, Liberia's reliance on the global capitalist system as the economic fire brigade undermined the prospects for autonomous capitalist development, and set to motion the process of incorporating the former into the latter merely as an appendage for the production of raw materials to supply the industrial-manufacturing machines of the metropolis. With the basis for autonomous capitalism eroded by the forces and dynamics of global capitalism, the members of the various factions of the caste-cum-class system turned to the state as the major employer, and particularly as the primary source for the private accumulation of wealth. Thus, the control of state power correspondingly occasioned the control of economic power. This set into motion a Darwinian struggle between the light-skinned and dark-skinned poles of the settler stock and the various factions of the dominant class for control of state power. The competition was waged through the instrumentality of rival political parties—the Republican, True Whig, and others. In short, rather than being an autonomous actor in the political economy, the state instead became the handmaid of whatever faction was in power.

State consolidation (1904–1950): With the limited jurisdiction of the settler state, coupled with its increased importance as the principal source of both political and economic power, the two rival poles of the settler stock agreed that the expansion of the construct was imperative both for the welfare of the settler stock and for the particularistic agendas of its rival poles and factions. Accordingly, the settler state accelerated the pace of its expansionist strategy in the hinterland. As expected, this aggressive policy of land grab was greeted with resistance by the various independent indigenous polities. However, through the use of a combination of force and questionable purchases, the settler state was able to acquire land. By the early 1900s, the settler state had expanded the ambit of its territorial jurisdiction virtually throughout the interior.

However, the settler state, tired of its tenuous control over the hinterland, undertook the process of designing and implementing a policy that would fully integrate the interior into the settler state and maintain the latter's stranglehold over the former. Toward this, the ruling True Whig Party and its presidential candidate Arthur Barclay designed a plan for the interior. In 1904, President Arthur Barclay outlined the plan ("The Barclay Plan") in an address to the legislature. The plan was composed of several interlocking elements. The centerpiece of the plan was the establishment of an administrative structure in the interior. Under the arrangement, the interior was divided into various districts headed by a commissioner. The commissioners reported to the secretary of the interior, who was the chief administrator of the hinterland. In turn, the secretary of the interior reported to the president. Also, the traditional chiefs of the various ethnic groups were subordinated to presidential authority through the hierarchical structure established by the plan. Accordingly, the traditional chieftaincy system was delegitimized as chiefs became reliant on the whims of the president as the basis of both their authority and their tenure. Although the organizational tapestry meant, among other things, the increase of presidential authority, the competing factions of the ruling class agreed on its necessity. This was because with the erosion of the prospects for autonomous development, the dynamics of the rivalry between and among various factions of the ruling class were affected in several ways. One of the major ways was that members of the ruling class became increasingly dependent on the state for employment. Hence, the viability of the state became indispensable to their survival. Also, the subaltern classes and the marginalized indigenes became quite strident in their respective protests against the exclusionary, segregative, repressive, and exploitative predilections of the settler state. Hence, the members of the ruling class concluded that a strong presidency was exigent for dealing with these threats to the survival of the settler state. Another conundrum was the persistent challenge posed by French and British imperialism to the sovereignty, political independence, and territorial integrity of the settler state. Again, there was consensus among the members of the ruling class that French and British imperialism was inimical to the very survival of the settler state; hence, a strong presidency was required to address the problem.

Another element of the plan was the arrogation to the president of Liberia the right to hold "presidential executive council" in any area in the interior on any matter of the chief executive's choosing. This plank in the blueprint helped establish the suzerainty of the central government in all policy matters at the local level, thereby effectively eroding the prospects for decentralization.

Also, two parallel legal systems were established: Western and traditional. The former, which was the dominant one, was mainly rooted in the urban areas. In the case of the latter, it was designed to adjudicate cases within the traditional or indigenous sphere. Accordingly, the courts of the traditional chiefs and the district commissioners were established.

Finally, the plan called for the establishment of a national military. Accordingly, in 1907, the Liberian Frontier Force (LFF) was established.[3] Clearly, the military was organized as the instrument of coercion of the settler state and its ruling class. Interestingly, the members of the military were primarily recruited from the subaltern classes, especially the peasantry. But, the military indoctrination program oriented them to be loyal and unquestionably obedient to the state, its custodians, and ruling class. As President Tubman, the architect of the modern authoritarian Liberian state put it, "The military has three functions: to obey, to obey and to obey" (Liberia: America's Stepchild, 2002). The LFF mandate consisted of three major functions. The overarching one was to protect the settler state from insurrectionist activities by the subaltern classes and the marginalized sectors of the indigenous stock. Second, the LFF was given the responsibility to collect taxes in the hinterland. The performance of this function was marked by vitriolic human rights abuses: The members of the LFF routinely beat and tortured scores of individuals who were delinquent in the payment of their taxes and/or who were considered subversive elements engaged in fomenting trouble for the settler state. The third function was to ensure that trade routes throughout Liberia, especially from the urban to the rural areas, were kept open.

Overall, the plan helped establish the primacy of the authoritarian Liberian state not just in the hinterland but throughout the body politic. Specifically, it institutionalized manipulation, intimidation, and violence as the dominant modes for conducting state-society relations. Also, the instruments of violence and exploitation galvanized by the plan made it possible for the succeeding regimes to continue the process of consolidating the power of the "Bula Mutarian state"[4] (Sawyer, 1973).

By 1926, the settler state experienced a major development: It was transformed into a neocolonial construct. The phenomenon was occasioned by the establishment of the Firestone Plantations Company, an American giant rubber corporation, as the first major foreign investment project in Liberia. The penetration of the embryonic Liberian peripheral capitalist economy by international finance capital through Firestone impacted the country's political economy in three major ways. First, it established what could be termed a "real private sector." This was because before the Firestone investment, the private sector essentially consisted of a small-scale retail sector. Second, the Firestone project established wage labor on a larger scale. Third, it occasioned the formation of a class system primarily wedded to the individual's relationship to the major means of production. Also, it added a foreign-based sector consisting of the owners of Firestone and subsequently those of other multinational corporations to the emergent Liberian ruling class. Overall, it finalized the process of Liberia's incorporation into the international capitalist system. Accordingly, the incipient neocolonial Liberian state became an instrument for promoting the interest of the ruling class.

Interestingly, the neocolonial construct and its new political economy were still bedeviled by the settler-indigene divide. So, realizing that ethnocultural antagonisms were anathema to the logic of capitalism, the Tubman regime, which came to power in 1944, took three major steps to address the perennial problem. The overarching measure was the granting of full Liberian citizenship to the members of the country's various indigenous ethnic groups. Another step was the acceleration of the pace of incorporating more indigenes to the ruling class both as state managers and as members of the local entrepreneurial wing. Also, the Tubman regime enunciated the "Unification and Integration Policy" as a framework for managing ethnic relations.

Another major challenge was harnessing Liberia's vast natural resources such as iron ore, diamond, gold, and timber for national development. Consistent with the imperatives of peripheral capitalism, the neocolonial Liberian state designed and implemented the open door policy as the dominant strategy for promoting national development. Under the policy, the country's economy and natural resources were further mortgaged to international finance capital. Consequently, there was an influx of various foreign-based multinational corporations and other businesses into the Liberian economy. With supercheap labor, lucrative investment packages, and a pliant neocolonial state, foreign-owned businesses such as the LMC, LAMCO, and the Bong Mining Company accumulated huge profits.

Postconsolidation: The "tugs and pulls" (1951–1989): The postconsolidation epoch of the Liberian state-building project focused on the problems of addressing the factionalization and fractionalization within the ruling class and the challenges posed by the subaltern classes. The Tubman regime played the pioneering role in addressing these two major lacunas. The issue of intra-ruling class factionalization was tackled in several ways. One measure employed was the humiliation and subsequent ostracization of the "renegade members" of the ruling class. Another step was banishment into exile. For example, on the eve of the 1951 presidential election, the leaders of the opposition Reformation Party were forced to flee the country (Kieh, 1988: 207). In his final preelection speech, President Tubman, the candidate of the ruling True Whig Party, charged that Didhwo Twe's, the presidential candidate of the opposition Reformation Party, "hands were stained with blood of treason, rebellion and sedition. He [Twe] has been unfaithful and recreant to his trust as a Liberian citizen" (Townsend, 1969: 115). Also, humiliation was used as a tool for dealing with some of the "renegade local bourgeoisies." For example in 1955, several rebellious members of the local ruling class were arrested, stripped of their clothing, and paraded naked through the streets of Monrovia, the capital city, and subsequently imprisoned under very harsh conditions. Another major measure was the establishment of a de facto one-party system under the suzerainty of the True Whig. In this case, membership in the True Whig Party became the sole route to the attainment of political and economic power in the country. Interestingly, the punitive tools were mixed with some "carrots." The dominant faction of the ruling class used financial (cash payments) and political bribes (appointment to positions in the state bureaucracy) as instrumentariums for arresting the rising tide of rebellion within the ranks of the ruling class. In the case of the subaltern classes, the Tubman government used state repression and patronage as the principal vehicles for cowing them into submission. To build the state's capacity to inflict violence and pain, a large security network consisting of agencies such as the Special Security Service, Executive Action Bureau, National Intelligence Security Service, the National Bureau of Investigation, and the Criminal Investigation Department was established. These security entities were complemented by the Armed Forces of Liberia and the Liberian National Police Force.

When President Tubman died in 1971, following his 27-year reign as the president of Liberia and the undisputed leader and spokesperson of the ruling class, he was replaced by William R. Tolbert, his deputy of 19 years. Cognizant of the deepening crisis of the neocolonial Liberian state, the Tolbert regime decided to liberalize the political space by, among other things, pledging to respect the practice of the constitutionally guaranteed political rights and civil liberties. As argued in Chapter 1, this development provided the fertile ground for the formation of three major national social movements—the MOJA, the APFA, and the PAL. In addition, various student and worker groups were organized throughout the country. Importantly, the various pressure groups individually and collectively launched political conscientization campaigns that were based on excoriating critiques of the pathologies of the ruling class. Importantly, the Tolbert regime's political liberalization program ignited a divisive debate within the ruling class. The so-called political reform faction led by President Tolbert argued that political reforms were indispensable to the survival of the state and the ruling class. However, the "pro–status quo faction" headed by Chief Justice James A. A. Pierre contended that the institution of political reforms would jeopardize the maintenance of the neocolonial state's stranglehold and ultimately undermine the dominance of the ruling class. Sensing and feeling the effects of his regime's political reform program, especially its implications for the future of the neocolonial state and its ruling class, President Tolbert abandoned the project and sought to adopt the repressive style of his predecessors, especially President Tubman. Unfortunately, it was too late, as the seeds of political reform were now fully planted and widespread. The April 14, 1979, crisis provided vivid evidence that the neocolonial state was in danger of collapse.

Taking advantage of the escalating crisis of legitimacy in which the neocolonial Liberian state was enveloped, the military staged a coup on April 12, 1980. The expected outcome was that the neocolonial state would have been deconstructed, rethought, and democratically reconstituted. Unfortunately, Samuel Doe and his military junta accepted the neocolonial construct as a given, and thus made no effort to reconstitute it. So, clearly their major interest was in regime change and not in state transformation. Disappointingly, even some of the leaders of the two major reform movements—MOJA and PAL—who were incorporated into the military-led leadership structure, were contented with the change of personnel. This provided ample evidence that the fundamental thrust of the reform movement of the 1970s was to liberalize the neocolonial state. Under the Doe military junta, the repressive capacities of the state were enhanced by, inter alia, the introduction of political murder as an instrument for dealing with those ousted disgruntled members of the ruling class who refused to accept Sergeant Doe's leadership of the compradorial class, the recalcitrant members of the ruling People's Redemption Council, and the so-called rebellious members of the subaltern classes. For example, several renegade members of the ruling military council led by Vice Chair General Thomas Weh Syen were arrested and imprisoned on the fabricated charge of "plotting to overthrow the Doe regime" and subsequently executed.

Having consolidated his status as the new leader and spokesperson of the ruling class, Sergeant Doe turned his attention to the consolidation of his power and rule by seeking the Liberian presidency during the 1985 postcoup election. Sergeant Doe manipulated the electoral process and ultimately rigged the election. Thus, on January 6, 1986, the military regime was officially transformed into a civilian one with Samuel Doe as the twentieth president of Liberia. However, there were no fundamental changes in the country's political economy. For example, the state continued to be authoritarian. The impact of this development on the citizenry was worsened by the continuing deteriorating social and economic crises. Significantly, the inability of the Doe regime to effectively manage and address the lingering crises of underdevelopment engendered by the state led to the further erosion of the regime's authority. By the late 1980s, there were glaring signs that the process of state collapse had reached its lowest point. Thus, the stage was set for Charles Taylor and his National Patriotic Front (NPFL) to launch the insurgency that ultimately degenerated into the first Liberian civil war. In 1990, the neocolonial Liberian state finally collapsed.

The Portrait of the Liberian State

The development of the settler and neocolonial Liberian state produced a portrait that embodied the essence or raisons d'être of the construct—the nature, mission, character, values, institutions, rules, processes, and policies. The substantive contents of the various aspects of the portrait reflected the particular complexion of the state—settler and neocolonial. In this part of the chapter, each aspect of the portrait is examined. In its settler form, the nature of the state was alien: It reflected the cultural and historical experiences of the United States and the settlers. This was reflected in the design of the major pillars of the settler state—the 1847 Constitution, the flag, the seal, and the motto. Interestingly, the transition to neocolonialism did not fundamentally alter the nature of the state. Basically, the nature of the Liberian state remained a reflection of the external realities.

Also, the mission of the settler state was threefold. At the core was the protection of the general and collective interests of the settler stock. For example, this was reflected in the state's designing and implementing of discriminatory policies against the indigenes who resided under its jurisdiction. Correspondingly, the state was charged with the task of protecting the settlers from rebellious and insurrectionist activities by the indigenes. Also, the state had the responsibility of privileging the members of the commercial wing of the ruling class in their competition with European merchants. Another essential element of the settler state's mission was to pander to the particularistic interests of the pole of the settler stock and faction of the ruling class that had control over the state's machinery at any given time. In its neocolonial complexion, the mission of the state was to foster the private accumulation of capital by the members of the ruling class, the protection of the interests of the external wing of the ruling class—the owners of foreign-based multinational corporations and other businesses—and facilitating the narrow interest of the dominant faction of the ruling class at particular junctures.

In terms of the character, the settler construct had multiple orientations, including authoritarian, repressive, predatory, criminalized, negligent, and prebendal. At particular conjunctures, one or more of the aspects of the state's character was ascendant (Agbese, 2007). In other words, the dominant aspect of the settler state's character at any given time was contingent on the imperative that needed to be addressed. For example, in cases in which the state's survival was threatened by the subaltern classes, the authoritarian and repressive aspects of the construct's character became dominant.

Over the course of its evolution, the Liberian state reproduced a set of values designed to both rationalize and sustain its existence. A full examination of the panoply of values is beyond the scope of this chapter. Instead, the chapter will discuss some of the major values that were reproduced by the imperatives of the development of the state in both its settler and neocolonial incarnations. The political economy of the settler state was based on two major pillars: caste and class. The resultant values were segregation and discrimination, the sanctity of private property, and limited government (until 1869). When the settler state was transformed into a neocolonial construct, class became the anchor of the political economy. Accordingly, the incipient values reflected the imperatives of the Liberian brand of

Setting the Stage: The Travails of the Liberian State

peripheral capitalism: the sanctity of private property and state power as a vehicle for the private accumulation of wealth. After the crackdown carried out by the Tubman regime, which resulted in the development of an authoritarian peripheral capitalist state, a corresponding set of values were reproduced. I refer to this set of values as the "Liberian Way." Since 1955, the Liberian Way has embodied the following politico-economic values:

- *The criminalization of the state*: The use of ones position in the state bureaucracy as an instrument for the private accumulation of wealth became canonized.
- *The abhorrence of competition*: The dislike of competition in the economic and political spheres—"a monopolist mindset."
- *Impunity*: State officials are not held responsible for their unsavory behavior—spanning a broad gamut of actions anchored on the abuse of power.
- *Masochism*: The practice of rewarding those who inflict pain and harm on citizens.
- *Sycophancy*: The tendency of engaging in acts of deception.
- *Flamboyance*: The obsession with form over substance.
- *Nepotism*: The use of nonmerit-based standards especially in the conduct of public affairs.
- *Antisystem*: The abhorrence for established rules and procedures.

The various public institutions were designed to serve as the superstructure of the state. In this vein, the performance of their respective functions was conditioned by the state's relationships with the various tiers of the caste system (under the settler state) and classes (under the neocolonial state). In both incarnations of the state, public institutions were designed to foster the interests of the dominant stock or class. For example, the settler state was used to impose the domination of the Americo-Liberians over the indigenes. Similarly, the neocolonial state was used on various occasions to suppress strike actions by workers in the interests of the external wing of the Liberian ruling class—the owners of Firestone Plantation Company, LAMCO, Bong Mining Company, and the like.

Also, the rules that were used to conduct the affairs of the state reflected the imperatives of the construct. That is, the rules, even if they appeared "democratic" on the surface conformed to buttressing the state's capacity to undertake both economic and political reproduction. Under the settler state, the rules were designed to ensure the operation of the embryonic peripheral capitalist system and its associated relations of production, and to foster the overall interests of the dominant stock and ruling class. Similarly, under the neocolonial state, the various rules governing issues such as the right of workers to organize and strike, private investment, and criticism of the government were designed to protect the interests of the ruling class.

Similarly, like the rules, the various processes governing issues such as adjudication, the awarding of state contracts, and employment in the public sector were reflective of the texture of the state. Both the formulation and the operation of the various processes were tailored to the interests of the various dominant forces that shaped the development of the Liberian state at various historical conjunctures. For example, during the initial stage of the state formation phase, the members of the Americo-Liberian stock—both light-skinned and dark-skinned—were guided by the doctrine of civic humanism. Among other things, the doctrine emphasized the ownership of private property, preferably in land, economic independence from the state, and the demonstration of ethical behavior in the conduct of both private and public affairs (Green, 1986). Accordingly, the various processes that were designed to serve as the crucibles for conducting the affairs of the state reflected the dictates of the doctrine. However, when the foundation of indigenous capitalism was destroyed by international finance capital, the emergent processes reflected the imperatives of the times.

In terms of public policies, both the settler and the neocolonial Liberian states designed approaches—political, economic, social, cultural, and so on —that ostensibly were to ensure the continual survival of the construct; to promote the interests of the settler stock and the ruling class as a whole; and to foster the particularistic agendas of the dominant tier of the caste-cum-class system and the faction of the ruling class at particular historical conjunctures. Although the various custodians of state powers and their respective regimes formulated and implemented policies based on the specific circumstances confronting the state, the commonality in policies of all of the regimes was that the maintenance of the settler and later neocolonial complexion of the state was paramount.

The Liberian State as the Arena of Social Struggles

Since the inception of the Liberian state, the construct has served as the battleground for social struggles, which were consequences of contradictions in the political economy. In the settler state, the social struggles pitted the Americo-Liberian stock against the various indigenous ones; the light-skinned against the dark-skinned settlers; one region against another; and various sections of the subaltern classes against the ruling one. For example, the light-skinned and the dark-skinned settlers were locked in fierce competition over the control of state power. Under the neocolonial or peripheral capitalist state, the struggles have been between the ruling class, on the one hand, and the various subaltern classes, on the other. For instance, on April 14, 1979, a coalition consisting of members of the petit bourgeois, working, peasant, and lumpen proletariat classes organized a massive demonstration to protest the antipeople policies of the ruling class.

Interestingly, the state played various roles in these struggles. Essentially, the specific role the state played was dictated by the stage of development of the formation and its political economy. For example, during the early years of the postindependence era, the relative autonomy of the construct gave it flexibility to mediate the conflicts between the two poles of the Americo-Liberian stock and the various factions of the dominant class. In these struggles, the state took actions against the interests of various factions, so as to serve the overall interests of the Americo-Liberian stock and the dominant class. In its neocolonial phase, particularly with the loss of its relative autonomy, ruling class power equals state power. That is, with the state as the primary source for the private accumulation of capital, the construct and the ruling class became fused.

Finally, the various contradictions that were inherent in Liberian state led to the steady germination and nurturing of multifaceted development crises—political, economic, social, and cultural—over the course of the evolution of the state. Since the contradictions that induced the crises of underdevelopment were so fundamental and intrinsic to the core of the formation, the state could not address them within the context of the construct. Accordingly, the state used an assortment of measures or "conflict inhibitors" to prevent an implosion. However, by 1989, the decimation of the fabric of the state occasioned by the contradictions and the attendant multifaceted crises of underdevelopment inherent in the formation reached an all time high. Thus, the stage was set for the occurrence of the first Liberian civil war.

Conclusion

This chapter, the epicenter of the book, has attempted to discuss the pedigree of the Liberian state. First, the chapter briefly examined the three clusters of indigenous polities—Kwa, Mande, and Mel—that were in existence in the Grain Coast, before the arrival of the repatriated African Americans and the establishment of Liberia. The central purpose was to decipher the conflicts that developed between the settlers or the Americo-Liberians and the indigenes as consequences of the two stocks' divergent approaches to statecraft and its attendant cultural, economic, political, and social systems.

Second, the chapter discussed the development of the Liberian state during the colonial and postcolonial—settler and neocolonial—phases. The emphasis was on the forces and factors that shaped each phase and the associated stages, the contradictions that emerged, the ways these contradictions were addressed, and the outcomes. In other words, consideration was given to issues such as the raisons d'etre for the creation of the colonial and postcolonial Liberian states—why and how was the state created during each of the phases? And what were the various dynamics that attended the process?—and the various challenges and opportunities.

Third, on the basis of the development of the Liberian state, a portrait of the formation encompassing its nature, mission, character, values, institutions, rules, processes, and policies was developed. The portrait reflected the imperatives of the various phases of the development of the states, especially the conjectural factors that shaped each stage. Ultimately, the portrait mirrored the vision of the dominant forces during the various phases of the development of the Liberian state.

Finally, the chapter briefly maps out the various social struggles that have taken place in the state arena. Specifically, the nature, forces, and dynamics of the various struggles were deciphered. Importantly, the role of the state as a mediator of conflicts—class and others—was examined. In each conflict, the role of the state was determined by the stage of development of the construct, including the caste and class forces.

Notes

1. The idea is borrowed from Samuel Huntington's seminal work on *The Clash of Civilizations*. When applied to the Liberian context, the term has a more expansive meaning: It refers to the multidimensional epic civilizational struggle—cultural, economic, political, social, and religious—between the indigenous Liberian ethnic groups on the one hand, and the repatriated African Americans or Americo-Liberians or settlers, on the other. The crux of the struggle was the dialectical tension produced by the effort of the settlers to impose, to paraphrase Edwin Wilmot Blyden, a "poorly learned version" of "American civilization" on the various indigenous ethnic groups, and the resultant resistance by these ethnic groups.
2. The "Greenleaf Draft" was written by Simon Greenleaf, Professor of Law at Harvard University.

3. Later, the name of the Liberian Frontier Force was changed to the Armed Forces of Liberia.
4. Bula Mutari is a Belgian expression that means the "crusher of rocks." Against this background, the application of the term to the Liberian experience is designed to underscore the authoritarian core of the post–"Barclay Plan" formation.

PART III: THE CRISES OF UNDERDEVELOPMENT

CHAPTER 4

The Crisis of Political Underdevelopment

Introduction

The relationships between and among the various tiers of the caste-cum-class structure during the era of the settler state and the class system during the neocolonial formation produced various contradictions in the Liberian polity. The state attempted to manage and resolve these contradictions at various conjunctures. But, given the characteristic nature of the state as the handmaid of the dominant ethnocultural stock and class, its policies instead sharpened these contradictions and generated the crisis of political underdevelopment. That is, as the settler state was established in response to the interests of the Americo-Liberian stock, state intervention in settler-indigenes conflicts was designed to protect and serve the overall interests of the former. Similarly, during its neocolonial phase, the Liberian state has always intervened on behalf of the dominant class. Significantly, these actions on the part of the Liberian state tended to exacerbate the political crisis underlying these conflicts. So, in essence, the political crisis that has bedeviled the Liberian state, since its creation in 1847, worsened as the formation evolved.

Against this background, this chapter examines the nature and dynamics of the state-generated political crisis that enveped Liberia from 1847 to 1989, and contributed to the country's first civil war. In other words, the chapter explores both the complexion and the substantive contents of the political crisis, their historical development.

The Constitutional Architecture

The 1847 Constitutional Order

The 1847 constitutional order was an attempt to replicate the American one. This was quite interesting because the settlers attempted to recreate the semblance of the American constitutional order that had not only excluded them but also regarded and treated them as subhumans. The Constitutional Convention examined the American federal constitution and the constitutions of some of the states in the American federation (Burrowes, 1998). The resultant constitutional framework was based on the "American presidential system of government" and its attendant doctrines of "separation of powers," "checks and balances," and "judicial review."

The 1847 constitutional order had several flaws that contributed to Liberia's perennial political crisis. The texture of the constitutional order did not represent the objective realities and the indigenous historical and cultural experiences of the country. One of the vivid cases was the wording of the preamble to the constitution: "We the people of the Republic of Liberia were originally the inhabitants of the United States of North America" (Constitution of Liberia, 1847). As Boley (1983: 28) observes, "[t]he Constitution of the First Liberian Republic did not evolve out of the natural conditions and surroundings and/or orientations of the Liberian experience." Instead, the settlers sought to impose a constitutional architecture on Liberia that reflected the historical and cultural experiences of the United States.

Furthermore, the settlers had limited knowledge of, and training in the operation of the "American presidential system of government." Therefore, they imposed a governmental framework borne out of the historical experiences and vision of another environment on theirs. Operationally, the settlers' limited knowledge of "American presidentialism" hampered their ability to both run the system and to apply it to the Liberian experience.

Another problem was that the constitutional order legalized the "apartheid-like" system by denying indigenous Liberians citizenship and thus the right to participate in the political process. Instead, citizenship was reserved for the members of the settler stock—light-skinned and dark-skinned—and the Congos. So, the indigenes became, to paraphrase Mamdani (1996), "subjects." As subjects, the indigenes were required to pay taxes and to perform an assortment of public works tasks without representation and compensation. However, in the early 1900s, citizenship was granted to indigenous Liberians on the basis of the exigencies of the development of the settler state. The major imperative was the effort by British and French imperialism to undermine the settler state by fomenting rebellion among the indigenes who were "subjects not citizens of Liberia." Hence, the granting of citizenship to the indigenes was designed as a response to the British and French imperial strategy of "divide, conquer, and rule."

Also, the constitutional framework was plagued with gender bias. The crux was that only men had the right to vote and to contest for public office (Constitution of Liberia, 1847, Article 1, Sec. 11). The discrimination against women reflected the chauvinistic orientation of the state-building project. A central element of the male-dominated cosmology was "gender roles." Matters such as statecraft were regarded as the exclusive domain of men. The major function of women was to "stand behind the men" by performing sundry utility functions—from the private to the public realm. Even after women were granted the right of suffrage in the mid-1940s, the praxis of entrenched male chauvinism made the legal change essentially nominal. Although women were thereafter granted the right to vote and to contest for public office, they did so under the suzerainty of men.

Class bias was one of the major flaws of the constitution. For example, only those who possessed property were eligible to vote (Constitution of Liberia, 1847, Article 1, Sec. 11). This meant that even if a citizen met the age eligibility requirement to vote, he or she had to be propertied, to exercise his or her franchise. Also, candidates for the presidency, the senate and the house had to fulfill various property requirements (Constitution of Liberia, 1847). In effect, the constitutional order privileged the propertied over the non-propertied.

Another shortcoming was the nurturing of "presidential imperialism." This was done through granting the president extensive appointment powers. For example, the president appointed virtually all local officials—superintendents, district commissioners, and the like. Beginning with the "Barclay Plan," even traditional chiefs were required to hold presidential commissions as the basis of their authority. That is, though the traditional chiefs were elected by their various ethnic groups, the president could remove them from office at his discretion. Moreover, under the constitution, the president had the authority to appoint both the commissioned and noncommissioned officers in the armed forces and the officers in the security establishment, as well as sheriffs, marshals, and bailiffs.

The 1986 Constitution

The 1986 Constitution attempted to address some of the flaws of the erstwhile constitutional order as a way of helping to address Liberia's perennial political crisis. One of the major ways was by changing the preamble to reflect the totality of the experiences of Liberia's various classes and ethnic clusters and groups (Constitution of Liberia, 1986). Also, the property requirement was removed as a basis for the eligibility to vote. Another effort was the establishment of various public commissions for curtailing the expansive realm of presidential appointive powers (Sawyer, 2005a; Sawyer, 2005b). However, the provision was removed by the Doe regime from the final draft of the constitution (Sawyer, 2005a; Sawyer, 2005b). Also, in the armed forces, presidential appointment was limited to commissioned officers from the rank of lieutenant and above.

Despite these efforts, the 1986 Constitution has some major flaws that contributed to the country's political crisis. Presidential appointive authority remained quite extensive. For example, the president retained the authority to appoint all local officials (besides mayors and other municipal officials)—county superintendents, assistant superintendents, district commissioners, and the like.[1] In addition, the president still appoints all the officers of the various security services as well as all sheriffs, marshals, and bailiffs.[2] Moreover, the president appoints virtually all civil servants.[3] Importantly, the retention of the extensive presidential appointment powers continued to give the president vast patronage powers and control over the legislative and judicial branches of the government. Another drawback is the continual monetization of the eligibility requirements for contesting the presidency and vice presidency. Under Article 52, candidates for the offices of president and vice president must, among other things, have a minimum of $25,000.00 in unencumbered real estate holdings (Constitution of Liberia, 1986). In a country enveloped by abject poverty and deprivation, only the economically well off can meet such a requirement. Hence, the two offices have class bias: Only the members of the ruling and petit bourgeois classes can contest the positions of president and vice president, because only they can afford the property requirement. Also, a major flaw of the constitutional order is that the president and the members of the legislature have very long terms of office. In the case of the president, the tenure is six years with eligibility to run for a second term; senators have unlimited terms of nine years each; and representatives have tenure of six years per term for an indefinite number of terms. Collectively, these extensive terms of office undermined accountability by insulating these public officials from periodic check and scrutiny by the electorate through the holding of elections at reasonably established time intervals. Moreover, these public officials developed a negligent attitude toward the needs of the citizenry. This was because they realized that their extensive terms of office were long enough for them to engage in the private accumulation of capital by pillaging and plundering public resources. So by the time elections came around, these officials could use their ill-gotten wealth to buy the votes of the poverty-stricken electorate.

The Governance System

The governance system reflected the imperatives of the state-building project in Liberia. That is, the types of governance system that were established at various time intervals were responses to the texture of the state and its relationships with the various forces that made up the caste-cum-class system during the settler phase and the class structure during neocolonialism. Against this background, between 1847 and 1989, there were three governance systems. The apartheid-like one was operational from 1847 to 1906. Under this arrangement, there was political liberalization and its associated freedoms of speech, assembly, association, thought, press, and religion within the strictures set by the discriminatory state construct. Only the citizens of Liberia—excluding the majority indigenous ethnic groups—could exercise these rights and freedoms. Clearly, this governance genre generated contradictions, especially as consequences of the antagonistic relationship between the state and its dominant settler stock, on the one hand, and the indigenous ethnic groups, on the other. The resultant conflicts were hoisted on the underlying political crisis that attended the state formation process from its inception.

The semblance of the liberal democratic system of governance was in effect from 1906 to 1955. Under this rubric, because citizenship was extended to the majority indigenous population after more than six decades of exclusion from the political process, the apartheid-like core was legally expunged. Accordingly, political rights and freedoms were extended to all citizens, irrespective of their ethnic and class backgrounds. Significantly, the semblance of a liberal democratic environment was subordinated to the imperatives of the neocolonial state and its peripheral capitalist economy. For example, the citizens' exercise of political rights and freedoms did not fundamentally alter the inequities and the associated exploitation that were inherent in the country's peripheral capitalist mode of production. In other words, the peripheral capitalist mode of production and its relations of production were "givens" around which the system of liberal democratic governance operated. In short, on the one hand, the system of liberal democratic governance created an environment in which Liberians exercised their political rights. But, on the other, the governance architecture promoted and defended an unjust, unfair, and exploitative socioeconomic system that is based on peripheral capitalism. In short, the various political freedoms were essentially procedural rather than substantive.

The post-1955 "Tubmanic crackdown" heralded the establishment of an authoritarian system of governance. Under this arrangement, suppression, repression, and state-sponsored violence, among others, became the dominant features of state-society relations. Basically, because the neocolonial state had assumed a "Bula Mutarian" orientation in its development, there was the need to correspondingly establish a governance architecture that could cater to the agenda of the state and its dominant class.

When William R. Tolbert ascended to the presidency, after serving as Tubman's vice president for almost two decades, he attempted to change the system of governance by introducing political reforms. One of the major "changes" was the decision that the state and its regime would respect the political rights and freedoms of Liberians. This occasioned a shift (temporary) in the governance system from authoritarianism to liberal democratic. As discussed in chapter 1, this development led, inter alia, to the birth of various national and sectoral social movements. When the Tolbert regime realized that its "political reforms" were detrimental to the imperatives of the neocolonial state and the interests of its dominant class, it reverted to the authoritarian system of governance. Amid the increased state of suppression, the neocolonial state and its ruling class were stunned by massive demonstrations organized by an alliance of the national and sectoral social movements on April 14, 1979. Characteristically, the neocolonial state and its custodians responded to the mass demonstrations with brute force. Among other things, several people were killed and wounded. The "post-April 14" era witnessed a wave of state-sponsored repression against the various national and sectoral social movements. The ostensible goal of the ruling class was to stop the process of the decomposition of the neocolonial state.

About a year later, a coup was staged by 17 noncommissioned officers led by Master Sergeant Samuel Doe. The fact that all of the coup-makers were members of the subaltern classes raised the expectation among Liberians, especially the national social and sectoral movements, that the putschists would democratically reconstitute the neocolonial Liberian state, including its authoritarian governance structure. But, within less than six months after the military coup, it became abundantly clear that the putsch was essentially a change of regime and thus did not represent an ideological shift. Accordingly, as it has been argued, the People's Redemption Council (PRC), the ruling military junta, retained the neocolonial state, including its authoritarian governance architecture. In fact, under the PRC, the authoritarian panoply was extended to include politically motivated murders. For example, in November 1985, Robert Phillips, an engineer who was a member of the opposition Liberian People's Party (LAP), was murdered by the Doe regime's death squad. Similarly, after the abortive coup on November 12, 1985, that was led by General Thomas Quiwonkpa, one of the leaders of the April 12, 1980, coup, a former senior member of the PRC and former Commanding-General of the Armed Forces of Liberia, the Doe junta undertook a "scorch the earth campaign" against Nimba County, the former general's home region. Hundreds of innocent people were killed. When Doe transformed himself from a military to a civilian despot in January 1986, the authoritarian governance system remained the framework for conducting the affairs of the state.

The Conflict of Interest in the Public Sector

Another major element of the crisis of political underdevelopment was the pervasiveness of conflict of interest in the state bureaucracy. The problem was manifested in many ways. One major way was that some government officials simultaneously engaged in private legal practice. For example, the Firestone Plantations Company, the giant rubber multinational corporation, retained the legal services of Richard Henries, Speaker of the House of Representatives, and Senator William V. S. Tubman, Jr., Chair of the Senate Foreign Relations Commission. These two government officials and others used their positions in the state bureaucracy to undermine the course of justice. This was because judges, in their attempts to protect their jobs, were fearful of ruling against the clients of prominent government officials. For example, in various cases involving aggrieved workers and the Firestone Plantations Company, the company's well-connected lawyers, who were also prominent officials of government, were able to get intimidated judges to rule in favor of the multinational corporation.

Also, various multinational corporations and other businesses rendered favors to government officials. For example, during the 1960s and 1970s, the Firestone Plantations Company allotted special trucks to transport the latex from the farms of presidents Tubman and Tolbert respectively. Both presidents, who simultaneously were "rubber farmers," used the presidency to get special treatment from Firestone. The fact that Firestone bore the cost of transporting the two presidents' latex gave them an advantage over the nonpolitically connected rubber farmers, who had to bear the cost of transporting their latex and other rubber products to Firestone for sale. Importantly, as a *quid pro quo* for the preferential treatment it accorded presidents Tubman and Tolbert, Firestone received sundry favors from the Liberian government. In addition, the relationships between Firestone and other multinational corporations operating in Liberia, on the one hand, and Firestone and Liberian government officials—including the president—on the other, were vivid demonstrations of the mutually reinforcing linkages between the economic and bureaucratic wings of the Liberian ruling class.

Moreover, the conflict of interest manifested itself in state officials using their positions to secure an unfair advantage for their private businesses vis-à-vis others. One way in which this was done was by government officials, who were simultaneously business people, using their positions to commandeer state contracts to their private firms. This was one of the major vehicles used by the members of the bureaucratic wing of the Liberian ruling class to engage in the private accumulation of wealth at the expense of the state. Also, state officials used their positions to undermine, undercut, buy out, and squeeze other firms out of business—a clear example of "monopoly peripheral capitalism" in the Liberian political economy. One of the major examples of this strand of the conflict of interest was exhibited in 1974, when Stephen Tolbert, the minister of Finance in the government of his brother President Tolbert, and owner of the giant Mesurado Group of Companies, tried to run Auriole Enterprises, which was owned by the prominent Weeks Family (part of the ruling class), out of business. Albert Porte, the late veteran crusader for democracy and social justice in Liberia, captured the essence of this genre of conflict of interest thus: "The Mesurado Group of Companies . . . is buying up, pushing out of business, and 'gobbling up' by questionable, unethical tactics many growing and well-established businesses, some of them Liberian-owned and managed(Porte, 1974: 1).

Fraudulent Elections

In Liberia, fraudulent elections were designed to serve two major purposes. In the bizarre "competitive" types, fraud was intended to give one faction of the ruling class an edge over the other faction or factions in their epic "life and death battles" for control of state power. Since the emergence of the state as the major employer and source for the private accumulation of wealth in 1869, fraud and chicanery became part of the electoral process as various factions and fractions of the compradorial sector of the ruling class tried to outmaneuver one another for control of the state machinery. This development was occasioned by the fact that the control of state power correspondingly meant the control of economic power. Hence, the political parties representing the various factions of the ruling class pursued different strategies ostensibly designed to win elections through fraudulent means. Several elections were instructive. During the 1923 presidential election, the ruling True Whig Party "won" 45,000 votes, after some 6,000 people had qualified as eligible voters (Buell, 1965: 714–715). Similarly, during the 1927 presidential election between Charles D. B. King, the incumbent and flag bearer of the ruling True Whig Party, and Thomas J. R. Faulkner, the candidate of the opposition People's Party, the qualified electorate was 15,000 (Brown, 1941: 62). The People's Party allegedly won 9,000 votes, while the ruling True Whig Party won 243,000 votes (Brown, 1941: 62). *The Guinness Book of World Records* lists the 1927 presidential election as one of the most fraudulent in the world. Similarly, during the 1955 presidential election, the incumbent President William V. S. Tubman, the presidential candidate of the ruling True Whig Party, "garnered" 244,873 votes, while the opposition "received" 1,182 votes. Again, in 1959, President Tubman "received "530,566 votes to 55 votes for W. O. Bright, the so-called independent candidate. During the 1985 electoral season, fraud was used in the various phases. The fraudulent process began with the appointment of the ad hoc elections commission without broad-based consultation. This was because given Master Sergeant Doe's desire to consolidate his rule, he appointed an election commission that was led by the late Emmett Harmon, a "grand master of political trickery." Under the leadership of Chairman Harmon, the election commission proceeded to organize a fraudulent electoral process. First, political parties were required to pay $150,000 as the fee for obtaining legal status. This financial requirement was enshrined in the elections laws because Chairman Harmon and the elections commission were aware that given their pathetic financial state, the two potential political parties—Liberian People's Party (LPP) and the United People's Party (UPP)—that would pose a threat to Sergeant Doe's presidential ambition could not meet the requirement. Second and related, when it became apparent that the two potential parties were able to mobilize the registration fee, Sergeant Doe moved to ban them from participating in the elections. Third, in order to give the electoral process, including the elections, legitimacy, Sergeant Doe instructed the election commission to permit the Liberian Action Party (LAP), an amalgam of members of the local bourgeois and petit bourgeois classes, to register. Given the class base of the LAP, it was not difficult for it to raise the required $150,000 registration fee. Fourth and interestingly, when Sergeant Doe realized that the LAP could defeat his National Democratic Party of Liberia (NDPL) by benefiting form the "protest votes," he financed the registration of the Liberian Unification Party (LUP) and the Unity Party (UP) founded by William Gabriel Kpolleh, a public school teacher, and Edward B. Kesselly, a member of the Liberian ruling class. In Doe's calculation, LAP, LUP, and UP would compete with one another and eventually divide the opposition vote. Hence, his "base of support" would then be sufficient for him to "win" the presidential election. Fifth, after the voting was done, the preliminary results indicated to Sergeant Doe that he had lost the presidential election to Jackson Doe (no relation), the candidate of the LAP and a longtime member of the ruling class. In his fury, Sergeant Doe ordered the burning of ballots belonging to the LAP (Seyon, 1988). Furthermore, in contravention of the elections laws, he ordered the chairman of the election commission to establish a 50-member vote counting committee; the membership of the committee was drawn primarily from a pool of Sergeant Doe's supporters (Seyon, 1988). Sixth, the so-called special vote counting committee declared Sergeant Doe the "winner of the presidential election" with "50.9%" of the votes (Seyon, 1988). In a classic display of chicanery, the results were certified by the election commission; and Sergeant Doe was officially declared the "winner" and the twentieth president of Liberia. But, independent assessments uniformly indicated that Sergeant Doe lost the presidential election to Jackson Doe, the candidate of the LAP.

Another major raison d'être for holding fraudulent elections in Liberia was that they served as instruments of legitimation, even within the framework of a one-party system. Basically, the ruling class used fraud to inflate the number of votes to assert the legitimacy of these noncompetitive elections. In turn, the fraudulent results were used to make the claim that the ruling class and its various regimes had mandates to rule from the "overwhelming majority" of the Liberian electorate. During the 1963, 1967, 1972, and 1975 presidential and legislative elections, the candidates of the ruling True Whig Party ran unopposed. Nevertheless, the elections were still fraudulent (Kieh, 1988a: 206). For example, there were no voters' registries, voters were allowed to cast ballots as many times as they desired; and the results exceeded the number of eligible voters (Kieh, 1988a: 206). For example, during the 1975 presidential election, the total votes of more than 700,000 "received" by President Tolbert, the incumbent and candidate of the ruling True Whig Party, dwarfed the number of eligible voters by approximately 200,000 (Kieh, 1988a: 206).

Cumulatively, the various fraudulent elections contributed to the political crisis that had enveloped Liberia over the years. One of the major effects was that Liberians became convinced that fraudulent elections were contests between and among various factions and fractions of the ruling class for control of the state power. And in all of the outcomes, the "winning faction or fraction" of the ruling class pursued an agenda that was primarily beneficial to the members of a particular faction or fraction. The members of the subaltern classes, the majority of the electorate, were being used as pawns in the "electoral games" between and among the various wings of the ruling class. Also, the subaltern classes came to the realization that since the elections were usually fraudulent, the electorate's will could never triumph. This widely held view helped to further erode public confidence in the state and its electoral process, thereby contributing to the country's political crisis.

The One-Party System

The imposition of a de facto one-party system under the suzerainty of the ruling True Whig Party in 1955 affected the Liberian polity in various ways. It consolidated the authoritarian system of governance as the framework for conducting the affairs of the evolving neocolonial Liberian state. Also, it helped to develop and foster the widely held belief that the ruling class had closed the final outlet for promoting mass participation in the political process. In addition, the one-party system dealt a fatal blow to the prospects of establishing meritocracy in the public sector. Consequently, the ruling True Whig Party became the bastion for dispensing prebends and patronage. Accordingly, those who had an interest in public service were forced to join the True Whig Party. Interestingly, the True Whig Party became a predatory force that used its domination of the state machinery to engage in "rent-seeking" behavior with groups and individuals that conducted business with the state. Also, state workers were forced to routinely "contribute" portions of their salaries to underwrite the operations of the True Whig Party.

Significantly, the impact of the excesses of the one-party state on the country's crisis of political underdevelopment and the ultimate stability of the state was so profound that it triggered dissension within the ruling class. By the mid-1970s, C. Abayomi Cassell, an "enlightened member" of the ruling class, led a brief effort to establish a competitive party system. Cassell and his fellow "enlightened members" of the ruling class were cognizant of the fact that the one-party system was helping to hasten the process of state decomposition. Accordingly, Cassell and company made the determination that by establishing a rival political party, the rising tides of state collapse could have been arrested. However, faced with strident opposition from the myopic members of the ruling class, who were contented with the status quo and impervious to the long-term implications for stability, Cassell abandoned his idea of forming a new opposition political party.

When President Tolbert assumed the leadership of the country and launched his so-called political reform program, there was hope among the various subaltern classes that the conditions would be created for the establishment of a competitive multiparty system. One of the major tests of the Tolbert regime's "political reform agenda" came in early 1980: The Progressive Alliance of Liberia (PAL), one of the country's national social movements, announced its plans to organize an opposition party to the ruling True Whig Party. Since there was no law banning the organization of opposition political parties, PAL followed the legal process for the organization of political parties as enshrined in the Constitution of Liberia and the Elections Laws of Liberia. Among other things, PAL collected the required 300 signatures of eligible voters—18 years and older and property owners—and presented its documents for probation to Judge Gladys Johnson of the Probate Court of Montserrado County. After reviewing the documents, Judge Johnson made the decision that all of the legal requirements had been satisfied. Accordingly, she probated the Progressive People's Party (PPP) as Liberia's first opposition political party in more than two decades. However, the ruling True Whig Party was quite unhappy with the development. One major indication was the fact that various barons of the ruling party berated Judge Johnson for helping "sow the seeds of instability" by registering PPP. In addition, two months after its legal registration, the True Whig Party–led National Legislature of Liberia banned PPP. In protest, PPP tried to organize a protest. In response, the Tolbert regime arrested and imprisoned the leaders of PPP on the charge of treason. Importantly, this action by the ruling class and its regime effectively ruined any hope about establishing a multiparty political system.

Using the excesses of the ruling True Whig Party as one of its reasons, the Liberian military staged a bloody coup on April 12, 1980 in which President Tolbert was killed. Thereafter, 13 high officials of the Tolbert regime and the ruling True Whig Party were publicly executed. One of the promises made by the new military junta led by Master Sergeant Samuel Doe was that the foundation for the establishment of a multiparty party system within a pluralistic political framework would be laid. So, when the ban on political activities was lifted in mid-1984, the expectation was that a vibrant multiparty system would be established. However, as has been argued, Sergeant Doe's ambition to become president within the larger context of the campaign for regime consolidation modulated the establishment of the "new multiparty system." So, by 1985, although there were three opposition political parties—Liberian Action Party (LAP), Liberian Unification Party (LUP), and the Unity Party (UP)—and the "ruling" National Democratic Party of Liberia (NDPL), the "culture of the one-party system" remained intact. This was because the Doe regime created hurdles and obstacles that made it very difficult for the opposition political parties to function effectively, and for the overall multiparty system to flourish. One of the major impediments was that the opposition political parties were denied the right to use public facilities for conducting their affairs. Also, media outlets were unwilling to serve as outlets for the dissemination of information about the opposition parties for fear of recrimination from the Doe regime. In fact, the *Daily Observer*, a major newspaper, experienced the Doe regime's "wave of terror," when it decided to publish news stories about the opposition: The newspaper's headquarters were destroyed by agents of the Doe regime. Another obstacle was the unmitigated "wave of repression" that was directed at the opposition parties. For example, some of the members of the opposition were arrested and imprisoned by the Doe regime. Others were forced go into exile. Also, the Doe regime prevented the opposition parties from cooperating. For instance, in 1986, the opposition parties attempted to organize a cooperative framework called the "grand coalition." Fearing the impact of such a mechanism, the Doe regime threatened the leaders of the opposition with arrest and imprisonment if they proceeded with the formation of the coalition. In addition, the officials and members of the opposition parties were routinely harassed and intimidated by state security agents and hired private thugs of the Doe regime. Another lacuna was that employment in the state sector—new and continuing—was contingent upon membership in the ruling National Democratic Party of Liberia (NDPL). The determination of membership in NDPL was made by the possession of and the display of the party's membership card, when required to do so. Since the state was the major employer, some members of the opposition party who had or were seeking employment in the public sector had to decamp to the ruling NDPL. This helped to erode the membership bases of the various opposition parties.

The "Hegemonic" Presidency

The "hegemonic" presidency was one of the major contributing factors to the crisis of political underdevelopment that plagued Liberia. The phenomenon was occasioned by a confluence of factors. The foundation for the establishment of the "hegemonic" presidency was laid by the "Barclay Plan" in 1904 (see chapter 3 for a detailed discussion of the plan). Fearful of the destabilizing effects of the rebellious activities of the various indigenous ethnic groups and the imperialist agendas of Britain and France on the settler state, the powers of the president were expanded. The Barclay Plan was the embodiment of the first systematic effort to expand the ambit of presidential authority. Specifically, the Barclay Plan established presidential suzerainty in the administration of the hinterland by, among other things, giving the president unfettered authority over the extensive local government administrative apparatus consisting of district commissioners, chiefs, and later superintendents.

Another source was the expansive appointment powers under the constitution. Under both the 1847 and 1986 constitutions, the president was given sweeping appointment powers covering the executive and judicial branches of government. In the executive branch, the president was given the power to appoint cabinet ministers, deputy and assistant ministers, the heads of various agencies, ambassadors and consuls, among others. In the judicial branch, the president had the power to appoint the justices of the supreme court, the judges of the subordinate courts, sheriffs, and bailiffs, among others. Sawyer (2005c: 3) summarizes the president's broad appointment powers thus:

> The President of Liberia exercises sweeping constitutional powers of appointment of executive and judicial officials—For example, except for mayors and traditional chiefs, all executive officers are appointed by and serve at the pleasure of the president; the entire judiciary is appointed by the president. A president who appoints prison wardens, sheriffs, district commissioners, county attorneys, the minister of justice, and all members of the judiciary has in his hands the legal authority to shape the rule of law and the course of justice.

The extensive scope of presidential appointment powers, especially in the absence of effective legislative oversight, made the president the hegemon in the state bureaucracy. As the hegemon, all public officials at all levels of the bureaucracy served at the will and pleasure of the president. So, the president could, inter alia, appoint anyone to any office, irrespective of qualifications and competence. Correspondingly, the president could dismiss any public official, including civil servants. Also, the president became a "Tammy boss" who controlled and dispensed patronage on his whims and caprices.

A compliant legislature contributed to the establishment of presidential suzerainty. The legislature did not provide oversight. For example, presidential appointments were made without the required "advice and consent of the Senate." In fact, presidential appointees to various positions in the executive and judicial branches were never subjected to confirmation hearings. Moreover, the president never consulted the Senate in the making of these appointments. The modus operandi was for the president to make an appointment and claim that it was done with the "advice and consent of the Senate." Also, the legislature transferred some of its powers to the president, in contravention of the constitution. For example, the "power of the purse" was under the purview of the president. For example, the president exercised sole control in determining periodic allotments of public funds to all agencies of government through a centralized warrant system of disbursements (Sawyer, 2005c: 3). Also, the legislature routinely granted the president "emergency powers," again in violation of the constitution. Under the 1847 Constitution, only the legislature could exercise "emergency power" under extraordinary cases. Under the illegally granted "emergency powers," the president was given carte blanche to violate political freedoms and civil liberties with impunity. For example, under the "Emergency Power Act," the legislature regularly granted the president the power to suspend the writ of habeas corpus (Cordor, 1979: 77). Also, the president was empowered to ban suspicious organizations and to create special courts to deal with offenders such as those counseling or influencing or attempting to incite violence that may subvert, disturb, and upset the economic, social, and political stability and security of the state (Cordor, 1979: 77). Also, law enforcement officers were empowered to search any house or place without warrant and to arrest and detain, for as long as the emergency powers were in force, without trial (Cordor, 1979: 77). Characteristically, various presidents used the "Emergency Power Act" to terrorize the opponents of the neocolonial state and its ruling class. For example, in some cases, student and labor leaders were arrested and detained for indefinite periods of time without trial.

Another factor was the one-party system. As the standard bearer of the True Whig Party, the president handpicked the party's candidates for the legislature. This included incumbents, who were desirous of retaining their seats. With such enormous powers, the president chose senatorial and representative candidates who were pliant, loyal, and obedient to his dictates. Since the legislative elections were noncompetitive, those chosen by the president as the candidate of the ruling True Whig Party automatically became senators and representatives. The power to choose the members of the legislature meant that presidential proposals were simply rubber stamped by the legislature. Moreover, the ruling True Whig Party had a rule that prohibited legislators, who were members of the party, from opposing proposals submitted by the president on either the floor of the Senate or the House of Representatives. Alternatively, legislators who had points of disagreement with presidential proposals were required by the party's rules to submit their views to the president. Similarly, under the "one-party dominant system" from 1986 to 1989, the legislature served as a "rubber stamp body" for President Doe's various proposals. This was because both chambers of the law-making body were dominated by the members of the ruling NDPL, who were selected personally by President Doe. The opposition members of the legislature were intimidated by the prospects of being victimized by state terror if they raised objections against presidential proposals. In addition, opposition legislators were fearful that given their small numbers they would have been impeached by the NDPL-dominated legislature, if they had opposed President Doe's various proposals. Wreh (1976: xi) laments the subservience of the legislature to the presidency thus:

> Under Tubman's rule, there was no countervailing power from the people or from the constitutionally created National Legislature . . . [an institution] which should

provide the checks and balances to the executive branch. . . . Unchallenged and unfettered, Tubman had everything to himself and ruled as he pleased.

Also, the judiciary was subservient to presidential authority. This was because positions of the judges were at the mercy of the president. With a weak and pliant legislature, the president could direct the legislature to impeach a judge without any problem; hence, the judges were quite fearful of issuing verdicts on the legal merits of cases in which the president had personal interests. Instead, judges crafted their verdicts in such cases around the outcomes preferred by the president. For example, it was quite common, especially during the Tubman regime, for the president to call a judge who was handling a case in which the former had an interest and dictate the verdict. With such an enormous leverage over the courts, the president was unrestrained by the constitutionally imposed limitations on his powers. This was because the president was assured that even if his actions were challenged under the "Doctrine of Judicial Review," the compliant judiciary would rule in his favor.

Another contribution was the factor of "deification of the president." Beginning in 1955, the president came to be portrayed as "omnipotent," "omniscient," and "omnipresent." The "deification syndrome" was demonstrated in various ways. Presidential edicts were accepted with unquestioned obedience because the president was regarded as "all knowing" and "incapable of making errors." Hence, it was regarded as "political heresy" to disagree with and/or disobey a decision of the president. Also, the president could interfere in people's personal matters—marital and others. Again, since the president was regarded as infallible, people were required to abide by his decisions, even regarding their private lives. Importantly, the "deification of the president" found expression in various realms. For example, as Liebenow (1969: 153–154) observes, "Government subsidization of the adulation of the president is everywhere, in the erection of his statutes at various points in the country, the naming of bridges, streets and public buildings after the president, his wife or his mother."

The Violation of Human Rights

One of the major dimensions of the character of both the settler and neocolonial Liberian state is repression. Historically, the state has intervened on the side of the dominant group. During the heyday of its settler phase, the state intervened on numerous occasions in attempts to cow the indigenous stock and the various subaltern classes under the caste-cum-class system into submission. For example, the state routinely used the military to subjugate rural dwellers who opposed tax policy, especially against the backdrop that virtually no benefits were being accrued to the rural areas. Similarly, the state employed force to collect taxes in the hinterland. This was principally done through the use of various repressive methods—beating, torture, and so on—by the military.

Also, before being granted citizenship, the indigenes were required to pay taxes, but without representation. Since the constitution did not regard the indigenes as citizens of Liberia (before 1905), they were debarred from participating in the political process through voting, contesting for public office, and involvement in any other political action. Despite this, the state coerced the indigenes to fulfill the tax obligations that were inherent in citizenship.

Similarly, the indigenes were forced by the state to provide their labor free of charge for various public projects. In addition to the exploitation of their labor, the state subjected the indigenes to inhuman working conditions such as exposure to hazardous materials that adversely affected their health. By and large, the various public works projects were undertaken to benefit the Americo-Liberian stock and the dominant faction of the ruling class. So, in effect, the indigenes were coerced to provide their labor for projects that did not improve their material conditions.

The establishment of the Firestone Plantations Company in Liberia in 1926 was fraught with various human rights violations. At the core of the abuses was the use of the power of the state to force farmers from their land to make way for the planting of rubber trees on one million acres. The affected farmers were never compensated for their lands by either the state or Firestone. Clearly, this violated the "law of eminent domain" because private land was seized by the state for use by a private multinational corporation. Also, the power of the state was used to forcibly recruit thousands of Liberians from the hinterland to work for Firestone. These people were forced from their villages, towns, families, and their vocations and transformed into the base of the emerging Liberian working class. Their living conditions were appalling. For example, the workers' quarters on the various divisions consisted of thatched roof mud houses with one long hallway, no electricity, no plumbing, and no running water. With regard to compensation, the workers, especially the tappers, were paid "chicken feed." For example, by 1980, the average rubber tapper was earning less than a $1.00 per day for eight hours of work involving tapping more than 400 rubber trees and physically transporting the latex to various central collection stations on the company's 45 divisions.

Another example of human rights violation was the Fernando Po Crisis. (Sundiata, 1980). In 1929, three prominent members of the bureaucratic wing of the ruling class—President Charles D. B. King, Vice President Allen Yancy, and Post Master General Samuel Ross—sent Liberians as slaves to labor on plantations owned by members of the Spanish bourgeois class in Fernando Po. As slave laborers, the Liberians were subjected to myriad inhumane treatments. The act and the attendant human rights violations were so egregious that the League of Nations launched an inquiry through the "Christie Commission." After an investigation, the Commission indicted the three Liberian compradors for their role in perpetrating the diabolical scheme. Eventually, all three officials were forced to resign. But, unfortunately, the three officials were not brought to justice. Also, the Liberian state did not pay damages to the exploited workers for the subhuman conditions to which they were subjected in Fernando Po.

In terms of the freedom of association, the state denied agricultural workers the right to unionize. This meant that the workers employed at the various rubber plantations could not establish labor unions to champion their causes. The decision by the state to deny agricultural workers their fundamental human right of the freedom of association was based on the personal interests of members of the ruling class, who were owners of rubber plantations: These members of the ruling class were fearful that if agricultural workers were allowed to exercise their freedom of association, the members of the agricultural sector of the ruling class would be forced to pay their workers decent wages and provide them with human living conditions. In terms of political associations, in 1951, the Tubman regime outlawed the Reformation Party, the principal opposition political party, and forced its leaders into exile. Four years later, the Tubman regime established a *de facto* one-party system in Liberia, thereby denying Liberians their right to organize political parties. Even in 1980, when the opposition Progressive People's Party was organized, the state took swift action to ban the party and to arrest its leaders on trumped-up charges. During the Doe regime, Executive Order #2 outlawed the establishment of student governments on the campuses of institutions of learning—from the elementary to the tertiary level. Also, the Liberian People's Party (LPP) and the United People's Party (UPP), the two most popular political parties in Liberia during the 1980s, were debarred from registration and participation in the 1985 presidential and legislative elections.

Also, the state routinely violated the rights of Liberians to express their views, including disagreement with state policies, freely without recrimination. Beginning in 1955, the state suppressed the right of Liberians to speak freely. Although the constitution guaranteed the freedom of speech, those who dared to exercise it, especially when it was the expression of views that were critical of the government, were harassed, intimidated, dismissed from their jobs, arrested, tortured, and imprisoned. For example, Albert Porte, the veteran human rights crusader, was arrested and imprisoned on various occasions during the 1950s and 1960s for criticizing the policies of the Tubman regime. Also, in 1978, the Tolbert regime ordered the arrest and detention of several leaders of the University of Liberia Student Union for the issuance of a statement critical of the visit of U.S. President Jimmy Carter to Liberia. During the same year, the Sedition Law was passed, which made it a crime to criticize an official of government. Similarly, during the Doe regime, several student leaders were arrested, detained, and sentenced to the firing squad by a military tribunal for criticizing the military junta. However, in the midst of the domestic and international pressure, the Doe regime was forced to release the students. In 1984, the ruling military regime enacted PRC Decree #88A, which made it a crime to criticize an official of government.

Another dimension of the violation of human rights was state's suppression of the freedom of assembly. For example, on April 14, 1979, the state employed the use of force to prevent a coalition of national and sectoral social movements from holding demonstrations to protest the state's decision to increase the price of rice, the country's staple food, and the general policies of the state. As a consequence of the state's action, hundreds of people were killed and wounded by state security personnel, who had been given "shoot to kill orders" by the president of Liberia. Subsequently, the state arrested and detained 33 leaders of the coalition on the charge of treason. After domestic and international pressures were brought to bear on the Tolbert regime, the pro-democracy activists were released. Also, in 1981 during the rule of the military junta, PRC Decree #12 made it illegal for workers to undertake strike action.

Similarly, during the period of the "post-Tubmanic crackdown," the state recurrently violated the right to the due process of law of those who were accused of committing "political crimes." One of the most famous cases was the "Fahnbulleh Trial." In 1968, Ambassador Henry B. Fahnbulleh, the Liberian plenipotentiary to East Africa, was accused by the state of high treason. The charge resulted from an alleged meeting between Ambassador Fahnbulleh and a Chinese diplomat. While the case was pending in the Supreme Court of Liberia, the ruling True Whig Party mobilized people to hold demonstrations condemning Ambassador Fahnbulleh. Wreh (1976: 111) describes the blatant violation of the "due process of law" thus:

> While the case was still subjudice, the counties of the nation were turned out, bearing resolutions denouncing Fahnbulleh. The people of Cape Mount County, Fahnbulleh's home county, were made to march in a mammoth demonstration in Monrovia to condemn, deprecate and denounce as vicious the plot of the former ambas-

sador and disassociate themselves from the iniquitous plan to overthrow a "stable and progressive government."

The judiciary ignored the miscarriage of justice and proceeded to find Fahnbulleh guilty of high treason (Kieh, 1989a: 43). He was sentenced to 20 years in prison (Kieh, 1989a: 43).

Table 4.1
Liberia's Human Rights Index, 1972–1989

Year	Political Rights	Civil Liberties	Status
1972–1973	6	6	Not free
1973–1974	6	5	Not free
1974–1975	6	3	Partially free
1975–1976	6	4	Partially free
1976–1977	6	4	Partially free
1977–1978	6	4	Partially free
1978–1979	6	5	Partially free
1979–1980	6	6	Partially free
1980–1981	6	6	Not free
1981–1982	6	6	Not free
1982–1983	6	6	Not free
1983–1984	6	5	Partially free
1984–1985	6	5	Partially free
1985–1986	5	5	Partially free
1986–1987	5	5	Partially free
1987–1988	5	5	Partially free
1988–1989	5	5	Partially free

Source: Compiled from Freedom House, *Freedom in the World Country Ratings, 1972–2002* (New York: Freedom House, 2002).

Table 4.1 provides Liberia's human rights index for about two decades. According to the data, during the first three years of the Tolbert regime, Liberia remained enveloped in morass of authoritarianism. But, during the last six years of the regime, there was some slight improvement in the areas of civil liberties. In the case of the Doe regime, state suppression of political rights was quite high from 1980 to 1985. During the same period, the violation of civil liberties was quite high from 1980 to 1983. From 1984 to 1989, state violation of political rights and civil liberties experienced a very small decrease (from a score of 6 to 5 for most of the period). However, because the decrease was not significant, state violation of human rights—including political rights and civil liberties—remained the norm.

Conclusion

The chapter examined the various dimensions of the crisis of political underdevelopment in Liberia. Specifically, it began with a discussion of the flaws in the 1847 and 1986 constitutions; the flaws include the denial of citizenship to the indigenes and the class and gender biases.

Next, the chapter mapped out the general outlays of the various governance systems—the apartheid-like, quasi-liberal democratic and authoritarian genres—that have been used to conduct public affairs in Liberia, since the creation of the state. Another major issue discussed was the adverse impact of conflict of interests on ethics in the public sector.

This was followed by an assessment of the effects of fraudulent elections in hastening the pace of state decomposition. The vagaries of the one-party system were examined, especially their roles in the suffocation of the development of political pluralism. Another issue was the cascading effect of the "hegemonic" presidency."

Finally, the chapter examined the violations of human rights—both "first" and "second "generation rights. The central conclusion is that the various dimensions contributed to the creation, maintenance, and exacerbation of the political crisis over the period of the development of the Liberian state.

Notes

1. The draft of the 1986 Constitution prepared by the Constitutional Commission had a provision under which the president was to appoint local government officials such as superintendents from a list of candidates vetted by the county council (Sawyer, 2005a; Sawyer 2005b). However, this was removed from the final version of the document by the Doe regime–controlled Constitutional Advisory Assembly.
2. Also, the draft 1986 Constitution included a provision for a Judicial Service Commission that would have attempted to establish a vetting system for the appointment of judicial officials by the president. At least, this would have helped to "check" presidential appointive authority. Again, this provision was removed from the final version of the document by the Doe junta-controlled Constitutional Advisory Assembly.

3. The draft 1984 Constitution stipulated the establishment of a Public Service Commission as the bulwark for the establishment and operation of a meritorious civil service. Characteristically, the Doe regime–controlled Constitutional Advisory Commission removed this proviso from the final version of the constitution.

CHAPTER 5

The Crisis of Economic Underdevelopment

Introduction

The founders of the Liberian settler state envisioned the establishment of a political economy built on the capitalist mode of production dominated by an indigenous entrepreneurial class. Consistent with the theology of classical market-based economics, there was to be a "minimalist state" with a limited regulatory role in the economy. In essence, the economy was to be controlled by private interests in the form of either sole proprietorships or corporations. Accordingly, the state was designed to protect the embryonic indigenous capitalist class from the imperialist forays of Britain and France, as well as from competition from the more affluent and strategically positioned metropolitan firms. This was the framework that guided the operations of the embryonic Liberian capitalist economy for the first two decades of the postindependence era (1847–1868). This period saw the emergence of an embryonic indigenous capitalist class that was engaged in a broad variety of businesses, such as agriculture and commerce. The booming domestic economy, inter alia, helped to boost the state's revenue base. Also, the state was relatively autonomous. This enabled it to become independent from the dictates of particular factions or fractions of the evolving local ruling class, so that it could effectively serve the general interests of the ruling class as a whole.

However, by 1869, the Liberian economy began to experience shocks and their associated problems. At the global level, on the basis of the cyclical imperatives of international capitalism, the prices of Liberia's major exports began to experience precipitous decreases. Similarly, at the domestic level, indigenous businesses began to lose market share to metropolitan competitors. Cumulatively, various indigenous businesses were forced to close down. For the state, this meant the corresponding loss of tax revenues. Significantly, the inability of the settler state to formulate and implement the requisite policies to address the effects of the economic shocks laid the foundation for the country's descent into economic crisis. Eventually, the emerging indigenous capitalist class disintegrated, thereby dealing a severe blow to autonomous capitalist socioeconomic development. Concomitantly, the state lost its "relative autonomy" and became a direct pawn in the resultant struggles between and among the various factions and fractions of the nonhegemonic ruling class (Gramsci, 1994; Fatton, 1988). Since 1869, the ruling class has taken various steps to address Liberia's economic problems; however, these measures have failed to address the country's underlying crisis of economic underdevelopment.

This chapter attempts to decipher the nature, depth, and dimensions of Liberia's crisis of economic development. The various efforts by the ruling class to address these problems are also considered. In short, the chapter's major question is, what were the scope and dynamics of Liberia's economic crisis of underdevelopment during the pre-1989 era?

The Structure of the Economy

The crisis of economic development was rooted in the structure of the Liberian economy—the mode of production, the relations of production, the role of the state, the mainstays of the economy, and the relationship to the international capitalist system. During the era of the settler state, the mode of production was embryonic peripheral capitalism. Under this arrangement, the major means of production—land and so on—were privately owned. From 1847 to 1869, the factors of production were controlled by an emerging indigenous capitalist class. After the collapse of this class for reasons explained earlier, metropolitan firms took control of and owned the major means of production.

The relations of production revolved around a class system embedded in a caste framework. In other words, given the attention paid to skin pigmentation and ethno-cultural background during this period, there was convergence between the skin color and class. Essentially, ethno-cultural factors overlapped with class (Burrowes, 1982). In effect, this meant that the light-skinned settlers occupied the upper tiers of both the overarching caste system and the class arrangement. Accordingly, the light-skinned settlers were at the commanding heights of the Liberian economy. Specifically, they controlled and dominated the major sectors of the economy, such as commerce. The middle tier consisted of the dark-skinned settlers, who were principally involved in the agricultural sector of the economy. In addition, an appreciable number of them were artisans. The lowest stratum had two tiers. The upper tier was occupied by the Congos or the recaptives. Occupationally, the majority of the members of this segment were indentured servants who worked in the homes of the settlers. The lower tier comprised the indigenes who were living under the jurisdiction of the Liberian state as "subjects" (Mamdani, 1996). Basically, these indigenes were laborers—forced, contract, and so on. Their labor was exploited by both the state and the members of the upper and middle tiers of the caste-cum-class system. Given the competing interests of the different strata, various contradictions ensued. In turn, these contradictions led to conflicts between and among the various tiers of the caste-cum-class system.

The settler state was a creation of the Americo-Liberians. As has been argued, like all other states, it was designed to serve the general interests of the settler stock. The state relied on taxes—business, hut, and so on—as the principal source of its revenues. The settler state performed several functions. Its core function was to serve the overall interests of the dominant class. This was reflected in its partisan interventions in the various class-based conflicts that occurred. Another function of the state was the maintenance of law and order. The state protected the persons and properties of the members of the upper and middle classes from the rebellious activities of the disadvantaged, exploited, and marginalized subaltern classes. Also, the state provided protection from the antiexpansionist countermeasures that were taken by the various independent indigenous polities in response to the territorial encroachment of the former. Another major role was the protection of the economic wing of the ruling class from the so-called competitive threats posed by metropolitan firms.

The mainstays of the economy were camwood and ivory. These products were sold to the metropolis in their raw and unprocessed forms. Consistent with the dynamics of the boom-and-bust cycle of capitalism, the emerging Liberian indigenous capitalist class accrued profits during the initial two decades of the postindependence era. In addition, water transportation was an important sector of the local Liberian economy. A portion of the emerging local capitalist class was well invested in this sector.

The relationship between the settler state and the global capitalist system was characterized by the domination of the former by the latter. The relationship had its genesis in the commencement of the process of formally integrating the settler state into the international capitalist system through trade. The global capitalist system provided the framework through which the settler state participated in the "international division of labor" and the "system of unequal exchange" with the metropolitan powers. As Amin (1974: 8) argues, "The underdeveloped countries form part of a world system, and that the history of their integration into this system forged their special structure—which henceforth has nothing in common with what prevailed before their integration in the modern world." The resultant special feature of the Liberian economy was its peripheral nature. In other words, with the commencement of the integration, the global capitalist system began to fashion the Liberian economy as an appendage. Internally, the conditioning occasioned a transformation of the Liberian economy that was consistent with the imperatives of the global capitalist system. Within the structure of the international division of labor, the settler Liberian state was assigned the role of producing raw materials such as camwood for consumption by the metropolis. This was linked to the system of unequal exchange, under which the raw materials produced by the settler Liberian state were priced lower than the manufactured goods from the metropolis. Accordingly, Liberia received less for its raw materials but was required to pay more for the finished products from the metropolitan powers.

Importantly, the emergence of the neocolonial Liberian state in 1926 witnessed the concomitant transformation of the structure of the economy. Although the mode of production remained peripheral capitalism based on private ownership, two of the major factors of production—capital and labor—experienced some changes. For example, there was an unprecedented infusion of private capital into the economy. Beginning with the Firestone Plantations Company, various multinational corporations—B.F. Goodrich, Bong Mining Company, Liberian Mining Company, and LAMCO—invested millions of dollars in the Liberian economy to facilitate their respective private investments. This, inter alia, helped to establish international capitalism's stranglehold over the Liberian economy. Also, the period heralded the origins of the Liberian working class and the system of wage labor.

The resultant relations of production were based on a class system that emphasized the individual's relationship to the major means of production and the state. Five major classes emerged: the ruling, petit bourgeois, working, peasant, and lumpen classes. The ruling class consisted of two sections: internal and external. The membership of the internal wing comprised state managers (the bureaucratic bourgeoisie) and private entrepreneurs from divergent ethnic, regional, religious, professional, and gender backgrounds. The external tier consisted of the owners of the multinational corporations, such as Firestone and Bong Mining Company, who owned and controlled the major means of production. Hence, a patron-client relationship existed between the external (patrons) and the internal (clients) wings of the ruling class. Accordingly, the principal role of the internal wing was compradorial: it created a conducive atmosphere for international capitalism. Specifically, the bureaucratic bourgeoisie section of the internal wing or the compradorial class served the interests of the external wing and international capitalism in general in two major ways. First, it used the power of the state to subordinate Liberia's development needs to the profit-seeking agenda of foreign capital. For example, it provided foreign businesses with tax breaks and duty-free privileges that deprived the country of revenues required for development. Between 1980 and 1984, of the $430 million that should have been paid on nonexempt items by foreign businesses, the Liberian government received a paltry 10% or $43 million (Jeffy Commission, 1985: 56). Similarly, the compradors allowed foreign businesses to repatriate their profits without restrictions. Second, and a corollary, the comprador class suppressed the rights of workers as a strategy for ensuring the accumulation of capital by foreign businesses. For example, the LAMCO Mine Workers' Union was denied legal status by the Liberian state from the early 1960s to 1970s. Also, from 1926 to 1980, the workers at Firestone were denied the right to form a single labor union. In addition, the state enacted several antilabor laws. The most draconian one was PRC Decree No. 12. This legislation, which was passed in 1980, made it a criminal offense for workers to strike. These measures enabled foreign capital to accelerate its maximization of profits by paying workers low wages and in most cases not providing them with fringe benefits. The compradors regularly employed the state's instruments of coercion—the police and the armed forces—to quell labor protests against foreign capital. Some of the most prominent cases were (1) the Firestone workers' strikes of 1961, 1964, and 1975; (2) the LAMCO workers' strike of 1978; and (3) the Bong Mining Company workers' strike of 1979. Cabral's (1969:101) general description of the compradors in the African context is germane to the Liberian case: "A pseudo-bourgeoisie controlled by the ruling class of the dominating country . . . thus the local bourgeoisie, however strongly nationalistic it may be, cannot effectively fulfill its historic function; it cannot freely direct the development of the productive forces."

The petit bourgeois class principally consisted of the intelligentsia and entertainers. The members of this class earned their livelihood by selling their labor to the ruling class. Significantly, in the 1970s, some members of this class forged an alliance with some members of the working and peasant class to institute political reforms in Liberia.

The working class was employed primarily in the agricultural and the mining sectors. The members of this class were responsible for the production of the wealth, which was privately appropriated by the owners of the multinational corporations. Because the members of this class were the most exploited, some of them sought additional income as farmers—hence, they simultaneously belonged to the peasantry.

The peasant class consisted of the farmers. Some of them earned their living mainly through subsistence agriculture; others (those who produced cash crops such as coffee and cocoa) sold their products to state enterprises and foreign businesses. Both the state and the forces of international capitalism exploited the peasants by underpaying them for their products.

The lumpen class comprised the unemployed and the hoi polloi. Some members of this class engaged in sundry criminal activities for economic survival. Given the precarious economic position of the members of this class, they were vulnerable to the manipulations of the ruling class. For example, the ruling class used the lumpens on various occasions as hired thugs to intimidate, harass and even harm those who were opposed to the vagaries of the ruling class. The most prominent case was the use of the lumpens during the 1985 national elections to terrorize voters, as a means of coercing them to vote for Sergeant Doe and his National Democratic Party of Liberia (NDPL).

The neocolonial Liberian state performed several functions. At the base was the protection of the interests of the members of the external wing of the ruling class. As has already been argued, this was achieved, among other ways, by giving the forces of global capitalism preferential treatment in the form of tax breaks, tax holidays, and duty-free privileges and by protecting multinational corporations and suppressing the Liberian working class by, inter alia, making it very difficult for the latter to strike. In those cases in which workers engaged in strike action, the state unleashed the full battery of its instruments of coercion to suppress the workers. Also, the state protected the members of the internal wing of the ruling class from mass protests by legislating repressive laws and unleashing its forces of terror when the state and its custodians were challenged by a subaltern class or classes. Interestingly, by the early 1970s, when foreign capital began to reduce its investment in the Liberian economy, the state sought to fill the void by trying to create jobs through the massive expansion of the public bureaucracy (the creation of several public corporations) and extensive borrowings from the metropolis.

With the "open door policy" and the attendant influx of foreign capital into the Liberian economy, the focus of the production process became oriented toward the needs of global capitalism. Specifically, Liberia became an export enclave or a "plantation" for the production of raw materials to feed the industrial and manufacturing complexes of the metropolitan powers. Accordingly, the Liberian economy had a narrow base that was reliant on the production of iron ore, rubber, and timber, all of which were exported in crude form (United Nations Development Program, 1999: 7). The extractive subsector as a whole accounted for almost 20% of GDP in the 1980s; it also accounted on average for approximately 70% of public revenue and approximately 60% of total export earnings (United Nations Development Program, 1999: 7). In a similar vein, iron ore accounted for 58% of total exports in 1988, followed by rubber at 29.2%, timber at 8.9%, diamonds and gold at 2.2%, and coffee and cocoa at 1.6% (United Nations Development Program, 1999: 7). The narrow base of the economy had some adverse consequences that worsened the crisis of economic underdevelopment. Liberia was largely dependent on global trade. Also, multinational corporations and other foreign businesses became the major sources of employment, state revenues, and domestic capital formation.

With the finalization of its incorporation into the global capitalist system as a peripheral state, Liberia joined the "club of subordinate players" whose relationships with the metropolitan powers were governed by the inequitable international division of labor and the system of unequal exchange. Accordingly, the international capitalist order conditioned the Liberian economy so that the latter could perform its subordinate role. Baran's (1988: 97) remarks on the deleterious impact of global capitalism on Africa and the third world in general are applicable to the Liberian case:

> [Capitalism] introduced [in Africa] and other third world [regions], all the economic and social tensions inherent in the capitalist order. . . . It substituted market contracts for such paternalistic relationships as still survived from century to century. It reoriented the partly or wholly self-sufficient economies of agricultural countries toward the production of marketable commodities. It linked their economic fate with the vagaries of the world market and connected it with the fever curve of international price movements.

So, as an appendage of the international capitalist system, the peripheral capitalist Liberian economy had certain basic characteristics. First, it lacked an industrial base. It was primarily an export enclave. It produced raw materials—iron ore, rubber, forest products—that were used to facilitate the development of the United States and the other advanced capitalist countries, while neglecting the production of goods and services for domestic consumption.

Second, the economy is dualistic: it is divided into monetized and traditional sectors. The former sector is quite small and is dominated by multinational corporations and other foreign businesses. It is the locus of economic activities. The latter revolves around subsistence agricultural activities. However, since the influx of private foreign investments in the mid-1920s, the rural peasants have been forced off their land so that foreign businesses can use it for the production of cash crops for export. For example, Firestone was given one million acres of land to grow rubber for export.

As a consequence, the peasants were constrained to engage in the production of some cash crops on the meager remaining available land to service the monetized sector of the economy.

Third, there are no intersectoral links among the various areas of the economy: the economy is disarticulated. Consequently, the limited technology that has been introduced by foreign capital is concentrated in the monetized sector, with no spillover to the traditional sector. In short, the use of the technology is tailored toward the specific activities of the multinational corporations; it is not designed to spur development in the broader economy.

Debt Bondage

In response to the economic crisis that engulfed Liberia at the end of the 1860s, the state managers relied on the international capitalist system to provide the panacea. One of the solutions used was the contracting of loans from the metropolis. For example, in 1871, Liberia borrowed $500,000 from Great Britain at an annual interest rate of 7%. The country's customs revenues served as the collateral. To make matters worse, Britain demanded that Liberia pay indemnity of approximately $300,000 for damages to properties of British traders in the Mano River belt, as a consequence of what the British government termed the "negligent behavior of Liberia." The British government was holding the Liberian government responsible for the losses incurred by the former's citizens as a result of protest activities by some members of indigenous polities in the area. So, after paying the indemnity, Liberia was left with less than half of the original amount of the loan. From the remaining amount, the Roye administration was accused of embezzling and mismanaging substantial portions; thus, approximately 25% of the original loan actually reached the Liberian state treasury. The issue of the loan sparked a conflict within the ruling class. The merchant wing, which was committed to autonomous capitalist development in Liberia, saw the loan and the increasing involvement of foreign capital in the Liberian economy and state as antithetical to its sectional interests. In the midst of Liberia's growing economic crisis, President Roye announced that the scheduled 1871 national elections would be postponed. Also, using the burgeoning economic problems as a cover, President Roye attempted to extend the presidential term of office from two to four years. Angered by President Roye's actions, the light-skinned wing of the ruling class undertook a campaign ostensibly designed to force President Roye out of office. The National Legislature, which was dominated by the light-skinned settlers, passed a joint resolution demanding President Roye's resignation. When President Roye refused to oblige, he was impeached and subsequently imprisoned. Later, he died under mysterious circumstances.[1]

Against the backdrop of the state's general lack of a viable strategy for mobilizing financial resources, the country was gradually engulfed in a "debt trap" (Payer, 1975). After a little more than three decades, Liberia again borrowed $500,000 from various British sources. As with the first loan, the terms of payment of this loan placed Liberia at a disadvantage and worsened the country's economic crisis. Six years later, Liberia contracted a third loan of $1.7 million from American, British, French, and German sources. In a classical display of neocolonialism, the four major metropolitan powers placed Liberia under their receivership. Liberia's customs revenues were directly collected by agents of the metropolitan powers, who were stationed at various ports of entry into Liberia.

Table 5.1
Liberia's External Debts, 1950–1985 (U.S. $ millions)

Year	Debt	Debt Servicing
1950	2.5	2.5
1955	8.7	3.7
1960	46.2	6.3
1965	64.2	23.2
1970	111.3	20.5
1975	267.7	30.1
1980	701.0	25.0
1985	1,155.0	38.0

Sources: Compiled from National Planning Office, Republic of Liberia, *Annual Report, 1960–1961* (Monrovia, Liberia: Government Printing Office); Ministry of Planning and Economic Affairs, Republic of Liberia, *Economic Surveys of Liberia, 1970–1985* (Monrovia, Liberia: Government Printing Office).

Again in 1926, as part of the Firestone Concession Agreement, Liberia was forced by the United States to borrow $5 million from the American-owned Finance Corporation at an interest rate of 7% (Boley, 1983). Concerned about Liberia's growing economic dependence on Britain and other European powers, the United States used the loan from the Finance Corporation in its inter-imperialist rivalry with its fellow metropolitan powers. In essence, the United States through Firestone and the Finance Corporation wanted to restore Liberia's dependence on American imperialism.

Given its incapacity and unwillingness democratically to reconstitute the neocolonial Liberian state, the country's ruling class became increasingly reliant on the loans from the metropolis as major sources of finance for national development projects. For example, as Table 5.1 shows, Liberia's external debt jumped from $2.5 million in 1950 to $46.2 million in 1960. Even in the midst of the so-called economic boom that was caused by the "open door policy," Liberia's external debt increased to $111.3 million by 1970 (Table 5.1).

With dwindling prices for its primary exports, cost-cutting measures by the multinational corporations, including the reduction of their work forces, and the attendant reduction of the state's revenue base, the Liberian economic crisis grew worse by the mid-1970s. Again, instead of rethinking and democratically reconstituting the neocolonial state and its associated policies, the Liberian ruling class relied on external loans. For example, between 1970 and 1975, Liberia's total external debt rose by more than 200% to $267.7 million (Table 5.1). With additional borrowings, including loans to cover the enormous financial cost of hosting the annual meeting of the Organization of African Unity (OAU, now the African Union), the country's external debt skyrocketed to $701 million by 1980.

Following the examples set by its civilian predecessors, the military junta, which seized power in a coup on April 12, 1980, continued the tradition of contracting loans to help fund nonrevenue-generating activities—mainly the conspicuous consumption habits of the members of the ruling class, including those added as a consequence of the coup. Moreover, the state's revenue base was woefully inadequate to underwrite the increases in the salaries of military and security personnel and civil servants decreed by the ruling People's Redemption Council, the ruling military body. So, by 1985, Liberia's total external debt stood at approximately $1.2 billion (Table 5.1). With Liberia's deteriorating economic conditions and the inadequacy of loans to address the problems, the ruling class turned to the International Monetary Fund (IMF). Characteristically, in 1981 and 1985, the IMF subjected Liberia to its "shock therapy," centered on, among other things, the decimation of the limited "social safety net" and the reduction of salaries in the public sector by between 16.7 and 25%. As in other peripheral capitalist states, the IMF's Structural Adjustment Program (SAP) worsened Liberia's economic crisis, as evidenced, for example, by the continuing deterioration in the standard of living of the majority of Liberians—the reduction of earning power, growing unemployment, and increasing levels of abject poverty.

Predatory Foreign Investment

With the determination made regarding Liberia's suitability for the planting of rubber and the subsequent discovery of natural resources such as iron ore, the country's ruling class made the decision that the attraction of private foreign investment would help provide solutions to the country's economic crisis. Against this background, in 1926, Liberia granted Firestone a concession agreement for 99 years for one million acres of land at two cents per acre. Under the terms of the agreement, the Liberian state agreed to supply 50,000 laborers annually under a contract system to work for the Firestone Plantation (Boley, 1983: 41). So, in effect, the Liberian state became a labor recruitment agent for Firestone. As Table 5.2 indicates, by 1960, total foreign direct private investment in Liberia stood at $437 million. Five years later, the amount jumped to $750 million. By 1975, the figure grew to an all-time high of $800 million.

Although foreign private investment contributed to the provision of employment for Liberians, its overall effects reflected the perennial economic crisis. The rentier aspect of the neocolonial Liberian state became ascendant, thereby deepening the country's dependence on international capitalism. The ruling class mortgaged the country's resources to international capitalism. In turn, the so-called royalties that were paid became major sources of rent and the bedrocks of the state's revenue base. For example, as Table 5.2 shows, in 1965, the rents from foreign private investments accounted for 81.6% of the revenue base of the Liberian state.

Another problem was that foreign private investment did not address human needs in Liberia. Despite the infusion of private capital and the concomitant growth of the Liberian economy, the material conditions of the majority of Liberians did not improve. Clower et al. (1966) characterized this phenomenon as "growth without development."

Also, multinational corporations such as Firestone exploited the labor of Liberian workers. For example, by 1980, the monthly salary of a rubber tapper was less than $30 per month. Moreover, a rubber tapper was required to tap 700 rubber trees within an eight-hour period, collect the latex, and physically transport it in aluminum buckets hoisted on a bar. Furthermore, Firestone's workers were subjected to inhumane living conditions such as mud huts with thatched roofs, cramped space, no running water and electricity, and a lack of indoor plumbing facilities.

Because the various multinational corporations exploited the labor of Liberian workers, they were able to make and repatriate huge profits. For example, between 1963 and 1976, LAMCO made more than $485 million in profits, from an initial investment of approximately $250 million. LAMCO paid the Liberian state less than $100 million in royalties. Consequently, LAMCO transferred more than $385 million to the metropolis as super-profits.

Table 5.2
Foreign Private Investment in Liberia, 1950–1985

Year	Foreign Investment (U.S. $ millions)	Royalties from Foreign Investment as a Percentage of State Revenue (%)
1950	40.3	4.0
1955	60.0	48.0
1960	437.0	57.0
1965	750.0	81.6
1970	775.0	65.8
1975	800.0	65.5
1980	702.3	55.0
1985	260.0	35.0

Sources: Compiled from National Bank of Liberia, *Annual Reports, 1973–1980* (Monrovia, Liberia: National Bank of Liberia); Ministry of Planning and Economic Affairs, Republic of Liberia, *Economic Surveys of Liberia, 1971–1980* (Monrovia, Liberia: Government Printing Office); Project Division, Ministry of Finance, Republic of Liberia, *Direct Foreign Investment in Liberia, 1978–1979* (Monrovia, Liberia: Ministry of Finance); National Investment Commission, Republic of Liberia, *Private Investment in Liberia, 1978–1979* (Monrovia, Liberia: National Investment Commission).

In addition, the various multinationals demonstrated virtually no sense of social responsibility. For example, beginning in the mid-1970s, some of the multinational corporations reduced their labor forces in their search for increased profits. The labor force in the mining sector dwindled from 14,200 in 1975 to fewer than 5,000 in 1985 (Kappel et al., 1986). During the same period, Firestone reduced its workforce by 17,000—from 22,000 to 5,000. Furthermore, others such as the Liberian Mining Company folded their operations. Under both sets of circumstances, thousands of Liberians were left unemployed. In a demonstration of the lack of sensitivity to the human condition, a hallmark of capitalism, the multinationals made no effort to help the affected workers to find other viable sources of livelihood.

Trade Dependence

The mainstays of the Liberian economy post-1944 were iron ore and rubber. These products were exported in their raw forms to help satisfy the demands of the industrial-manufacturing complexes in the metropolis. The prices for the two commodities were set by the metropolitan powers. Importantly, these two commodities accounted for the bulk of the country's exports and foreign exchange earnings. For example, by the late 1980s, iron ore and rubber accounted for approximately 88% of Liberia's total exports (United Nations Development Program, 1999). Also, these two commodities accounted for almost 90% of the state's total revenue base (United Nations Development Program, 1999). Against this background, a dependency chain was established: the state relied on iron ore and rubber as its principal sources of revenues; the prices for iron ore and rubber were determined by the metropolis. So, the fate of the Liberian economy was determined by the metropolitan powers. Liberia's dependence on trade as an export enclave made it extremely vulnerable to the fluctuations that characterized the global capitalist system. Accordingly, the prices of the two commodities on which the country's economy was dependent were susceptible to changes in demand in the metropolis. When demand was high, the prices of the two commodities experienced a boom; conversely, when the demand was low, the prices of rubber and iron ore experienced a decline. For example, in 1980, the continuing decline in the prices of the two major exports was the major contributing factor to Liberia's terms of trade loss, which stood at $126.2 million (National Bank of Liberia, 1981).

The Criminalization of the State and the Private Accumulation of Wealth

As with the other manifestations of the crisis of economic underdevelopment in Liberia, the use of the state as an instrument for the private accumulation of wealth was a consequence of the evolutionary imperatives of the peripheral capitalist formation. For example, during the initial two decades of the development of the settler state, the members of the ruling class sought to accumulate wealth in the private sector. Accordingly, it was difficult to recruit members of the ruling class to work in the state bureaucracy. In essence, there was a consensus among the members of the ruling class that private entrepreneurship was the "legitimate" vehicle for the private accumulation of wealth. Significantly, the ruling class took some steps to help ensure that the state was not directly used as an instrument for primitive accumulation. One of the major methods employed was the establishment of limited tenures of office for the president, vice president, legislators, and other elected national officials.

However, when the economic base of the ruling class began to crumble in 1869, the state became the major employer and source of personal wealth. Therefore, the control of the state's machinery became a life-and-death struggle between various factions and fractions of the ruling class. Mayson (1976: 3) provides a vivid picture of the "scramble for state power":

> The settlers, particularly those residing in Monrovia, resorted to staking claims on the government bureaucracy as a means of livelihood. Whereas in former times it was difficult to get any of the respectable settlers to take up positions in government, now government jobs became the thing to have. . . . Monrovia at this time became a one industry town, that industry being government. All of the important settlers saw it as a right to have a job in government.

Against this backdrop, the members of the ruling class laid the foundation for the criminalization of the Liberian state in their quest for the accumulation of private wealth. Effectively, the state became like a warehouse from which each member of the ruling class collected his or her share of the loot (Fanon, 1965). The "buffet service" commenced with the 1871 loan that was contracted from Britain: various members of the bureaucratic wing of the ruling class took their shares of the loan. The little that was left was too paltry for meaningful national development. Thereafter, the members of the ruling class used the state in various illicit ways to accumulate wealth privately. Subsequently, the members of the subaltern classes, who occupied various positions in the state bureaucracy—the military, the police, security organizations, and the civil service—began to follow the example of the members of the ruling class. They too used their respective positions in the state sector to accumulate wealth. Overall, the emergent pervasive view and practice was that having a position, especially in a "lucrative sector" of the state bureaucracy, was the fastest and cheapest way to accumulate capital and get wealthy. So, each regime perpetuated the culture of corruption that was the bedrock of the private accumulation project. The resultant effect was the diversion of state funds to personal use through various corrupt means. For example, as Ballah (2003:11) argues, "By the end of his rule, Doe and his cronies had stolen a reported $300 million in public funds."

The Mismanagement of State Economic Resources

The mismanagement of state economic resources was another major dimension of the economic crisis that engulfed Liberia as a consequence of the imperatives of the state. Essentially, this entailed the allocation and use of state resources for nonproductive purposes—those that did not help create wealth and meet the basic human needs of the Liberian people. For example, during the Tubman administration, a 463-ton presidential yacht was purchased at a price of more than $1 million (Wreh, 1976: 18). Its upkeep required an international crew, a separate bureau within the Ministry of Foreign Affairs, and a budget of $125,000 per annum (Wreh, 1976: 18). Later, two other vessels were purchased for presidential cruises at the cost of $1.2 million each (Kieh, 1989: 43).

Similarly, during the Tolbert regime, more than $100 million was borrowed from the metropolis to finance the hosting of the 1979 Summit of the Organization of African Unity. The bulk of the money was used to construct luxurious villas and to purchase a fleet of Mercedes cars for the convenience of the visitors. Such a large sum of money was lavishly spent amid deteriorating economic and social conditions in Liberia. For example, thousands of Liberian workers had been laid off by various multinational corporations that folded their operations in Liberia and others that were engaged in so-called cost-cutting measures. The state undertook no effort to assist these affected workers. Moreover, civil servants were not being paid on time. In the social realm, there was a pressing requirement to construct new health facilities and schools to meet the needs of the Liberian people.

The Doe regime followed the tradition of wasteful and frivolous spending established by its predecessors. One of the major hallmarks of economic mismanagement during the rule of Doe and his military junta was the regular purchasing of new vehicles for members of the ruling People's Redemption Council (PRC), who had frequent accidents.

The Decline in Real Income

Beginning in the 1970s, there was a precipitous decline in real income. For example, real wages in the agricultural sector decreased by more than 50%, those in the mining sector by more than 40%, and those of civil servants by approximately 33%. In Monrovia, the capital city, approximately 60% of the working people earned wages below the official poverty line of $125 a month established for an urban family of four people (Tipoteh, 1986: 126). A similar trend continued during the 1980s. One of the major reasons was that the Liberian government, as part of the International Monetary Fund's Economic Recovery Program, reduced the salaries of public sector employees by 16.7% and 25% in 1981 and 1985 respectively. This meant, for example, that the average state employee, who was earning $200 per month in 1980, saw his or her salary decreased by 41.7% in 1985. The reduction in real income meant that it became quite difficult to purchase various essential commodities that were indispensable to people's well-being. This was because real wages were insufficient to pay for the costs of these commodities. The situation became especially difficult with the recurrent increases in the prices of basic commodities such as rice. Likewise, it became a challenge for workers who did not own their own homes to meet their rental obligations. Also, parents found it increasingly difficult to underwrite the educational and medical expenses of their families.

Unemployment

Given the orientation of the Liberian state, the custodians of state power failed to formulate and implement effective strategies for creating jobs that would have met the human needs of Liberians of working age. As Table 5.3 shows, despite occasional reductions, the rate of unemployment in the country was quite high. Although the rate of unemployment dropped from 40% in 1950 to 25% in 1955, having a quarter of Liberians of working age unemployed posed serious challenges. One of the challenges was the emergence of a lumpen class. A substantial number of the members of this class resorted to various criminal activities—selling illegal drugs, counterfeiting, robbery, and so on—as a means of earning a livelihood. Another problem was the migration of people from rural areas to the urban centers. Because the limited employment opportunities were concentrated in the urban centers, people moved to the cities, especially Monrovia, in search of employment. Cumulatively, migration led to overcrowding, housing shortages, increased sanitary problems (especially in light of the inadequacy of the facilities), and increase in crime.

In an attempt to address the high tide of unemployment, the state took two major steps. First, the state sought to attract multinational corporations and other businesses, as these would create jobs. As Table 5.3 indicates, by 1960, the height of the influx of private investment capital, the unemployment rate stood at 20%—a reduction from 25% five years earlier. But, as the subsequent periods indicate, the rate of unemployment experienced a sustained increase over the next two decades. This development was caused by the confluence of three major sets of factors. The first factor was that despite the influx of private investment capital, not enough jobs were created to absorb the large pool of unemployed people. Moreover, the various multinational corporations and other businesses wanted small workforces to increase their profits. A related point was that various multinational corporations, such as Firestone, undertook various labor reduction schemes ostensibly designed to reduce their labor costs. One of the major outcomes was the retrenchment of thousands of workers, contributing to the high rate of unemployment. Another factor was that by the mid-1970s, some of the multinational corporations in the mining sector closed their operations, claiming that the reduction in the price of iron ore in the global capitalist marketplace had adversely affected their capacity to generate profits. Accordingly, it was no longer economically tenable to maintain their operations. Again, thousands of Liberian workers were laid off, thereby contributing to the rise in unemployment.

Table 5.3
The Rate of Unemployment in Liberia, 1950–1988 (%)

Year	Unemployment Rate
1950	40.0
1955	25.0
1960	20.0
1965	35.0
1970	40.0
1975	48.0
1980	50.0
1988	36.2

Sources: Compiled from National Planning Office, Republic of Liberia, *Annual Report, 1960–1961* (Monrovia: Government Printing Office); Ministry of Planning and Economic Affairs, Republic of Liberia, *Economic Surveys of Liberia, 1970–1985* (Monrovia: Government Printing Office); UNDP, *Human Development Report, 1990* (New York: Oxford University Press, 1990), p. 156.

The second measure employed by the Liberian state, beginning in the mid-1970s, was an exponential increase in the size of the public bureaucracy in terms of agencies and positions. But this step was limited because the state could not create the required number of jobs in the public sector to absorb thousands of unemployed people. Importantly, the state's capacity was hindered by the decline in its revenue base occasioned principally by the decline in the prices of iron ore and rubber. That is, the state did not have the financial resources to pay its new employees even if it could have created the massive number of jobs required to absorb all the unemployed.

Inequities in Income and Wealth

The distribution of income and wealth captured the essence of the class-based character of the Liberian state. As Table 5.4 shows, income was distributed in a skewed manner that favored the upper class. For example, in 1985, the upper or ruling class, which accounted for 5% of the national population, received 68% of the national income. On the other hand, the lower classes, which accounted for 75% of the population, received a meager 20.2% of the national income. By the end of the 1980s, Liberia's Gini Coefficient was 0.53 (Peters and Shapouri, 1997: 45).

Table 5.4
Liberia: The Distribution of Income, 1960–1985 (%)

Year	Lower Classes in Population	Lower Classes' Share of National Income	Upper Classes in Population	Upper Classes' Share of National Income
1960	73.7	24.6	3.9	60.4
1965	73.7	24.6	3.9	60.4
1970	73.6	25.0	4.0	60.0
1975	73.6	25.0	4.0	62.0
1980	74.2	23.7	4.0	65.0
1985	75.0	20.2	5.0	68.0

Source: Compiled from the Ministry of Planning and Economic Affairs, Republic of Liberia, *Economic Surveys of Liberia*, 1970–1985 (Monrovia: Government Printing Office).

Similarly, there were inequities in the distribution of wealth. For example, before 1980, the members of the ruling class, consisting of 4% of the population, owned and controlled approximately 60% of the wealth, whereas the subaltern classes, 96% of the population, struggled over the remaining 40% (Kieh, 1997: 27; Movement for Justice in Africa, 1980). By 1985, the expanded ruling class, comprising approximately 6% of the population, owned and controlled about 70% of the national wealth (Kieh, 1997: 27).

Conclusion

This chapter examined the various dimensions of the crisis of economic underdevelopment generated by both the settler and neocolonial Liberian states. In this vein, the chapter began by probing the structure of the Liberian economy. It then mapped out other aspects of the economic crisis—the debt bondage, predatory foreign investment, trade dependence, the criminalization of the state and the resultant culture of corruption, the related mismanagement of state economic resources, the decline of real income and the associated downturn in the standard of living, the high rate of unemployment and the failed efforts by the state to reverse the trend, and gross inequities in income and wealth.

Cumulatively and in concert, these various dimensions of the economic crisis contributed to the creation of two Liberias: one Liberia consisted of the wealthy, who lived well, while the other comprised those who lived precariously on the periphery in a state of poverty, malaise, deprivation, and neglect. Importantly, the members of the latter group had no vested interest in the maintenance of the status quo. Instead, they longed for change of any type, as long as it led to the removal of the ruling class and its regime. Also, the pathetic economic conditions of large segments of the members of this group predisposed them to joining insurgency groups. As a consequence, the crisis of economic underdevelopment helped to provide two major ingredients that were pivotal to the occurrence of the first Liberian civil war: mass resentment of the ruling class and its regime and mass sympathy for the use of violence against the ruling class and its regime.

Notes

1. The light-skinned settlers, who regained control of the state machinery as a result of President Roye's so-called impeachment, claimed that the president drowned while trying to escape from prison. The counterclaim was that President Roye was assassinated at the behest of some members of the light-skinned segment.

CHAPTER 6

The Crisis of Social Underdevelopment

Introduction

Keeping with the negligent dimension of its character, the Liberian state has never made social development a priority. Although, the ruling class and its various regimes have recurrently paid lip service to social development as the foundation of national development, the rhetoric has never been translated into practice. Accordingly, over the years, the country has been gripped in a crisis of social development. Consequently, life for the majority of Liberians, especially in the subaltern classes, in the Hobbesian parlance, became "poor, nasty, brutish, and short" (Hobbes, 1996: xii).

The sordid state of social development in Liberia is vividly reflected in the educational system; health services, and related human survival areas—sanitation, access to clean drinking water, life expectancy, and mortality—the lack of adequate housing; and the challenges of gender relations. Importantly, the social development crisis has contributed to and exacerbated the broader pantomimes of human development. As the United Nations Development Program (2006: 38) notes, "Liberia's human development index has, for some time, been at the bottom of the list of countries with the lowest human development indices."

The focus of this chapter is to examine the various dimensions of Liberia's social development crisis—education, health services, and related human survival issues; housing; and gender relations. In other words, the chapter seeks to address this critical question: What are the dimensions and depth of Liberia's crisis of social underdevelopment?

Education

Fundamentally, the Liberian state has never been interested in the education of its citizens. This is because the country's ruling class has always been fearful that education would enable the members of the various subaltern classes to develop the requisite knowledge base and skills that would lead them to critically examine the anti-people and antidevelopment policies of the state. In turn, the subaltern classes could then galvanize the majority of the population against the ruling class. Moreover, the ruling class was concerned that educated members of the subaltern classes could be perceived by the mass public as alternatives for the leadership of the country. Consequently, the state did not make public education—from the elementary to the tertiary level—a priority. Hence, the weak government commitment was the main reason for Liberia having one of the weakest public educational systems in Africa (United Nations Development Program, 2004: 1).

The ills of the Liberian public educational system were reflected in several indices. At the core was inadequate access. This was manifested by the fact that all those who wanted to enroll in schools could not do so owing to the inadequacy of the number of schools. For example, at the tertiary level, since 1862, the University of Liberia has been the only four-year public institution in the country. The university lacked the capacity to enroll qualified students, especially the thousands who graduated from various high schools around the country annually. At the secondary level, the limited access adversely affected the ability of thousands of young men and women to enroll in high school. Similarly, at the primary level, scores of eligible children could not enroll in school. For example, the net enrollment at the primary level in 1989 was 32% (Government of Liberia, 2004: 20). Also, the problem of access was a major challenge in the rural areas. Because of the urban bias in the construction of the limited number of public schools that were available, thousands of school age children in the rural areas, particularly at the primary and secondary levels, could not enroll in school. For example, by 1988, approximately 0.5 million children of school age were not enrolled (United Nations Development Program, 1990: 132). Importantly, the problem of access in the rural areas was reflected in three major ways. It was quite common to have comparatively large population centers with hundreds of eligible students without the availability of any school in these areas—public or private. The other scenario was to usually have an elementary school without middle and secondary schools or elementary and middle schools without a secondary school. In such cases, those students who completed the elementary and middle school levels then had no access to secondary school. Another situation was the severe limitation of the number of public secondary schools. Basically, each county, outside of Montserrado County (the center of political power), had one high school located in its administrative capital city. The single high school was intended to serve the whole of the population of those counties. Clearly, this made it very difficult for eligible high school students, who resided outside of the county capital, to enroll in high school. This is because it would have required that these students relocate to the county capital city. The problems associated with such a venture made it quite difficult for these eligible students to enroll in secondary school; hence, hundreds of them were forced to end their educational sojourn either at the elementary or at the middle school level.

Interestingly, the state responded to the access to educational opportunities conundrum, which it created through its negligent policy, by enacting a "compulsory education policy" in 1868, 1912, 1937, and 1966 (Azango, 1968). The policy was professedly designed to compel children between the ages of 7 and 14—the primary and middle school levels—to enroll in school. But, the irony was that the state did not construct more schools to accommodate the growing student population. So, even if the policy had been stringently enforced, the number of schools available would not have been enough to accommodate all of the eligible students at these two levels. The reality therefore was that the policy was never enforced. Thus, the policy was more of a hoax designed to bamboozle the members of the subaltern classes into believing that the state and its ruling class were interested in the education of their children. Also, the state launched the "free education policy" covering from the primary to the secondary levels and the "subsidized education policy" covering the college and university levels. Under the policy, tuition was waived for students enrolled in public schools from the elementary to the high school levels. As for the "subsidized education policy," it entailed the reduction of the tuition at the William V. S. Tubman College of Science and Technology (a two-year public institution) and the University of Liberia. But, the common problem for the two policies was that they did not help to address the access conundrum. Instead, they simply enabled those students who were already enrolled to remain so. In addition, the policies benefited those students who had the opportunity to enroll in the limited number of elementary, junior high, and secondary schools and college and university.

Also, the educational system was primarily designed to reproduce the dominant peripheral capitalist ideology and its relations of production. This was done through the use of two major instruments. Distortion was used to "exalt" capitalism and to denigrate competing systems such as socialism. For example, capitalism was glorified as the only system that provides individuals with the opportunity to excel. Also, capitalism was made coterminous with democracy. In addition, alternative systems such as socialism were vilified as atheistic, undemocratic, and based on a form of "crude equality." Socialism was usually presented in the Liberian educational system as follows: Under socialism, individuals are required, for example, to share their spouses and their clothes with others. This form of cynical distortion was tailored to appeal to the students' crude sense of individualism. Interestingly, the students usually accepted these distortions as facts and embarked upon their reproduction in the families, communities, and the entire country. The related instrument was "brainwashing." Teachers transmitted capitalist propaganda in a very uncritical manner and conditioned students to accept them without questioning it. Particularly, in the absence of alternative explanations and viewpoints, the students parroted the pro-capitalist and antisocialist claims. The net effect was that students accepted the capitalist mode of production and its relations of production as providential and the "natural order of things." Accordingly, they became largely docile and compliant. The few teachers and students who dared challenge the distortion and "brainwashing" projects were branded as "troublemakers."

Clearly, the lack of access to educational opportunities contributed to Liberia's growing illiteracy rate, which stood at an alarming 65% in 1980 (see Table 6.1). This adversely affected the country's development in several ways. First, the lack of education robbed thousands of Liberians of the knowledge base and skills they required to effectively participate in the affairs of the country. For example, a vast majority of illiterate Liberians did not have the tools that could allow them to perform their civic responsibilities, including holding the ruling class and its regime accountable. Thus, the ruling class used mass illiteracy as a tool of manipulation. For example, the vast numbers of illiterate members of the subaltern classes were recurrently manipulated by the ruling class. One of the tools of manipulation that was recurrently used was the propaganda that the educated citizens, who were challenging the authoritarian rule of the ruling class, were "troublemakers." Unfortunately, the bulk of the illiterate Liberians came to believe the propaganda. In turn, this helped to undermine the struggle for reforms in the country because it drove a wedge between the subaltern classes and the pro-reform groups. Second, mass illiteracy deprived the country of the skilled human capital it needed to foster national development. Third, illiteracy made it quite difficult for those affected to be competitive in the small job market. Hence, this contributed to the high rate of unemployment and poverty.

The related problem was that within the context of limited access to educational opportunities there was gender bias. The limited educational opportunities were allotted to males. For example, in 1989, the ratio of girls to boys in primary education was 39.4%/60.6% (Government of Liberia, 2004: 22). Similarly, during the same period, at the secondary level, the secondary school ratio of girls to boys was 33.3%/66.7% (Government of Liberia, 2004: 22). Overall, this development was made possible by the fact that the Liberian polity was dominated by males and the ideology of "hegemonic masculinality."

Table 6.1
Liberia's Illiteracy Rates, 1950–1985

Year	Illiteracy Rate (%)
1950	90.0
1955	88.0
1960	87.4
1965	85.0
1970	79.2
1975	79.0
1980	65.0
1985	77.0

Sources: Ministry of Planning and Economic Affairs, Liberia, *Economic Surveys of Liberia, 1970–1985* (Monrovia, Liberia: Government Printing Office); and United Nations Development Program, *Liberia's National Human Development Report, 2006* (New York: Oxford University Press, 2006), p. 1.

Also, education was designed to reproduce peripheral capitalism and its relations of production. This was done in several ways. At the core was the presentation of capitalism as providential. That is, students were made to believe that the capitalist mode of production was designed by God; hence, human beings had no choice but to accept it and operate within its framework. Moreover, capitalism was depicted as the best socioeconomic system ever designed in the history of the human race. Accordingly, its so-called virtues, among others, of individualism and the capacity to rise from "rags to riches" were exalted. Furthermore, alternative systems such as socialism were vilified as atheistic and undemocratic. The distortion of the facts and "brainwashing" were used to socialize students. In addition, books that exalted capitalism were selected as the textbooks for the various courses from the primary to the university level. One of the major resultant effects was that students uncritically accepted the "capitalist theology" without question. In turn, they transmitted these views to the members of their respective families and communities as facts. Thus, a critical mass of docile and compliant citizens was created. Significantly, this helped to undermine the development of the requisite solidarity within the subaltern classes that was exigent for waging a successful struggle against the ruling class. Interestingly, those teachers who subjected capitalism to critical analysis and exposed students to an alternative sociopolitical system such as socialism were branded as "communists," who were bent on teaching "foreign ideology." Similarly, students who adopted this method of critical inquiry were classified as "troublemakers."

In a similar vein, the curricula were irrelevant because they sought to teach Liberian students about the historical, cultural, economic, political, and social experiences of the United States and other metropolitan powers. For example, the textbooks and the topics covered in courses in literature, history, and the social sciences were based on conditions in the metropolis rather than those in Liberia and the periphery. For example, at the elementary level, students learned about the climatic conditions in the United States. Clearly, this was not relevant to the prevailing conditions of the society in which they lived. Also, at the secondary levels, the courses in literature and the social sciences focused on actors, events, and issues in the United States and Western European states. Although efforts were made by some Liberians to write and produce books in the language arts, history, and the social sciences that sought to reflect the realities in Liberia, the dominance of the metropolitan-centered curricula remained intact. Ultimately, the Liberian educational system trained students in curricula that had no relevance to the cultural, historical, economic, social, and political experiences of Liberia.

Another challenge was the quality of instruction, especially at the primary and secondary levels. Owing to the very poor compensation packages and working conditions for public schoolteachers, many qualified Liberians sought other employment opportunities. Thus, it was commonplace for the state to employ unqualified teachers with both limited formal education and training. This problem was particularly common in the rural areas. The major resultant effect of this development was that students who were enrolled in such institutions did not acquire the academic skills and training that were required for their respective grade levels. Moreover, the problem became more acute when the students graduated from high school: Due to poor training, it became quite difficult for them to be competitive in the very small job market.

Also, overcrowding was a major problem. Because the number of schools was not adequate to accommodate the large numbers of school-age children, especially at the primary level, it was commonplace for students to be packed into classrooms beyond their capacities. In such cases, students had to either stand up or find places to sit in the very limited space that was available on the floor. Clearly, this created a poor environment that made it quite impossible for effective learning to take place.

The inadequacy of logistics, equipment, and supplies was a major problem. For example, various public schools at all levels throughout the country did not have sufficient chairs in the classrooms to accommodate students. For instance, at the University of Liberia, it was a regular challenge for students to find seats for courses with large enrollments. Linked to the problem of insufficient seating was the inadequacy of space. The number of classrooms was usually inadequate. And the existing classrooms did not have variations in size to accommodate difference class sizes. In addition, public schools lacked basic instructional equipment, which adversely affected the learning process. Moreover, there was inadequacy of basic school supplies such as blackboards and chalk. This made it very difficult for teachers to provide the desired excellent instruction. The problem was so acute that in some cases students were required to either buy the school supplies and/or pay fees to teachers to purchase them. Also, it was common for teachers to require students to purchase class notes. These problems helped to corrupt the public educational system. This is because the payment of fees for sundry requirements became a major determinant of students' "academic success" rather than actual performance.

Health and Related Issues

The inadequate and poor health facilities and related conditions throughout Liberia reflected the fact that the lives of Liberians, especially the members of the various subaltern classes, hung in a precarious balance. At the core of the country's health problem was the issue of limited access to facilities and services. For example, by 1985, only 35% of the population had access to health services (Ministry of Planning and Economic Affairs, 1985). That meant that the majority of the population—65%—had no access to health services. Even the minimal health services that were available were heavily concentrated in Monrovia, the capital city, and the urban centers.

Similarly, the health care infrastructure—the number of public hospitals and clinics—was woefully inadequate. For instance, the country had one major public hospital, which was located in Monrovia. The remaining public "hospitals" were based in the capital cities of the various political subdivisions—one "hospital" per political subdivision. Thus, only those residing in the administrative centers of the various political subdivisions had a modicum of access to the woefully inadequate health facility. Accordingly, thousands of rural dwellers, including those in large population centers, had no access to health services. Importantly, the limited health care infrastructure was dominated by private ownership, a reflection of the peripheral capitalist mode of production. By 1989, approximately 60% of the limited number of hospitals, health centers, and clinics were privately owned (Ministry of Health and Social Welfare, Liberia, 2005).

Another problem was that the number of health professionals in the various public health facilities was seriously inadequate. For example, in 1980, there were fewer than 8,000 doctors in the entire country with a population of more than 1.5 million people (Ministry of Planning and Economic Affairs, 1985). During the same period, the ratio of population to hospital bed was approximately 650 (Ministry of Planning and Economic Affairs, 1985). In 1989, there were an estimated 3,526 health workers in the public sector (World Health Organization, 2003: 2). Overall, there were 237 physicians/specialists, 656 nurses, and nurse midwives, 2,782 trained traditional midwives, and 1,381 other supporting personnel in the entire health sector (World Health Organization, 2003: 2). Clearly, when juxtaposed with the population of Liberia—about 2.5 million people—the number of health care professionals was quite inadequate to attend to the needs of the people. A related problem was that some of the most qualified health care professionals worked in private health care facilities. This was because the private medical facilities had comparatively better salaries and benefits packages than the Liberian state.

Also, there was a chronic lack of equipment and supplies. The various public health facilities lacked even the basic medical equipments required for diagnosis and treatment of people with various ailments. Moreover, there was a lack of essential medical supplies. In addition, there was a prevalent inadequacy of drugs. Even if they were available, there was usually the problem that some of these were past their expiry date. This was exacerbated by the fact that the privately owned pharmacies, which comparatively had more drugs than the public medical facilities, charged high prices. Given the prevalence of poverty in the country, several patients could not afford to purchase these drugs. This made them vulnerable to death. Clearly, the lack of basic equipment and medical supplies made it quite difficult for the appropriate diagnosis and treatment of illnesses.

The health problems were compounded by various related challenges. One of the conundrums was food insecurity. Given the high rates of poverty and unemployment, a substantial portion of the population had difficulties meeting their food needs. That is, they did not have the economic access to sufficient and nutritious food to meet their basic dietary needs for an active and healthy life (Flores, 2004: 13). One of the effects of the limited access to adequate and nutritious food was mass undernourishment. For example, the number of undernourished Liberians rose from 0.4 million in 1971 to 0.7 million in 1989 (Flores, 2004: 75). Also, in 1985, about 1.1 million Liberians did not have access to safe drinking water (United Nations Development Program, 1990: 132). In the rural area, only 23% of the population had access to safe drinking water (United Nations Development Program, 1990: 132). Against this backdrop, the majority of rural dwellers got their drinking water usually from contaminated streams and rivers that were used both as laundry and as lavatory facilities. As the World Health Organization (2005: 14), observes, "Households disposed of their human waste in bushes, polyethylene bags, streams, rivers, ponds, beaches or holes in the ground." The contamination of these waterways by human waste made people vulnerable to water-borne diseases such as hepatitis A and typhoid fever. To make matters worse, many Liberians did not have proper sanitation. For example, there were limited garbage disposal facilities throughout the country and inadequate sewage and drainage systems throughout the country. In cases where they were available, the systems were not maintained and did not function properly. One of the consequences was the recurrent spillage of raw sewage into the streets. In addition, a very large number of homes in the country, especially in the rural areas, did not have lavatory facilities.

Cumulatively, the health and related problems affected the life span of Liberians. For example, as Table 6.2 shows, despite the modest increases over the years, life expectancy was low. Even the peak of 55 years attained in 1985 was far below the life expectancy of various countries. This was reflected in the high crude death rate of 13.7 per 1,000 registered between 1982 and 1986 (World Health Organization, 2003: 1). In the same vein, by 1989, the maternal mortality rate was 578 per 100,000 (World Health Organization, 2003: 1). Also, from 1960 to 1985, the infant mortality rate experienced a steady increase (see Table 6.2). By 1985, approximately 24 babies out of every 100 live births died before they reached their first birthdays. Put in a larger context, in 1989, the infant mortality rate was 157 per 1,000, and the under-five mortality rate was 235 (United Nations Children Fund, 2006: 1). As has been previously argued, the horrendous health and related conditions were the major contributing factors to the short life span for adults and babies. Moreover, the inadequacy of the health infrastructure created the conditions for people to die from even basic curable diseases.

Importantly, even the members of the ruling class were fully cognizant of the fact that the health conditions and infrastructure were horrendous. But, rather than using the state's resources to improve these conditions, the members of the ruling class chose to use these resources to pay for the health care needs of their families. For example, during the Tubman era, the president took regular "health trips" to Europe for routine medical checkups. At times, these trips lasted a period of a month each. Similarly, during the Tolbert era, the president went for regular medical checkups in the United States and various European states. Moreover, the wives and female relatives of the members of the ruling class were sent to the United States and Europe to give birth. In essence, the members of the ruling class were fearful of the consequences of the poor health conditions and infrastructure on their personal well-being; so, they used state resources to attend to their health needs, while neglecting those of the vast majority of Liberians.

Table 6.2
Life Expectancy and Infant Mortality Rate, 1960–1985, Liberia

Year	Life Expectancy (Years)	Infant Mortality Rate (Per 1,000 Live Births)
1960	41.0	12.6
1965	43.0	15.0
1970	45.0	21.8
1975	49.0	21.5
1980	50.2	22.0
1985	55.0	23.8

Sources: Compiled from the Ministry of Planning and Economic Affairs, Liberia, *Economic Surveys of Liberia, 1970–1985*, (Monrovia, Liberia: Government Printing Office); United Nations Development Program, *Human Development Report, 1990*, (New York: Oxford University Press, 1990), pp. 134–142.

Overall, the sordid state of health and related services helped to diminish the human capabilities of the members of the subaltern classes and made it impossible for them to develop to their full potential and lead healthy, long, and creative lives. In short, the policies of the settler and the neocolonial state were not designed to address the social welfare needs of the members of the subaltern classes.

Housing

There is a paucity of data on housing issues in Liberia before the country's first civil war. However, the data gathered collected from observation indicate that there were three major problems in the housing sector. First, there was inadequate housing, especially in the urban areas. For example, in 1988, there were 500,000 dwellings in Liberia (Encyclopedia of Nations, 2006: 1). However, the majority of these dwellings were both inadequate in terms of space and not suitable for human habitation. This resulted in overcrowding, especially in the urban areas. In comparatively large urban centers such as Monrovia, it was common for large numbers of people to share a single bedroom. The majority of the dwellings were in the informal sector, which provided 70% of the housing stock before the first civil war (United Nations Human Settlement Program, 2006: 6). In response to the inadequacy of housing, the state initiated the low cost housing scheme in the 1970s. Under the program, public housing complexes were constructed in Barnesville, Gardnersville, New Georgia, and Sinkor. However, the scheme was plagued with several problems. First, the scheme did not serve its purpose of providing affordable and livable housing for low income earners. This was because the housing units were mainly occupied by people in the middle stratum of the income structure. Second, characteristically, the program was Monrovia-based, and did not extend outside of the capital city and its environs. For example, no effort was made to construct public housing for the rural low income earners and the poor. Third, the number of houses constructed in the various estates was not sufficient to address the housing needs of the population.

Second, a substantial number of the houses throughout the country lacked some of the basic amenities such as running water, plumbing, lavatory facilities, and electricity. Therefore these houses were not conducive for human habitation. For example, on the Firestone Plantations, the company's workers lived in thatch-roofed mud houses without the aforementioned facilities. In addition, rooms were not designated, and inner layout was simply a hall-like space. It was left to the workers to use cardboard and other materials to divide the hall-like space into various tiny rooms.

Third, the failure of the state to make housing a priority led to the development of various slums, especially in Monrovia, the capital city. As the United Nations Human Settlements Program (2006: 6) notes, "The [Liberian state's] inadequate response to shelter needs resulted in the proliferation of unplanned settlements and services, starved communities, and enclaves of residential communities and slums characterized by congestion, makeshift buildings, unsanitary conditions and insecure tenure status."

By 1989, the number of people living in slums was one million, approximately 50% of the national population (United Nations Human Settlements Program, 2006) For example, West Point, located on the Atlantic Ocean, is an expansive slum community. Characteristically, West Point has the basic features of a ghetto. The community is overcrowded. Specifically, these residents were cramped into a very limited land mass. One of the resultant effects of the space crunch was the great difficulty encountered in moving around the community. That is, the very limited space militated against the freedom of movement. Another problem was that most of the "houses" were unsuitable for human habitation. This was because they were essentially structures built with defective pieces of corrugated zinc. One of the major consequences was the vulnerability of the residents to the heavy rain during monsoons. The related problem was that scores of residents regularly contracted cold-related illnesses such as pneumonia. Similarly, the houses did not have plumbing and lavatory facilities; hence, the residents constructed, for example, makeshift lavatory facilities on the Mesurado River, which runs through the community. Also, the portions of the Atlantic Ocean beach were used as lavatory facilities as well. This created health hazards in the community because these waterways—the Atlantic Ocean and the Mesurado River—were also used as sources of drinking water and seafood.

Gender Relations

Gender relations in Liberia took place within the patriarchal context created by the settler and the neocolonial state. Under this arrangement, hegemonic masculinality was the overarching operational architecture. That is, gender relations were based on the unbridled suzerainty of males. As Kieh and Railey (1993: 192) argue, "Men occupy the upper echelon of the social structure, control the political and economic systems and dominate relationships—both marital and non-marital." Male dominance was reflected in the operation of the polity in virtually every sphere.

Importantly, hegemonic masculinality was propagated through a process of socialization. The various agents of socialization—family, school, work, and peers—inculcated in the minds of both males and females a set of values as the guideposts for conducting gender relations. Given Liberia's professed claim of being a "Christian state," one of the major values was that biblical teachings required that in a marital relationship the wife should be subservient to her husband. Also, African patriarchal traditions were used to justify the "superior-subordinate relationship." Another value was that men are naturally strong and women are inherently weak. This belief was used to justify male domination of the state bureaucracy. The male claim was that because of women's so-called fragile emotions, especially in the face of challenges and problems, females were unsuitable for certain leadership positions in the state bureaucracy.

Significantly, the context conditioned the conduct of gender relations in various areas in the settler and the neocolonial state and the associated political economy. During both phases of the Liberian state, the peripheral capitalist mode of production impacted men and women differentially. The overarching impact was that the mode of production reenforced and institutionalized patriarchy. For example, under the settler state, the constitution denied women the right to vote and to seek elected office. From the male chauvinistic perspective, the basic roles of the women were to perform domestic services—cooking and cleaning—and child bearing. In the traditional setting, women had the additional responsibility of farming, and men helped to clear the fields for planting and engaged in fishing, hunting, and the cultivation of crops (Moran, 1990). At the level of the state bureaucracy, women were assigned the role of performing the menial and mundane tasks such as the preparation of the food for various public events. The business of the running the affairs of the state was within the exclusive province of the males.

Even after the Liberian state metamorphosed into a neocolonial formation, women were denied legal equality under the constitution in areas such as the right of suffrage and the right to seek elected public offices, until 1945. One year after ascending the presidency, Tubman spearheaded the effort to amend the constitution so that women could have the right to vote and to seek and hold elected public office. However, the granting of "legal equality" to women in some of the major areas was not motivated by the Tubman regime's interest in promoting gender equality. Instead, the decision to grant women legal equality was dictated by the factional competition within the ruling class for the control and domination of the state. As the leader of one of the factions, President Tubman used his power to effect the change in the 1847 Constitution because women represented a major political constituency.

Although the granting of suffrage and the legal right to seek and hold elected offices witnessed the rise of women to various elected and appointive positions in the state bureaucracy, it did not fundamentally alter the predominantly male chauvinistic attitude and its overarching hegemonic masculinality. For example, the criteria for recruiting women to the state bureaucracy was based less on qualifications and more on the female's relationship to the power structure (both familial and social) and her acceptance of the rules of the male-dominated political culture (Kieh and Railey, 1993: 195).

Importantly, women were subjected to various forms of abuse as manifestations of the male-female power relationship. A major type of abuse was the pervasive practice of male supervisors in the public bureaucracy requiring female job seekers or staff members eligible for promotion, salary increase, or other rewards to have sex with them as the *quid pro quo* for favorable action by the supervisor (Kieh and Railey, 1993). Women who refused such demeaning propositions were denied favorable action, irrespective of their qualifications. Also, women were subjected to physical abuse. The most common form was beating by spouse, boyfriend, or another male. Given the culture of male suzerainty, the state did not enact laws designed to punish males who physically abused women. Another form of abuse was sexual predation. Under this genre, males, who were substantially older than their victims, preyed on underage—younger than 18 years—girls. Again, in a permissive environment conditioned by hegemonic masculinality, older men, several of them members of the ruling class, used minors as sex tools. Although, there was an "age of consent statute," the threshold age of 13 established by the dominant male members of the ruling class, made a mockery of the statute. Moreover, the statute was never enforced. Accordingly, men had carte blanche to exploit girls younger than 13 years.

Conclusion

The chapter examined the dimensions of the crisis of social development in Liberia. The first issue that was addressed was public education. The central argument was that the various pantomimes—the inadequacy of access and the educational infrastructure—of the country's educational system reflected the decision of the state and its custodians not to develop an educated and skilled citizenry. This was motivated, among other things, by the ruling class's belief that a largely uneducated population would not pose challenges to the excesses of the class.

Similarly, the horrendous conditions of the country's health services and infrastructure demonstrated the core of the negligent dimension of the state's character. For example, the majority of Liberians had no access to health services. Even the existing services were quite limited. The poor state of the health infrastructure contributed to, inter alia, low life expectancy and high infant mortality rates.

Another issue that was addressed was the vexatious problem of inadequate and poor housing. One of the major manifestations of the problem is the existence of various urban ghettos, particularly around Monrovia, the capital city. In these shanty towns, people live under deplorable conditions. In turn, these conditions pose major health hazards to the health of the residents.

The issue of gender relations was examined. It is argued that gender relations in Liberia were hoisted on hegemonic masculinality and its associated tapestry of male chauvinism and dominance. This framework was strengthened and institutionalized by the settler and neocolonial state and provided the arena in which gender relations were conducted. Against this background, patriarchy and male dominance pervaded gender relations in all spheres in Liberia.

CHAPTER 7

The Crisis of Cultural Underdevelopment

Introduction

The foundation for the cultural crisis in Liberia was laid in 1820 on the arrival in Liberia of the African-American repatriates or the settlers. The settlers came to the Grain Coast with the agenda of subjugating the various indigenous ethnic groups they met in the area. Having been exploited, abused, and marginalized by the vagaries of plantation-based slavery in the United States, the settlers came with an "imperial mentality:" They envisaged a situation in which they would establish suzerainty over the various indigenous ethnic groups within the framework of a master-servant relationship akin to the one to which they were subjected to in the United States. In short, the settlers were interested neither in the fostering of the bonds of kinship with the indigenes nor in acclimating to the sociocultural and political environment. Instead, the settlers firmly believed that because they had lived in the United States, they were therefore familiar with the cultural and political systems of a so-called superior society; hence, they wanted to recreate the so-called superior American civilization in the Grain Coast.

Significantly, when the settlers declared Liberia an independent state in 1847, the cultural crisis became formalized within the state. The settler state, which emerged in response to the needs of the Americo-Liberians, was the embodiment of the cultural divide between the African-American repatriates and the indigenes. This was because the settlers, among other things, deposited their cultural vision into the formation of the state. Accordingly, the state became an instrument for establishing the cultural domination of the settlers over the indigenes. As Sawyer (1992: 1) notes, "the question of settler dominance—the primacy of Liberia's settler society over the indigenous African communities—[was] the central issue in Liberian society." When the settler state was transformed into a neocolonial construct, the divide between the Americo-Liberian and indigenous stock remained, although no longer as the major antagonistic relationship. Class contradictions and their attendant conflicts became the epicenter of the struggles that occurred within the arena of the state.

In this chapter, the various dimensions of the cultural crisis will be examined. Specifically, the following questions will be addressed: First, how did the Liberian state condition ethnic claims? Second, what were the nature and dynamics of ethnic relations? Third, how did the state respond to these ethnic conflicts?

The Liberian State and Ethnic Claims

Both the settler and the neocolonial Liberian state conditioned the claims that were made by various ethnic stocks and groups. During the settler state, the construct was used by the dominant Americo-Liberian group in various ways. Within the territorial confines of the settler state, the construct was used to suppress and repress the indigenes who were living under its jurisdiction as "subjects" rather than as "citizens" (Mamdani, 1996). For example, although the indigenes were not regarded as citizens of the Liberian settler state, they were required to pay taxes and to perform sundry services for the state. When the indigenes protested, the repressive arsenal of the state was used to cow them into submission. The type of repression meted out against the indigenes ranged from flogging to imprisonment. At the external level, the Americo-Liberians used the settler state to undermine and ultimately destroy the various independent indigenous polities and to impose their vision of state-building on them. Specifically, the power of the settler state was used by the Americo-Liberians to take the land of the various indigenous ethnic groups; to exploit their labor; and to impose the Americo-Liberian version of "Western civilization" on them. Even when the indigenes were integrated into the settler state, beginning in 1905, the Americo-Liberians continued to use state power to ensure that their vision of the political economy and cultural institutions and values would undergird state-building in the integrated construct. These developments generated protests from the indigenes. However, the indigenes' claims of "Americo-Liberian imperialism" were rebuffed by the state because the construct was an instrument of the settlers. Accordingly, the indigenes were placed at a disadvantage because the state that they expected (naively) to be an "impartial mediator" was instead an instrument of Americo-Liberian domination. So, the indigenes' claims were conditioned by their two-headed struggle with the dominant settler stock and the partial settler state.

During the neocolonial phase, the state became nonamenable to promoting the particularistic agendas of dominant ethnic groups and stocks. This was because the formation's peripheral capitalist mode of production was tailored toward classes as the bedrocks of the relations of production. So, in essence, the perennial ethnic contradictions and their attendant antagonisms were antithetical to the class-based logic of the country's new peripheral capitalist mode of production. However, the new class-based ideology did not obliterate the settler one, which was based on the "superior-inferior myth." This was because the development of the settler ideology of superiority, which was used as the compass to navigate their relationship with the indigenes, did not synchronize with the transformation of the state and its mode of production. Accordingly, despite the transition from the settler to the neocolonial state in 1926, the settler stock still maintained its consciousness of ethnocultural superiority vis-a-vis the indigenous one. In short, the settler ideology was not aligned with the material transformations that had occurred in the country. But this was not peculiar, because the two phenomena—settler ideology and the transformation of the political economy—developed at distinct paces; hence, to have an alignment with the emergent dominant material transformation, the settler ideology had to exhaust the travails of its historical trajectory. Against this background, a major debate emerged within the dominant settler stock. On the one hand, there was the view that with the material transformation of the Liberian state, settler domination was no longer possible; in effect, it had become a relic of the past. In contradistinction, the other perspective was that despite the material transformation of the Liberian state, settler hegemony was still possible. This schism between the two poles of the settler stock was the centerpiece of the Americo-Liberian-indigene relationship from 1926 to 1980. The post-1980 coup epoch of the neocolonial Liberian state witnessed the birth of the instrumental use of ethnicity. I explore this issue in detail later, when I discuss the relationship between the Krahn and Gio/Mano ethnic groups.

Ethnic Relations: Forces and Dynamics

Liberia's crisis of cultural underdevelopment was primarily manifested in the relationships between and within so-called dominant and subordinate ethnic stocks and groups. Against this background, the focus is on the relationships between the settler and indigenous stocks, between the two poles of the settler stock, between the Krahn and Gio/Mano ethnic groups and among the various ethnic groups that constitute the indigenous stock. The various stocks and ethnic groups and their constituents, the issues, and the dynamics are examined.

Table 7.1
Liberia's Ethnocultural Composition

Ethnic Group	Percentage of the Population[a]
Kpelle	20.0
Bassa	16.0
Gio	8.0
Kru	8.0
Grebo	8.0
Mano	7.0
Lorma	5.0
Krahn	5.0
Gola	5.0
Kissi	4.0
Mandingo	3.0
Vai	3.0
Gbandi	3.0
Belle	0.5
Dei	0.5
Mende	0.5
Americo-Liberians	2.0
Caribbean Origin	0.5
Other Africans	1.0

Note: [a]The data are based on the 1974 national census of Liberia (the most recent in the country's history).

Source: Compiled from the Ministry of Planning and Economic Affairs, Republic of Liberia, *1974 Census of Liberia* (Monrovia, Liberia: Government Printing Office, 1975).

Table 7.2
Liberia's Indigenous Ethnic Clusters

Mande Cluster	Gbandi; Gio; Kpelle; Lorma; Mano; Mandigo; Mende; Vai.
Mel Cluster	Gola; Kissi.
Kwa Cluster	Bassa; Belle; Dei; Grebo; Krahn; Kru.

Source: Compiled by the author.

The Settlers versus the Indigenes

As has been argued, the settler-indigenous divide was the locus of Liberia's cultural crisis for almost a century. The conflict between the two stocks evolved through two major epochs: the settler state and the neocolonial one. The former era had two phases: the segregated phase (1847–1905) and the integrated phase (1905–1926). Each epoch and the associated phases shaped both inter and intraethnic relations in Liberia.

The two stocks in the country's major cultural conflict were the settlers or the Americo-Liberians and the indigenes. The settlers were African-Americans who were repatriated from the United States, where they were enslaved. The settler stock consisted of two poles: the light-skinned or mulatto and dark-skinned. After a brief period in Sierra Leone, the repatriates settled in the Grain Coast, which they later named Liberia. After about two and a half decades of colonial rule under the American Colonization Society (ACS), the settlers established the Liberian state. The indigenous stock comprises 16 ethnic groups, each with its own culture (see Table 7.1). The various indigenous ethnic groups can be classified into three cultural clusters: Mande, Mel, and Kwa (see Table 7.2). These groups were already occupying the Grain Coast, when the repatriates arrived. Each indigenous ethnic group had its own independent polity replete with systems—cultural, economic, political, religious, and social.

During the first phase of the settler state (1847–1905), the conflict between the two stocks revolved around the issues of culture, economics, and politics. Overall, the conflict was anchored on the settler-based ideology of superiority. That is, since they had lived in the United States, although as slaves, the settlers believed that they were superior to and more civilized than the indigenes. As Brown (1941: 125–126) notes, "The American-Liberians [the settlers] considered themselves a "superior people;" thus, there was no sense of feeling of oneness with the Africans [the indigenes]." Accordingly, the settlers used derogatory terms such as primitive, heathens, bush niggers, rustic people, and uncivilized to describe the indigenous people (Cordor, 1980: 35). In addition, the appellations "civilized or kwi" and "country" were developed by the settlers to describe themselves (civilized or kwi) and the indigenes (country). Driven by the ideology of the superior-inferior myth, the settlers sought to impose their brand of Western civilization on the indigenes who resided within the jurisdiction of the Liberian state and those who were citizens of independent indigenous polities. One of the important dimensions of settler "cultural imperialism" was the effort to impose a particular brand of "American Christianity." The basic argument that the settlers used for doing so was that the various indigenous religions were paganistic and their customs reflective of heathenism. Hence, the settlers sought to Christianize the indigenes by, among other things, converting them to the "settler cum American brand of Christianity." Among other things, this brand of Christianity rationalized discrimination, segregation, marginalization, and exploitation, a far cry from the egalitarian, prosocial justice, and propeople theology that was preached, promoted, and practiced by Jesus Christ, the founder of Christianity. Also, the settlers denounced polygamy as the basis of the institution of marriage, and tried to impose monogamy on the indigenes. However, this development further reflected the gap between the settlers' pious "Christian rhetoric" and praxis: The settlers exhorted the indigenes to have one wife, on the one hand, but they themselves subscribed to the admonition in theory only because it was common for married male settlers to have several concubines (many of whom were their *de facto* wives). Another manifestation of the cultural divide was the settlers' insistence that the indigenes changed their ethnically based names to so-called English ones. Accordingly to the settlers, this was a major determinant in the battery of stipulations for an indigenous to become civilized. Similarly, the settlers made English the official *lingua franca*, and relegated the various indigenous languages to the periphery of the communications sphere. Accordingly, the indigenes were forced to learn English. Also, the settlers imposed their style of dress on the indigenes. For example, the tailcoat and the top hat and the "American-styled female regalia" became the national dress for men and women respectively; this dress code was a must while attending state functions. Cumulatively, settler cultural imperialism sought to recreate the United States in Liberia. As Dunn and Holsoe (1985: ix) observe, "[The life style imposed by the settlers] reminded one more of a society on the other side of the ocean than those much closer at hand." Characteristically, the indigenous people resisted settler cultural imperialism. This was because the culture and values of the settler community came into sharp conflict with theirs (Fahnbulleh, 1985: xv).

The economic dimension of the conflict between the two stocks revolved primarily around the exploitation of labor, the mode of production, and the issue of land. Within the domain of the settler state, the Americo-Liberians were pitted against the indigenes who were resident in the formation. As argued earlier, within the overarching caste system, skin pigmentation, and ancestral origins overlapped with class. Thus, the indigenes who resided within the settler state were subjected to double exploitation as members of the lowest tier in the caste system and the bottom level in the subaltern classes. In other words, on the basis of their skin color and ancestral origins and their places within the class structure, the indigenes were subjected to the most vitriolic forms of oppression. For example, as members of the lowest stratum of the subaltern classes, the indigenes' labor was exploited by the members of the settler stock and the ruling class. As indentured servants and laborers, the indigenes lived and worked in the homes and businesses of various members of the settler stock and the ruling class. Various forms of exploitation included long working hours, deplorable working conditions, and no compensation. The other aspect of the economic conflict was between the settlers and the indigenes, who lived outside of the settler state. The thrust of the conflict was a land grabbing campaign launched by the settlers. The campaign sought to dispossess the indigenes of their land so that the settlers could use it to pursue their private business interests. The settlers' capitalist orientation as expressed through the efforts to privatize the ownership of land was at variance with the indigenes' communal mode of production and its attendant collective ownership of the major means of production, especially land. Although the indigenes resisted, they were subdued by the relative superior strength of the settler state.

Politically, the settlers and the indigenes had diametrically opposed positions on various issues. On the issue of citizenship, the settlers denied citizenship to those indigenes who were resident in the state. Instead, citizenship was restricted to the settlers and their descendants (Nass, 2000: 9). For their part, the indigenes maintained that they were entitled to the citizenship of Liberia. Also, both disagreed on the national symbols. For their part, the settlers designed national symbols that solely reflected their cultural and historical experiences. For example in the flag, the eleven stripes represent the settlers who signed the declaration of independence; and the red signifies the valor of only the settlers. Similarly, the national emblem, which primarily consists of a ship on the ocean, represents the settlers' journey to the Grain Coast (later Liberia). The motto, "the love of liberty brought us here," pertains only to the settlers. However, the indigenes argued that the various national documents and symbols should be designed to represent the experiences of both the settler and indigenous stocks. The settlers refused to consider the indigenes' grievances. Another issue was "taxation without representation." On the one hand, the indigenes were denied citizenship, yet on the other hand, they were required to pay taxes such as the obnoxious hut tax to the settler state (Nass, 2000: 9).

By the time the settler state entered its second phase (1905–1926), the multifaceted conflict between the settlers and the indigenes had crystallized and this was reflected in various wars. With the incorporation of the various independent indigenous polities into the expanded settler state, the Americo-Liberians still faced the challenge of dealing with the various indigenous groups. With the control of the state, the settlers pursued the incorporation of the indigenes on their terms. For example, the indigenes were required to accept settler cultural institutions and values as the bedrocks of the national order. Although the indigenes continued to resist, the settlers with the state at their disposal were able to institutionalize their cultural institutions and values through legislation.

Economically, the peripheral capitalist mode of production was imposed as the national framework. One of the major resultant effects was the privatization of sizeable portions of indigenous land that was previously owned collectively by the communities. Also, as members of both the lowest tier in the caste system and the class arrangement, the indigenes were on the margins of the system. Basically, they served as an "army of reserved labor" for state projects and the small number of businesses—mainly farms— owned by members of the settler stock, especially the ruling class.

In the political sphere, the settler state granted citizenship to the indigenes. But, this decision was driven more by the imperatives of British and French imperialism than the desire of the settlers to forge the bonds of national unity. But, even with *de jure* citizenship, the indigenes remained *de facto* second-class citizens. This was clearly reflected in the fact that they had no representation in the various institutions of the state. The state bureaucracy was dominated by the members of the settler stock.

During the neocolonial phase (up to 1989), the settler-indigenous conflict was supplanted by a class one. But, as I have argued, the emergent dominant class conflict did not end the settler-indigenous one. This was because the development of the settler-indigenous conflict and the material transformation of the state occurred at different paces. Culturally, the settler-imposed institutions and values remained intact. However, during the Tolbert regime, efforts were made to replace the settler dress style with the indigenous one. Also, it was no longer a taboo to speak indigenous languages and to have indigenous names. For example, President Tolbert spoke in Kpelle during his inaugural address in 1972. Moreover, the state took some modest steps to develop Kpelle, the largest ethnic language, as the national one. However, the efforts were never successful.

In terms of economics, the class conflict superseded the traditional ethnic one. Essentially, this was because class replaced ethnicity as the overarching economic tapestry. Accordingly, the establishment of panethnic classes consisting of settlers and indigenes at various tiers ended the practice of the overlap between skin pigmentation and the individual's relationship to the major means of production. In short, the focus of the struggle shifted to the contradictions between and among classes and the resultant conflicts.

At the political level, beginning in 1944, various steps were taken to fully integrate some of the indigenous members of the ruling class into the state machinery, as ways of addressing the perennial grievance of the indigenes regarding political marginalization. Also, efforts were made to elevate some of the indigenous members of the *petit bourgeois* class to the ruling class. Again, this was another manifestation of the effort by the ruling class to incorporate indigenes into the bureaucratic wing of the class.

Significantly, the April 12, 1980 coup represented a watershed period in that it effectively ended the tension between the lingering effects of the settler-indigenous conflict and the imperatives of class-based peripheral capitalism. This was because for those in both the settler and the indigenous communities who hung on to the conflict the coup represented the end of settler domination of the Liberian state bureaucracy. However, two years after the coup, the Doe regime engineered an ethnic conflict between the Krahn ethnic group and the Gio/Mano ethnic groups (see the section on the Krahn and Gio/Mano Divide for details). Despite the Doe regime's efforts at the instrumental use of ethnicity, class contradictions and their associated conflicts became increasingly important.

The Light-Skinned versus the Dark-Skinned Settlers

Although the two poles—the light–skinned or mulatto and the dark-skinned—of the settler stock were united in their conflict with the indigenes, there were differences between them. As Osaghae (1998: 134) correctly notes, "the class treatment of the Americo-Liberian group has, however, tended to gloss over the historical fact that it was never a homogenous group." The light-skinned pole's ancestral origin was traced in part to the white male plantation owners in the United States. Academically, the members of this pole were relatively more educated. Professionally, they were lawyers, preachers, and entrepreneurs. In class terms, they occupied the upper echelon of the socio-economic system of the settler state. The dark-skinned repatriates came from comparatively lower educational background. In career terms, they were primarily artisans and self-employed small business owners.

Significantly, the pivot of the conflict between the two poles was skin color. Light-skinned settlers believed that because of their white ancestral origin, they were superior to the dark-skinned repatriates. Accordingly, the light-skinned pole advocated for a division of labor under which they would be responsible for managing the affairs of the state and its economy and the dark-skinned settlers would work in the agricultural sector. Importantly, the differences in skin color overlapped with class. Accordingly, the light-skinned repatriates occupied the upper class, and the dark-skinned settlers were in the middle tier. The differences in skin pigmentation and class between the two poles of the settler stock framed their respective positions on various national issues. For example, the light-skinned settlers advocated for early independence from the American Colonization Society (ACS), whereas the dark-skinned pole wanted a delay in the declaration of independence. This was because the dark-skinned sector argued that the light-skinned pole wanted the early granting of independence so that they could dominate the government of the emergent Liberian state. Similarly, the two poles disagreed and were locked in conflict over the location of Liberia College (now the University of Liberia). The light-skinned pole wanted the institution to be established in Monrovia, the capital city, because it was the cornerstone of its political base. Conversely, the dark-skinned sector wanted the institution established outside of Monrovia, preferably around the settlements in the St. Paul River area, the fulcrum of its political support.

The differences and their associated conflicts propelled the two poles to organize two opposing political parties, which they used as their political vehicles for contesting for state power. Interestingly, the two settler poles' control of state went through various cycles. For example, first the light-skinned pole controlled state power from 1847 to 1870, which was followed by the dark-skinned sector controlling state power from 1870 to 1871. Again, the light-skinned pole took control of the state's machinery from 1871 to 1884. Then, from 1884, the dark-skinned settlers controlled state power. Despite the cyclical nature of the control of state power, the light-skinned pole remained the dominant class until 1926.

Interestingly, as I argued earlier, despite the differences and the attendant conflicts between them, the two poles constituted a united front in their conflict with the indigenes. The dark-skinned settlers identified with their light-skinned kin rather than with the indigenes with whom they shared a subordinate position vis-a-vis the light-skinned pole for several reasons. First, both the light-skinned and the dark-skinned settlers had a common origin from the American South. Hence, there was a feeling that the two poles of the settler stock needed to build bonds of solidarity in dealing with the indigenes, who they perceived as their common enemies. Second and related, the members of the dark-skinned pole were socialized to believe that despite their subordinate position in relationship to the light-skinned, they were superior to and more civilized than the indigenes. Third, historically, the dark-skinned settlers and the indigenes had separate political and economic existence. Fourth, the dark-skinned pole was part of the larger settler stock that exploited the labor of the indigenes who resided within the jurisdiction of the settler state. Fifth and related, the dark-skinned settlers were part of the larger effort to expand the territorial expanse of the settler state. Among other things, this meant dispossessing the indigenes in the hinterland of their land, thereby expanding the ambit of the antagonistic relationship between the indigenes and the settler stock as a whole. In essence, the indigenes saw the dark-skinned pole an integral part of the settler stock that disrespected their cultures; dehumanized, exploited, cheated, and marginalized them; and plundered and robbed their land.

Intra-Indigenous Schisms

Like the settler stock, the indigenous one also did not constitute a cultural monolith. In addition, the various indigenous ethnic groups and their various sects had divergent economic, social, and political interests and agendas. Importantly, the pursuance of the respective agendas often led to conflicts, including wars.

Even in their collective conflict with the settlers, the various indigenous groups simultaneously pursued their particularistic agendas. This was because the conflict with the settlers affected the indigenous ethnic groups in diverse ways, thereby providing each group with distinct sets of opportunities and challenges. For example, in bargaining with the custodians of the settler state, each ethnic group did so on its own behalf rather than for the totality of the indigenous collectivity.

Also, the advent of the neocolonial state did not fundamentally alter the self-interest logic of the various ethnic groups. In fact, the neocolonial Liberian state became increasingly irrelevant as Liberians relied on their respective ethnic groups as sources of solidarity and other types of support. For example, some ethnic groups organized development associations to fill the vacuum left by state neglect. In the pursuance of their various development projects, each ethnic group focused primarily on its own people. Moreover, even some of the various sects within some of the ethnic groups established separate "home town associations" as "engines of community development," against the backdrop of the neocolonial Liberian state's refusal to cater to the basic needs of its citizens across the ethnic spectrum.

The Clash Between Class and Ethnicity

Despite the material transformation of the Liberian state and the attendant emergence of classes and class-based conflicts as the bedrocks of the political economy of the neocolony, some settlers and indigenes remained steadfast in their resolve to continue the settler-indigenous conflict. So, for these hard-core ethnicists, the April 12, 1980, coup represented what Liebenow (1980) calls the "dissolution of privilege" for the settlers. For the settlers who refused to come to grips with the fact that the transformation of the Liberian state in 1926 made class ascendant, the coup represented the *coup de grace* for the stock. Similarly, for the indigenes who shared the same perspective, the coup represented the emergence of indigenous domination of the polity. In fact, various groups of indigenous women reflected this belief in the song they composed and sang to greet the coup: "Country woman born soldier, Congo woman (settler) born rogue" (Liberian Market Women Group, 1980).

However, to the disappointment and chagrin of the indigenous ethnicists, the postcoup reality reflected class realignments. For example, in the ruling class, Master Sergeant Doe emerged as the chief spokesperson of the bureaucratic wing. Moreover, the leading members of the bureaucratic wing were recruited from both the settler and ethnic stock. Hence, the empirical evidence made it abundantly clear that classes were the centrifugal forces of the neocolonial political economy. In short, the coup did not alter the fundamentals of the peripheral capitalist mode of production and its relations of production, which have been in effect since 1926. But rather, the coup ended the settler-indigene conflict, which had become secondary with the transformation of the material base of the state.

The Krahn-Gio/Mano Divide

Faced with the perennial state-generated crises of underdevelopment and incapable and unwilling to address them, the Doe regime decided to pursue a diversionary strategy that would shift attention away from the crisis of the state and its military regime. Accordingly, beginning in 1982, the Doe regime conveniently identified the Gio/Mano ethnic groups of Nimba County as the principal enemies of the regime. The problem commenced when Sergeant Doe and his erstwhile pal and confidante extraordinaire General Thomas Quiwonkpa, a member of the Gio ethnic group, became locked in a conflict driven by personality differences. Briefly, General Quiwonkpa was one of the leaders of the coup that brought Sergeant Doe to power. After the coup, General Quiwonkpa became commanding-general of the armed forces and the fourth–highest ranking member of the People's Redemption Council, the ruling military council. Importantly, along with Sergeant Doe, General Quiwonkpa was the major executor of the American plan to purge the ruling military council of so-called communists and supporters of Libya (Discussions, 1983–1984). In this vein, both Sergeant Doe and General Quiwonkpa, with the backing of the United States, orchestrated a "fake coup," in which they implicated General Thomas Weh Syen, the vice chair of the ruling military council and vice head of state and other members of the military council, who were regarded as "supporters of Libya" (Discussions, 1983–1984). After a "kangaroo trial," General Weh Syen and the others were summarily executed (Discussions, 1983–1984).

Amid the increasing crisis of the neocolonial state and the horrendous performance of the Doe regime, the United States shifted its support from Sergeant Doe to General Quiwonkpa (Discussions, 1983–1984). Angered by the American action, Sergeant Doe decided to remove General Quiwonkpa from his leading role in the military regime (Discussions, 1983–1984). Accordingly, Sergeant Doe demoted General Quiwonkpa from his powerful position as commanding-general to the largely ceremonial position of secretary-general of the ruling council. General Quiwonkpa refused to oblige. Consequently, Sergeant Doe ordered his arrest and detention. However, General Quiwonkpa was taken out of Liberia by the United States and temporarily resettled in the Baltimore, Maryland, area (Discussions, 1983–1984). Thereafter, Sergeant Doe elevated his conflict with General Quiwonkpa over power to an ethnic one between their respective ethnic groups: Sergeant Doe began to convince some members of his Krahn ethnic group that the Gio/Mano ethnic groups were determined to oust him (Doe) and his Krahn ethnic group from power. With no base of support in the country, the instrumental use of ethnicity became Sergeant Doe's "strategy of regime survival."

After the fraudulent presidential election held in October 1985, in which Sergeant Doe was declared the winner and the "new civilian president of Liberia," General Quiwonkpa led an abortive coup on November 12, 1985. After foiling the coup, the Doe regime embarked on a military campaign against the Gio/Mano ethnic groups and their county (Nimba). Consequently, hundreds of members of the Gio/Mano ethnic groups were killed and villages, towns, farms, and other properties were destroyed. Eventually, General Quiwonkpa was captured and killed. Characteristically, Sergeant Doe (later President Doe, beginning in 1986) used the failed coup as a new propaganda weapon for mobilizing members of his Krahn ethnic group against the Gio/Mano ethnic groups. Even as the state began to approach its final collapse in 1989, President Doe again laid the responsibility on the Gio/Mano ethnic groups. In this vein, several members of the Gio/Mano ethnic groups were arrested, detained, and murdered. In one case, hundreds of young Gio and Mano children were loaded up in trucks in Nimba County and taken to the Camp Schefflin Military Barracks, where they were buried alive (Interviews, 1998–1999).

State Intervention

The state's response to the conflicts between, among, and within Liberia's various ethnic stocks and groups was contingent on the formation's stage of development and its relationship to the various cultural groups and classes. During the first phase of the settler state (1847–1905), the state intervened in the settler-indigenous conflict and the light-skinned versus dark-skinned rivalry in various ways. In the case of the former, the state recurrently intervened on the side of the settlers. For example, the state used various draconian measures, including torture and imprisonment, to suppress the rebellion of the indigenes who were residing within the jurisdiction of the settler state. These indigenes regularly protested the inhuman treatment—the denial of their basic human rights, including slave labor and its vagaries—that they received from the settler stock. In terms of the settler stock's conflict with those indigenes who were outside of the ambit of the settler state, the state intervened on behalf of the Americo-Liberians as well. For example, the state used its military might to seize the land of various indigenous groups; subsequently, the land was turned over to the settlers, who used it to engage in private business activities. In terms of the light-skinned versus the dark-skinned settlers' conflict, the state intervened in various ways. During the epoch of relative autonomy (1847–1869), the state's intervention in the intrasettler dispute was designed to serve and protect the interests of the settler stock as a whole. Importantly, since the state was independent of the control of both poles of the settler stock, it was thus able to take action against the particularistic agendas of the two poles in its effort to serve the broader agenda of the stock as a whole. However, when the state lost its relative autonomy in 1869, it then sided with the faction of the settler stock that controlled the bureaucratic apparatus at the time. For example, from 1870 to 1871, in its various interventions in the disputes between the two poles, the state sided with the dark-skinned settlers; this was because the dark-skinned settlers controlled state power. But, when the light-skinned pole wrestled away power from the dark-skinned faction in 1871, the state swung its support to the former.

During the second phase of the settler state (1905–1926), the various inter and intraethnic conflicts continued. In fact, the settler-indigenous conflict was broadened with the incorporation of the previous independent indigenous polities into the settler state, and the consequent granting of citizenship to the indigenes. Despite these developments, the settler stock and its dominant class continued to control the machinery of the state. Accordingly, in the various conflicts with the indigenes over issues such as political representation and the parochial and segregative core of the various national symbols, the state sided with the settler stock. In fact, the state took steps to consolidate settler domination. For example, the state encouraged Americo-Liberians to establish enclaves in various indigenous communities. The central purpose was to promote the settler vision of state-building. Similarly, the state promoted various apprenticeship programs, in which members of the indigenous ethnic groups were to "learn various skills from the Americo-Liberians." Also, the state established public schools in various indigenous communities to promote settler cultural imperialism through indoctrination. Interestingly, there was the lack of adequate funds, equipment, supplies, and instructional personnel to run these schools. This was because the state was less interested in educating the indigenes. Instead, its purpose was to ensure that these schools inculcated in the minds of young indigenes the settler vision of state-building and its foundational values. Another major step taken by the settler state was the restructuring of the interior administration in 1914. The crux was the creation of chiefdoms within the various indigenous communities. The chiefdoms became the principal administrative units. One of the resultant requirements was that chiefs—paramount, clan, and town—be elected. The election of chiefs and the requirement that they hold presidential commissions as the basis of their authority contravened the traditional method for ascendancy to the chieftaincy within the various indigenous ethnic groups. However, these devices served the purpose of the Americo-Liberians because they finalized the subordination of indigenous political authority to the settler state. As for the light-skinned versus the dark-skinned conflict, beginning in 1884, the state became an instrument of the latter pole. This was because the dark-skinned faction controlled state power for the duration of the settler state.

During the neocolonial phase (up to 1989), the state was faced with the imperatives of a class-based system and the lingering legacies of the settler-indigenous conflict, and after 1980, the Doe regime induced the Krahn and Gio/Mano conflict. With the finalization of Liberia's incorporation into the international capitalist system, the emergent neocolonial state was tailored toward serving the interests of the ruling class, whose members (local wing) came from both the settler and indigenous ethnic stocks. In other words, the transformation of the material base of the Liberian state created new class-based alliances that transcended the old settler–indigenous divide. However, as I have argued, given the fact that the development of the ideology of ethnic dominance did not synchronize with the material transformation of the Liberian state, the settler-indigenous conflict continued to fester. Particularly, the conflict remained a nagging issue because, *inter alia*, the various national symbols—the flag, emblem, motto, and national anthem—remained representative exclusively of the historical and cultural experiences of the settler stock, the political structure of the state and the distribution of positions in the state bureaucracy was decidedly skewed in favor of the settler stock.

Against this backdrop, from 1944 to 1980, the state took various steps to address the settler-indigenous divide and to consolidate the material transformation of the state. The open door policy was designed, among other things, to formally incorporate the indigenous ethnic communities into the emerging peripheral capitalist economy, particularly through the penetration of foreign capital.

Another policy enunciated by the state was the coexistence of the indigenous traditional and Western legal codes. This policy created two legal systems. One was national in scope, and the other was applicable to the governance of the affairs of the various indigenous ethnic groups. In rationalizing the policy, President Tubman, in his inaugural address in 1944, "averred that customary tribal laws so far as they are humane and reasonable, would be adhered to in the administration of the hinterland under tribal authorities" (Lowenkopf, 1976: 55).

The Unification and Integration Policy that was designed to serve as road map was obliterating the last vestiges of discrimination and segregation and the attendant acrimony in the settler-indigenous relationship. In launching the policy at the First National Unification Council held in 1954, President Tubman outlined the contours of the policy thus:

> For more than 80 years since the Founding Fathers settled here, we have tried to destroy each other by internal wars. Both sides have failed. Destroy all the ideologies that tend to divide us. Americo-Liberianism must be forgotten and all of us must register a new area of justice, equality, fair dealing, and equal opportunities for every one from every part of the country regardless of tribe, clan, section, element, creed or economic status. (Lowenkopf, 1976: 55).

Also, to address the political structural imbalance between the settlers and the indigenes, four new indigenous-based political subdivisions were created in 1964—Bong, Grand Gedeh, Lofa, and Nimba. These counties were carved out of the three provinces—Central, Eastern, and Western—that comprised the principal political units of the various indigenous ethnic communities inhabited by the Kpelle, Krahn, Belle, Gbandi, Kissi, Lorma, Gio, and Mano ethnic groups. The professed purpose was to give the indigenes in these areas equal political status with the other subdivisions in the Liberian body politic.

In addition, several indigenes were appointed to various positions in the executive (cabinet, junior cabinet, and others) and judicial (justices of the Supreme Court, judges of subordinate courts, and other positions) branches of the government. Also, several indigenes were elected to the National Legislature as senators and representatives. Although, the legislators were legally elected, in practice, from 1955 to 1980, they were appointed from a list of contestants in the True Whig Party by the president of Liberia in his capacity as Standard Bearer of the ruling party. Subsequently, the candidates were rubber stamped by the party's local caucuses and national leadership and elected unopposed in the legislative election. This measure was taken to help address the problem of the skewed distribution of jobs in the public bureaucracy, which tilted heavily in favor of the settlers.

During the Tolbert regime, additional policies were introduced. One of the policies was designed to give the indigenes authority in the House of Representatives. Accordingly, two new positions of first and second deputy speakers of the House of Representatives were created on an ethnoregional basis. The position of first deputy speaker was assigned to the old counties of Montserrado, Bassa, Cape Mount, Maryland, and Sinoe, the political bases of the Americo-Liberian stock. The second deputy speakership was assigned to the new counties of Bong, Grand Gedeh, Lofa, and Nimba, the major hubs of the indigenous population.

Another policy was the creation of the position of first and second vice national chairs of the ruling True Whig Party, the de facto one party at that time. The criterion for assigning the two positions was the same as the one for the two deputy speakerships. Again, the intention was to help address the festering problem of indigenes occupying high positions in the structural arrangements. Importantly, this change helped to increase the indigenes' access to the largesse of the state bureaucracy. This was because the second vice national chair of the ruling party became one of the patrons with the responsibility of the distribution of positions in the public sector.

Also, in 1979, a policy was introduced that sought to ensure that the settler stock and all of the various indigenous ethnic groups were represented in the cabinet. Given the number of indigenous ethnic groups (16) and the factions within the settler stock, the cabinet was expanded with the creation of new ministries. The hope was that this would close the final chapter on the age-old settler-indigenous conflict, and consequently align ethnic relations with the material transformation of the Liberian state that commenced in 1926.

The postcoup phase of the neocolonial state (1980–1989) witnessed the introduction of another ethnic conflict between the Krahn ethnic group, on the one hand, and the Gio/Mano ethnic groups, on the other. Having lost its popular appeal, support, and legitimacy, the Doe regime characteristically resorted to the manipulation of Krahn and Gio/Mano primordialism. As has been argued, President Doe convinced a number of his kith and kin in the Krahn ethnic group that his regime was their government; thus, if the regime was undermined and deposed, it would engender catastrophic consequences for the Krahn ethnic group as a whole. Correspondingly, the Doe regime identified the Gio/Mano ethnic groups as the principal opponents of the regime and the Krahn ethnic group. Accordingly, the Doe regime formulated and pursued several policies. It placed the leadership of the armed forces of Liberia in the hands of a trusted Krahn as chief of staff of the armed forces. The related strategy was that the regime recruited scores of Krahns into the officer corps and the rank and file of the military.

Another policy was the dismissal and/or nonappointment of people from the Gio/and Mano ethnic groups to important and sensitive positions in the state bureaucracy, unless they had proven their loyalty to the regime beyond every doubt. For example, in 1982, the Doe regime dismissed scores of members of the Gio and Mano ethnic groups from various positions in the state bureaucracy, including the military and security services. The most important personnel action by the regime was the demotion of then Brigadier-General Thomas Quiwonkpa from his position as commanding-general of the armed forces and the fourth highest ranking official of the ruling military council to the ceremonial position of secretary-general of the ruling council and the sixth highest ranking member of the council. General Quiwonkpa refused to accept the demotion and to take up his new assignment. Infuriated by this action, the Doe regime sought to bring one of its former prominent leaders to book. Accordingly, General Quiwonkpa fled Liberia, and thereafter commenced leading the efforts to oust the Doe regime through the use of force. Importantly, the demotion of General Quiwonkpa and the massive dismissals of members of the Gio and Mano ethnic groups from the state bureaucracy set the stage for the Krahn versus Gio/Mano ethnic conflict that was crafted by the Doe regime.

Also, the regime's internal security policy focused on the harassment and intimidation of opinion leaders, and at times ordinary members of the Gio and Mano groups. Since the Doe regime had identified the Gio and Mano ethnic groups as the primary enemy, it used the machinery of the state to make life unbearable for and to instill fear in the minds of the members of these ethnic groups. One of the principal strategies used by the Doe regime was the manufacturing of various "Gio and Mano led rebellions and coup plots" against his regime. In turn, these concocted plots were used to harass, arrest, torture, and imprison members of the Gio and Mano ethnic groups.

The crowning point of the Doe regime's instrumental use of ethnicity was the use of the state's coercive apparatus to undertake a "scorch the earth" campaign in Nimba County, the hub of the Gio and Mano ethnic groups, in late 1985. The failed coup against the Doe regime on November 12, 1985, led by former Brigadier-General Thomas Quiwonkpa, one of the major leaders of the April 12, 1980 coup that brought Doe to power, a prominent leader of the ruling military junta and a onetime confidante of Doe and a member of the Gio ethnic group, provided the Doe regime with the opportunity it needed to engage in "ethnic scapegoating." Since the abortive coup was led by a member of the Gio ethnic group, the Doe regime made the broad assertion that the putsch was the centerpiece of the plan by the Gio and Mano ethnic groups to oust him, a Krahn, from power. Accordingly, the Doe regime unleashed the fury of the state's repressive machinery on Nimba County, resulting in the deaths of hundreds of members of the Gio and Mano ethnic groups and the destruction of property. Significantly, this action by the Doe regime set into motion the development of an antagonistic relationship between the Krahn ethnic group (Doe's ethnic group), on the one hand, the the Gio and Mano ethnic groups, on the other.

Conclusion

The chapter has attempted to examine some of the major dimensions of the crisis of cultural underdevelopment in Liberia. The chapter began with a discussion of the ways in which the settler and neocolonial Liberian state conditioned the making of ethnic claims. Essentially, this phenomenon was contingent upon the stages in the development of the state and its relationship with the various ethnic stocks.

Another issue addressed in the chapter concerned ethnocultural conflict. Specifically, this was done in the context of the settler-indigenous divide; the light-skinned versus the dark-skinned settlers' dispute; conflicts between and among the various indigenous ethnic groups; and the conflict engineered by the Doe regime between the Krahn and Gio/Mano ethnic groups.

Finally, the chapter discussed the intervention of the settler and the neocolonial Liberian state in the various conflicts. Characteristically, the type and orientation of the state's intervention in these conflicts was dependent on the particular historical juncture in the development of the state's material base and the consequent impact on the various groups. This is critical because the essence of state intervention in conflicts is to protect and defend the overall interests of the dominant class.

CHAPTER 8

From the Crises of Underdevelopment to Civil War

Introduction

The multifaceted crises of the state initially enveloped Liberia from the moment the first group of repatriated freed African-American slaves from the United States arrived in Liberia. As argued, for more than a century and three decades, the Liberian ruling class was able to use what I termed "conflict inhibitors" as the *deus ex machina* for preventing the outbreak of violent civil conflict. Importantly, once the conflict inhibitors' effectiveness was undermined, the mass discontent that had been percolating under the facade of stability imploded first into the April 14, 1979, mass demonstrations and eventually the April 12, 1980 military coup.

However, the Doe military junta, which subsequently metamorphosed into a civilian regime, demonstrated its lack of will to rethink, deconstruct, and democratically reconstitute the neocolonial Liberian state. This failure was reflected in the horrendous performance of the regime in all areas (Kieh, 1996a; Sawyer, 1987a; Wonkeryor, 1982). This made Liberia, to paraphrase Zartman (1989), "ripe for war." In essence, the decades of state failure provided the contingent conditions, and the sordid performance of the Doe regime served as the necessary factor for creating the conditions for civil war.

Against this background, this chapter explains the following: First, it briefly discusses the way the crises of the state were used as the pretext for the civil war. Second, it examines the various warlordist militias in terms of their composition, ideology, military doctrine, fighting capabilities, and relations with the larger society. Third, it explores the roles of the patrons who supported the various militias. Fourth, it assesses the efforts of the peacemakers to resolve the war. Fifth, it discusses the dynamics of war. Sixth, it examines the way the war led to the final collapse of the state. Seventh, it assesses the cost of the war.

The Crises of the State: The Pretext for the Warlordist Militias

The crises of the state provided the pretext that was used by the National Patriotic Front of Liberia (NPFL) to initiate the civil war in Liberia. That is, the Taylor–led NPFL used the legitimate grievances of the subaltern classes of Liberia to dislodge the Doe regime from power. Similarly, the other militias used the legitimate grievances of the Liberian people as a pretext for prosecuting the war. In reality, the various antigovernment forces in Liberia participated in the war because they wanted to gain control of state power and use it for the private accumulation of wealth. In other words, although there were legitimate mass grievances, the war, unfortunately, was motivated by greed for political power and wealth. The Taylor–led NPFL and the other warlordist militias had absolutely no interest in the democratic reconstitution of the neocolonial Liberian state. Davis et al. (1997: 2) provide an excellent summation of the common motivation of the warlords: "Neither political philosophy nor long-running historical tribal clashes were at the roots of the [Liberian civil] war [Instead, it was motivated by greed]."

Clearly, the manner in which the various militias executed their war agendas confirmed the fact that all wars were propelled by the acquisitive impulse. Given Liberia's wealth of natural resources—diamond, gold, rubber, and timber— and the collapse of the state, a militia served as an effective instrument for unbridled plundering and pillaging. In fact in the Hobbesian-like "state of nature" that was created by the civil war, the more powerful a militia, the greater its capacity to pillage disproportionate amounts of Liberia's resources (Hobbes, 1661). For example, given the fact that the NPFL was the most powerful militia, Charles Taylor, its leader, was able to illegally amass huge wealth through the sale of diamond, gold, rubber, and timber (Reno, 1996, 1998).

The Civil War: The Forces and Dynamics

The civil war was designed and shaped by a broad constellation of forces: the military of the incumbent president Samuel Doe, the various warlordist militias, the patrons who supported the various militias, and the peacemakers. Between 1989 and 1994, the number of militias in the war increased from two to seven. The precipitous increase was propelled primarily by the desire of would-be warlords to acquire wealth. In other words, having observed the phenomenal increase in the amount of territory with natural resources—gold, diamond, and so on—under the control of the Taylor-led NPFL, the potential warlords were convinced that they too could successfully pursue the "warlord logic": They could organize a militia; acquire some weapons; take and hold territory, and the attendant natural resources; and become political actors.

In this section of the chapter, the various warring factions are assessed in terms of their agendas, recruitment bases, capabilities, external support, fighting technique, roles in the war, and relations with civil society. In other words, what were some of the major attributes of the various warring factions? Also, the roles of the various patrons and the peacemakers in the war are examined.

The Warlordist Militias

The National Patriotic Front of Liberia (NPFL)

The late Brigadier-General Thomas Quiwonkpa, former commanding general of the armed forces of Liberia, organized the NPFL in 1984.[1] The purpose of the group was to overthrow the government of Samuel Doe. Accordingly, in 1985, using neighboring Sierra Leone as a launch pad, the NPFL launched a coup attempt under the leadership of General Quiwonkpa. Unfortunately, Sergeant Doe foiled the coup, and General Quiwonkpa and several of his lieutenants were arrested and killed. However, some of the remnants of the NPFL fled to Sierra Leone and Côte d'Ivoire.

After Charles Taylor, the former director-general of the General Services Agency and deputy minister of commerce, industry, and transportation, fled Liberia in 1983, amid charges of embezzlement, he made several stops in Côte d'Ivoire, Ghana, and the United States. During his visit to Côte d'Ivoire, he met with the remnants of the NPFL. Using money and by murdering the new leaders of the group (Moses Duopu and others), Taylor was able to install himself as the head of the NPFL. Taylor was able to bribe several of the original members of the NPFL to support him as the leader. Also, he arranged for the incumbent leaders who posed a threat to his leadership to be eliminated. Subsequently, he used ethnicity as a tool for the recruitment and the mobilization of resources. For example, he capitalized on the differences that ensued after the abortive 1985 coup between the Gio and the Mano ethnic groups (General Quiwonkpa's ethnic groups) and the Krahn ethnic group (President Doe's ethnic group) to recruit fighters from the Gio and Mano ethnic groups.[2] Taylor assured the Gio and Mano fighters that by joining him, they would have the opportunity to exact revenge on President Doe and his Krahn ethnic group.

Clearly, the agenda of the NPFL was to make Taylor the president of Liberia, and to make him wealthy, through the plundering and sale of Liberia's natural resources. The NPFL recruited its fighters primarily from the Gio and Mano ethnic groups; other fighters were recruited from the various ethnic groups. Also, the NPFL recruited several "child-soldiers." The NPFL was the best equipped of the militias: It had an assortment of conventional weapons.

The NPFL's fighting techniques consisted of immersing its fighters into the civilian population, as a way of launching attacks without detection; hitting selected targets and fleeing; and engagement in selective battles for short periods of time. In terms of relations with the civilian population, the NPFL fighters robbed, plundered, tortured, killed, raped women, and destroyed various public and private facilities.

The Independent National Patriotic Front of Liberia (INPFL)

The Independent National Patriotic Front of Liberia (INPFL) was a breakaway faction of Taylor's NPFL. Organized in 1990, and led by Prince Johnson, one of Taylor's confidantes, the establishment of the INPFL reflected a split between Prince Johnson and Charles Taylor over the complexion of the post-Doe era.

The INPFL's agenda was twofold: The removal of the Doe regime, and the prevention of Taylor from succeeding Doe as president. Compared with the other warlords, Prince Johnson was less interested in political power and the acquisition of wealth. The fighters were recruited from all ethnic backgrounds. The INPFL had some conventional weapons, which were captured from, the NPFL and the Armed Forces of Liberia, and received from the United States and Economic Community of West African States Monitoring Group (ECOMOG). The INPFL's fighting techniques were similar to those of the rival NPFL. Although it committed its own share of atrocities, the INPFL had a relatively better relationship with civil society than the other warring factions had.

In 1992, Prince Johnson and Charles Taylor concluded a *modus vivendi*, under which their two militias agreed to cooperate in taking over Monrovia. Under the operation dubbed "Octopus," both the NPFL and INPFL were to launch a joint military assault against ECOMOG. However, Prince Johnson reneged at the eleventh hour. Consequently, the NPFL overran the INPFL's Cadwell base, and killed some of its fighters. Prince Johnson surrendered to

ECOMOG and was given sanctuary in Nigeria. Thus, the INPFL ceased to exist in October 1992.

The United Liberation Movement for Democracy in Liberia (ULIMO)

The ULIMO was organized in 1991, following the capture and subsequent killing of President Doe by the NPFL. The group consisted of some of the former officials of the Doe regime, including his closest allies. Initially, General Albert Karpeh, former minister of defense in the Doe military junta, led the group. Subsequently, in a power struggle that ensued, General Karpeh was killed and replaced by Alhaji Kromah, former minister of information and director-general of the Liberian Broadcasting Corporation under the Doe regime, and Raleigh Seekie, a former official in the public financial sector under Doe. The power struggle within ULIMO continued, resulting in the division of the militia into two factions: ULIMO-K led by Alhaji Kromah, and ULIMO-J led by Roosevelt Johnson, a former low-level civil servant in the Doe regime. The two factions used ethnicity as the bait for their recruitment: ULIMO-K appealed to the members of the Mandingo ethnic group, and ULIMO-J appealed to the Krahn ethnic group. Also, most of the fighters of ULIMO-J were soldiers in the Armed Forces of Liberia. The two militias' agendas, fighting techniques, and relations with civil society mirrored those of the NPFL. In terms of capabilities, although ULIMO-J had few conventional weapons, it nevertheless had the best fighting force, as demonstrated during the April 6, 1996, round of the civil war.[3]

ULIMO-K had limited fighting capabilities in terms of weapons and personnel. Its fighting techniques and relations with civil society were similar to those of its counterparts —NPFL and ULIMO-J.

The Liberian Peace Council (LPC)

George Boley, former minister of state for presidential affairs, minister of post and telecommunications, and chairman of the national investment commission during the Doe regime, organized the LPC in 1991. Its fighters were principally recruited from the Armed Forces of Liberia. Like ULIMO-J and ULIMO-K, it used ethnicity as the basis for recruitment: It appealed to "Krahn nationalism" as the vehicle for recruiting fighters. The agenda was similar to those of the NPFL, ULIMO-J, and ULIMO-K. Its leaders wanted to gain political power, and to get rich. Like ULIMO-J, it had limited fighting capabilities. Also, its fighting techniques were similar to those of all of the other militias. Like the NPFL, ULIMO-J, and ULIMO-K, it gained notoriety for harassing, brutalizing, and killing civilians, and for burning down homes, private businesses, and public buildings.

The Lofa Defense Force (LDF)

François Massaquoi, a former civil servant during the Tolbert and Doe regimes, organized the LDF in 1991. The militia was purportedly organized to protect Lofa County, the largest region in Liberia, and the home of the Belle, Gbandi, Kissi, and Lorma ethnic groups from attack by the other militias. However, in reality, like the other militias (excluding the INPFL), the LDF was organized as an instrument for François Massaquoi and the other ethnic entrepreneurs to negotiate and secure political positions in the various interim administrations. As an organization, the LDF was very small. Its fighters were recruited mainly from the Lofa region. The LDF was tangentially involved in the prosecution of the civil war. Thus, by 1991, the LDF ceased to function.

The National Patriotic Front of Liberia-Central Revolutionary Council (NPFL-CRC)

The NPFL-CRC was a breakaway faction of the NPFL. Established in 1994, its leadership consisted of erstwhile confidantes of Charles Taylor—Samuel Dokie (late), J. Lavela Supuwood, and Tom Woweiyou.[4] Its fighters consisted of defectors from the NPFL and its capabilities were quite limited. The agenda and fighting techniques of the NPFL-CRC were similar to those of the NPFL, ULIMO-J, ULIMO-K, and the LPC. In terms of relations with civil society, they were relatively harmonious.

The Armed Forces of Liberia

When the civil war erupted in 1989, the Doe regime was faced with several serious problems. First, the Liberian military had small selectively trained units that were not sufficient to contain and crush the NPFL. In other words, overall, the military was not well trained.

Second, since the rise to leadership positions in the military historically has been dictated by personal connections, and not merit, the military top brass was not prepared to provide the requisite leadership. In fact, Lieutenant-General Henry Dubar, the chief of staff of the armed forces of Liberia, fled Liberia, at the onset of the civil war.

Third, historically, the military has been undisciplined; and this affected its ability to wage a successful counterinsurgency strategy. For example, the soldiers continued to harass and brutalize civilians, especially those who were suspected of being sympathizers of the "rebels." Thus, more time and energy were spent on terrorizing civil society than that spent on the war itself.

Fourth, the Doe regime recruited several criminals, who were serving prison terms in the military, to both buttress the ranks and to replace defectors. These criminals did not have the minimum or basic military training; hence, they were liabilities.

Fifth, the Doe regime did not have the support of the majority of the population, as evidenced by the fact that the legitimacy of the regime finally eroded by 1981. The erosion of the regime's legitimacy was caused by its failure to set into motion the requisite modalities for addressing the neocolonial state and its pantomimes. Thus, when the NPFL launched its ostensibly designed rebellion to depose the Doe regime, the majority of the Liberian population was supportive. This was not because the NPFL presented a viable alternative, but rather, the mass support was propelled by exhaustion and frustration with the excesses of the Doe regime; hence, there was the dangerous inclination to support the removal of the Doe regime from power by any means and group. Importantly, the lack of mass support for the Doe regime undermined the effectiveness of the pursuance of the regime's counterinsurgency strategy.

Sixth, the majority of the soldiers were ill equipped. Given its extreme paranoia, the Doe regime provided weapons only to those who were determined to be loyalists. Hence, several soldiers went to the battlefront without the necessary weapons.

Seventh, the Liberian military did not have an effective counterinsurgency doctrine. Accordingly, the NPFL was able to undertake successful ambushes and rapidly gain territory. The various ambushes resulted in the death and capture of hundreds of Liberian government soldiers.

The Patrons

Various patrons—states and private individuals—and groups supported the warlordist militias. Five states played pivotal roles in providing support to the various militias. Libya supported the NPFL in two major ways. It played a critical role in training the initial 150 commandos of the NPFL, who constituted the core of the militia's fighters that initially attacked Liberia. Also, Libya supplied weapons to the NPFL. Libya supported the NPFL for several reasons. First, Libya held a grudge against the Doe regime for refusing its many overtures in the early 1980s, after the military coup in Liberia. Libya's hope was that the Doe regime could become its surrogate in the West African subregion. But to Libya's chagrin, the Doe regime became a client of the United States. Thus Libya's support for the Taylor-led NPFL was designed to teach the Doe regime a lesson. Second and a corollary, given Libya's antagonistic relationship with the United States then, the opportunity to contribute to the removal of a trusted American client regime from power was viewed as a major victory in the quest to diminish American influence in Africa. Third, Libya viewed its collaboration with the NPFL as an opportunity to "settle an old score with Nigeria." During the Chadian civil war in the 1980s, Nigeria played a pivotal role in the evacuation of Libyan dissidents from Chad, after the defeat of the pro-American faction led by Hisan Habre (Kieh, 1992a). Accordingly, Libya saw its support of NPFL as an opportunity to undermine the efforts of the ECOWAS peacekeeping force led by Nigeria, which intervened in the Liberian civil war.

Côte d'Ivoire, Liberia's eastern neighbor provided support for the NPFL in four major areas. It provided its territory as a bridgehead from which the NPFL launched its insurgency against the Doe regime. Also, Cote d'Ivoire provided a "safe haven" for Charles Taylor, the leader of the NPFL, and his principal lieutenants. In addition, Cote d'Ivoire provided safe passage for the transshipment of arms bound for the NPFL and for the illegal sale of Liberia's resources that were plundered and pillaged by the militia. Moreover, the country served as the NPFL's "window to the world." That is, Cote d'Ivoire served as the point of contact of any travel undertaken by officials of the NPFL and in the militia's development of an expansive web of international connections. Significantly, Cote d'Ivoire supported the NPFL for two major reasons. Then Ivorian President Felix Houphouet-Boigny had harbored a grudge against the Doe regime for the military coup in Liberia that led to the overthrow of the Tolbert regime and the subsequent killing of President Tolbert and his son Adolphus Benedict Tolbert. The vendetta was informed by the fact that Presidents Boigny and Tolbert were personal friends and in-laws. Adolphus Benedict Tolbert was married to President Boigny's daughter. Accordingly, since 1980, President Boigny had been looking for an opportunity to exact revenge against the Doe regime; hence, the support for the NPFL provided that opportunity. The other reason was driven by Ivorian national interests. That is, the Ivorian support for the NPFL was designed to help bolster Cote d'Ivoire's advantage in its competition with Nigeria for leadership in the West African subregion. The belief was that a Taylor-led government in Liberia would be aligned with and supportive of Ivorian interests. This was against the backdrop of Nigeria's opposition to the NPFL's effort to cease state power through the force of arms.

For its part, Burkina Faso also supported the NPFL. As Whiteman (1991: 401) notes, "The relationship between Burkinabe President Blaise Compaore and NPFL–leader Charles Taylor predated the Liberian civil war: Burkina Faso picked up Taylor when Ghana passed him on in 1987." In terms of support, Burkina Faso served as a conduit for shipping arms from Libya to the NPFL; provided military training and advisers, and gave sanctuary to Taylor and his lieutenants (Kieh, 1992: 133). The Burkinabe support for the NPFL was based on three factors. The core factor was that various Burkinabe government officials were privately accumulating capital from the commissions they were paid by Charles Taylor; hence, the support for the NPFL was a profitable venture personally. Another reason was Burkina Faso's desire to become a subregional player in West Africa; thus, it saw the Liberian conflict as an opportunity to take a side and become a "power broker" (Whiteman, 1991: 401). Finally, the Burkinabe president is yet another son-in-law of the then Ivorian President Boigny who used the familial ties to gain Burkina Faso's support for Taylor's NPFL (Kieh, 1992: 133).

Sierra Leone played a role during the initial phase of war in supporting the formation of ULIMO. The militia was organized to counter the NPFL. The group was organized by former officials of the Doe regime, who had been given sanctuary in Sierra Leone as the collapse of the Doe regime became imminent. Sierra Leone's action was based on self-interest: Because Taylor was supporting the rebel Revolutionary United Front (RUF) in its bid to oust the Momoh regime from power, the latter's support for ULIMO was designed as a "strategy of containment." Essentially, the Sierra Leonean government entertained the hope that ULIMO would serve as an effective check on the NPFL, thereby undercutting its capacity to support the RUF.

The United States' involvement in the Liberian civil war was based on a policy of inconsistency characterized by recurrent vacillations. At the onset of the civil war, the Bush administration decided to continue its support for the Doe regime, its client. Toward this end, American military advisers were dispatched to Liberia to help the Doe regime suppress the insurgency (Kieh, 1992a: 133). However, after an avalanche of pressure from Liberians and various human rights organizations was brought to bear on the Bush administration, the military advisors were withdrawn (Kieh, 1992a: 133).

Interestingly, when it became quite apparent that the collapse of the Doe regime was imminent, the United States decided to assess its policy of blanket support for the Doe regime. One of the outcomes was the Bush administration's admonition to President Doe to call "early presidential election" (the election was scheduled for October 1991). Clearly, this strategy was designed to placate the NPFL and the majority of Liberians, who saw the United States as an obstacle to the removal of the Doe regime from power. This was followed by a visit to Liberia by Herman Cohen, the American assistant secretary of state for African affairs (Kieh, 1992a: 133).

During the trip Assistant Secretary Cohen held discussions with both President Doe and warlord Taylor, the leader of the NPFL (Kieh, 1992a: 133). President Doe refused to comply with the American call of the holding of "early presidential election." So, amidst the scoring of one military victory after another by the NPFL, and not wanting to alienate the militia, the United States withdrew its support from the Doe regime. The shift in policy was reflected in the Bush administration's call for President Doe to resign and go into exile. The United States promised to provide safe passage for President Doe, his immediate relatives, and senior advisors. But, again, President Doe rejected the American proposition, opting as he put it, "to fight until the last man." Having dispensed with its ally, the United States then engaged in the process of finding a new client to support in the civil war. At that time, Washington had two major options. The first one was to support Charles Taylor and his NPFL. However, the United States refused to pursue this option because of Taylor's links to Libya and the attendant issue of unreliability as a client. The other option was to support Prince Johnson and his breakaway INPFL. In the end, the Bush administration chose this option. As a demonstration of support for Johnson's INPFL, its emerging client, American marines began to train the group's fighters and to deliver arms and other supplies to them (*West Africa*, 1990: 2330). Also, the United States provided the group with helicopters to airlift its fighters closer to the Liberian presidential mansion (*West Africa*, 1990: 2330). The rationale was to give the INPFL a strategic advantage over the rival NPFL in the final battle to cease control of the mansion and wrestle away state power from the Doe regime. Another demonstration of American support for the INPFL was reflected in the provision of intelligence that the militia used to capture Doe and subsequently kill him.[5] Characteristically, as the commission of human rights abuses by the INPFL became embarrassing, the United States decided to withdraw its support from the INPFL. The next turn was to support, howbeit grudgingly, the ECOWAS.

Also, private individuals and groups provided support for the various militias. For example, several leading members of the True Whig Party–led deposed ruling class provided financial support to the NPFL. This was because Taylor promised to exact revenge on Doe for depositing their government, and to restore them to power in Liberia. Others, especially some Liberians based in the United States, supported the INPFL, ULIMO-J, ULIMO-K, and the LPC. Among these individuals was a cadre of "wartime capitalists" who saw their provision of support as an investment in getting financial returns from the natural resources these groups were pillaging and selling illegally.

The Peacemakers

There were two groups of peacemakers involved in the civil war: the Religious Leaders of Liberia (RLL)(the name was later changed to the Inter-Religious Council of Liberia (IRCL) and the ECOWAS. The former group was an amalgam of Christian and Islamic leaders, who organized themselves into a mediation group designed to seek an end to the civil war. Before the formation of the RLL, the Liberian Council of Churches (LCC), the Christian-based organization of members of the clergy, served as the principal forum for the clergy's involvement in seeking an end to the civil war. On January 20, 1990, the LCC issued a statement expressing its concern about the military situation and the killings in Monrovia (Liberian Council of Churches, 1990: 1).

Operationally, the RLL formulated and promulgated a peace plan that, *inter alia*, called for a ceasefire between the military forces of the Doe regime and the NPFL and the holding of peace talks between the two groups. Subsequently, the group engaged in active mediatory efforts that involved the holding of separate meetings with President Doe and warlord Taylor. Faced with the imminent demise of his regime, President Doe was more amenable to the group's peace plan. On the other side, the Taylor-led NPFL was opposed to the Religious Leaders' peace plan because it was seen as an obstacle to the NPFL's military conquest and subsequent seizure of state power. Interestingly, though, the NPFL gave the clerics the false impression that it was interested in the resolution of the conflict and thus accepted the terms of the group's peace plan. On the basis of the assurances from the two belligerents, the Religious Leaders organized a peace conference in neighboring Sierra Leone. A delegation from the Doe regime attended the talks; however, the Taylor-led NPFL failed to send representatives. This action on the part of the NPFL severely undermined the peace plan and effectively rendered it moribund.

With the collapse of the Religious Leaders' peace plan and the escalating level of violence, the ECOWAS decided to intervene in the civil war. This ignited a heated debate among the organization's membership. On the one hand, the pro-intervention group led by Nigeria made the argument that the war had generated a humanitarian crisis evidenced by the deaths of hundreds of civilians and burgeoning refugee problem. Moreover, the pro-interventionists asserted that the war posed a major threat to peace and stability in the subregion. On the other hand, the anti-interventionist group countered by asserting, among other things, that the civil war was an internal affair. Furthermore, ECOWAS's Charter did not clothe the organization with the authority to intervene in civil conflicts. This point was particularly poignant against the backdrop of the organization being an economic one.

Without settling the debate and its attendant legal, political, and military issues, the pro-interventionist group under Nigeria's leadership made the determination that the organization would intervene. Against this background, a two-pronged approach was designed. One dimension focused on peacemaking and the other on peacekeeping. The two strategies were pursued concurrently, For example, while the organization was convening the First All Liberia Conference in Banjul, the Gambia in mid-1990, involving various Liberian political parties and interests groups, it was simultaneously developing the modalities to dispatch a peacekeeping force to Liberia. Accordingly, after the close of the First All Liberia Conference, ECOWAS intervened in Liberia with a peacekeeping force. Throughout the war, ECOWAS recurrently used the two approaches as mutually reenforcing modalities. In addition, when it appeared that the NPFL was bent on undercutting efforts to resolve the war, ECOWAS added peace enforcement as a third approach to its battery of conflict management tools. Under the latter approach, the peacekeeping force undertook military action against the NPFL for inducing its compliance with the terms of the various peace accords.

The Dynamics of the Civil War

The war began on December 24, 1989, when a group of fighters from the NPFL led by Charles Taylor, a former official of the Doe regime, launched an attack from Cote d'Ivoire, Liberia's eastern neighbor. Using Ivorian territory as a launch pad, the NPFL quickly took control of various towns in Nimba County. This was made possible by the high degree of mass disenchantment with the policies of the Doe regime. In other words, the Doe regime had become so illegitimate that most Liberians were prepared to support any kind of change. The mass disaffection was pivotal in helping the NPFL to recruit fighters, to collect intelligence, and to secure safe havens in their various battles with Doe's forces. Despite the support of civilians, NPFL fighters committed various human rights violations—rape, beatings, torture, and murder—in an indiscriminate fashion. The NPFL's military successes in Nimba were replicated in the adjacent counties of Lofa, Bong, Rivercess, and Grand Bassa. Later, the NPFL successfully took control of more territories. By early March 1990, the NPFL was in control of approximately 90% of Liberia's territory.

Interestingly, as the NPFL scored one military victory after another against Doe's troops, dissension began to set in. The problem was caused by two sets of factors. It became clear to some of Taylor's top lieutenants, including Prince Johnson, that the war was not designed to oust a repressive regime to democratically reconstitute the Liberian state. Instead, the war was designed to make Charles Taylor the president of Liberia. Taylor's penchant for selling Liberia's natural resources in the territories under his militia's control and using the revenue for private accumulation offended some of his lieutenants, who saw the war as one of liberating the Liberian masses. Another issue was Taylor's tendency to order the murder of popular members of his militia, whom he perceived as posing threats to his omnipotence. For example, Taylor ordered the murders of Cooper Teah and Edmond Johnson, two very popular commanders of his militia. Taylor's ostentatious lifestyle in the midst of a war further helped convince his skeptical commanders that the war was about the deification of Taylor. In the midst of the "tug and pull" within the ranks of the NPFL, Prince Johnson, one of the top commanders broke away and organized the rival INPFL.

As Taylor's NPFL continued to make advances and the Doe forces struggled to hold on to state power and the attendant vitriolic human rights abuses and anarchy, the ECOWAS intervened in the war in May 1990. ECOWAS's initial approach was the use of mediation through the holding of the Banjul Meeting as a medium for trying to arrest the tide of violence in Liberia. The Banjul Meeting was a national conference that brought together all of the stakeholders in Liberia. Unfortunately, Taylor's NPFL refused to attend the conference. The rationale was that Taylor was convinced that his militia was on the verge of winning a military victory and taking over control of Liberia; hence, he saw ECOWAS's mediation efforts as a hindrance to his overall objective of capturing state power.

Exacerbated by the rising level of violence, ECOWAS intervened in the war with a peacekeeping force (ECOMOG). The military intervention by the regional body was welcomed by Prince Johnson's INPFL and Doe's forces, but opposed by Taylor's NPFL. Accordingly, Taylor's NPFL attacked the peacekeeping force. In the end, the peacekeeping force prevailed, and was able to push Taylor's forces out of Monrovia, the capital city, and to confine the INPFL to Cadwell, a suburb of Monrovia.

By September 1990, a major development occurred in the war: President Doe was captured, tortured, and killed by Prince Johnson's NPFL. Doe's death witnessed an increase in the level of violence, as Doe's loyalists burned down public buildings and murdered those suspected of supporting Taylor's NPFL. Subsequently, the remnants of the Doe forces regrouped and organized two new militias: The ULIMO and the LPC. Later, ULIMO splintered into two groups: ULIMO-J and ULIMO-K.

In late December 1990, ECOMOG was able to establish a security zone in Monrovia and its environs, and to maintain a modicum of "peace" for almost two years. But in October 1992, the Taylor–led NPFL launched a military offensive against Monrovia. Code-named "Octopus," the military offensive was designed to overrun ECOMOG's position and ultimately seize control of state power. ECOMOG was able to repel the attack. This decisive war led to the disintegration of the INPFL, which had collaborated with the NPFL in planning the attack and using its Cadwell base as a sanctuary for NPFL fighters. However, the INPFL reneged on the arrangement at the last moment.

From late 1992, ECOWAS continued to make concerted efforts designed to end the war. This was evidenced by the holding of numerous peace conferences. While ECOWAS was engaged in peacemaking efforts, the NPFL and ULIMO-K collaborated and launched a massive military attack on Monrovia in April 1996. After sitting on the sidelines and watching the bloodletting between the NPFL and ULIMO-K on the one hand, and ULIMO-J and the LPC, on the other, ECOMOG finally intervened and brought the situation under control.

After several failed agreements (16 of them), the Abuja II Accord succeeded in formally terminating the war in 1997. This was followed by the holding of presidential and legislative elections in July 1997. Given its dominant military position, Charles Taylor and his National Patriotic Party (the off-shoot of the NPFL) won the elections by more than 75% of the vote. Subsequently, Charles Taylor became the president of Liberia, and Liberia's "Third Republic" was ushered in on August 2, 1997.

State Collapse

The collapse of the Liberian state began in November 1985, following the abortive coup attempt against the Doe regime. The coup occurred as a protest against the rigging of the October 1985 national elections in Liberia. By all independent accounts, Doe and his National Democratic Party of Liberia (NDPL) lost the presidential elections to Jackson Doe (not a relative) and the Liberian Action Party.

However, using the power of incumbency, President Doe was able to manipulate the results of the elections. The resultant mass disenchantment and campaign of terror waged by the Doe regime occasioned the beginning of the collapse of the state's authority: Opponents of the regime—the student and labor movements and other civil society organizations, opposition political parties, and others—engaged in the mass mobilization of the citizenry to resist the authority of the state and its illegitimate regime. To make matters worse, the state's ability to pay government workers regularly and to provide basic social services for the populace fuelled the resistance to state authority.

By the beginning of the war in December 1989, the Liberian state had partially collapsed. The process of collapse was accelerated as the NPFL wrestled away territory from the Doe regime. With the loss of territory came the disintegration of state institutions and processes. That is, as the NPFL took control of Nimba and other regions of Liberia, the state institutions in those areas collapsed and the state's capacity to make and enforce laws and to collect taxes became nonexistent.

In September 1990, the Liberian state experienced final and total collapse, when President Doe was captured, tortured, and killed by Prince Johnson's INPFL. The aftermath was marked by the complete disintegration of state institutions throughout Liberia. In fact, Taylor and his NPFL established an alternative government in Gbarnga, the militia's "capital city." The so-called Taylor–led government was referred to as the National Patriotic Reconstruction Assembly government. Moreover, the NPFL made efforts to establish alternative state structures at the local level throughout the country. Interestingly, no country in the world recognized Taylor's so-called government.

In essence, the civil war hastened and ultimately occasioned the total disintegration and collapse of the Liberian state. The violence and anarchy that the war unleashed and the corresponding incapacity of the state to respond, resist, and overcome the challenge led to the acceleration of the pace of the final phase of the state's collapse.

The Cost of the Civil War

Like every civil war, the Liberian one exacted multiple costs. As Pottenbaum and Kaubur (2001: 1) note "Civil wars inflict serious human, social and economic damage on the countries involved. Against this backdrop, this section of the chapter examines some of the costs incurred during the first Liberian civil war—human, economic, political, social, and infrastructural. In terms of the human loss, there are various estimates on the total number of civilians who were killed: The estimates ranged from 150,000 to 200,000 (Lincoln, 1991; *Armed Conflict Event Data*, 2006). The various warlordist militias were collectively responsible for the killing of civilians. Some of the civilians died as part of targeted killings that was carried out by the various militias, while others were caught in various crossfires. Also, thousands of civilians were wounded and maimed; however, there are no available data on the numbers. Given the insecurity conundrum created by the war, scores of Liberians fled the country in search of safety. During the course of the war, an estimated 850,000 Liberians became refugees in the neighboring countries of Côte d'Ivoire, Guinea, and Sierra Leone, as well as in Ghana, Nigeria, and Togo (Kieh, 1996b; United Nations Mission in Liberia, 2006). Similarly, the war forced droves of other Liberians throughout the country to flee their homes and become internally displaced. By the end of the war in 1997, there were an estimated 1 million internally displaced persons (USAID, 2006). Some of these individuals were housed in makeshift camps throughout the country by international organizations, while others sought shelter in ransacked public and private buildings. One of the major dimensions of the human tragedy wrought by the war was manifested by the "culture of vitriolic human rights abuses." All warlordist militias—NPFL, INPFL, LPC, ULIMO-J, and ULIMO-K—committed various human rights abuses against civilians. These abuses took the form of rape, robberies, beatings, tortures, forced labor, and killing (Human Rights Watch, 1996: 1).

The economic consequences of the war were evident at various levels. First and foremost, all economic production in the various sectors—iron ore, rubber, logging, and so on—ceased. In the absence of state authority, the various warring factions used the opportunity to engage in illegal economic production as part of the process of the private accumulation of capital for their leaders. For example, the Charles Taylor-led NPFL, the largest and most powerful militia, engaged in the illegal production of rubber at the Firestone Plantations Company, the largest rubber firm in the country; undertook the illicit mining of minerals—diamond and gold—and engaged in logging activities. Second, the war adversely affected food production. According to the Food and Agriculture Organization (1996: 1), by 1995, rice production (the country's staple food), dropped by approximately 80% from the pre–civil war level. Cassava production was similarly affected, falling by as much as 50% (Food and Agriculture Organization, 1996: 1). Third, by 1997, exports fell to $25 million—a precipitous decline from $440 million in 1988 (World Bank, 2006). Fourth, there was massive capital flight, especially in the retail industry that was dominated by Lebanese merchants.

Also, the war decimated the country's already underdeveloped infrastructure. For example, the national hydro plant and water purification systems were destroyed. In addition, the electric poles were stripped of the copper wire and destroyed in some cases. Also, bridges were blown up as part of some of the group's fighting tactics. Public and private buildings were destroyed. As for the roads, which were already in a deplorable state, the years of warfare made them even more impassable.

Similarly, health facilities, including hospitals and clinics—both public and private—were destroyed. Clearly, this aggravated the health crisis in the country by substantially decreasing access. Consequently, hundreds of people died, in some cases from curable diseases.

Like the other sectors, the war adversely affected the country's environment in various ways. For example, it was common practice to use various waterways as disposal sites for dead bodies. Dead bodies were also left to decay on various tracts of land throughout the country.

Conclusion

The chapter examined the first Liberian civil war that was the by-product of the multifaceted crises of underdevelopment generated by the failure of the Liberian state to be relevant to the lives of the majority of the Liberian people. First, the study discussed the forces and dynamics that shaped the irregular warfare. Several forces shaped the war: the regime of Samuel Doe and several militias—the NPFL, INPFL, ULIMO-J, ULIMO-K, LPC, LDF, and NPFL-CRC. Each warring faction had a leader, a semblance of an organizational structure, a recruitment pattern, and antagonistic relations with the larger society. Also, each insurgency group prosecuted the war without a formal doctrine.

Second, the chapter discussed the roles played by various patrons—Libya, Burkina Faso, Sierra Leone, and the United States—in supporting the armed factions. Libya and Burkina Faso supported the Taylor-led NPFL; Sierra Leone initially supported ULIMO, which subsequently splintered into two factions; and the United States initially supported the Doe regime and its Armed Forces of Liberia; but later, it shifted its support to Prince Johnson's INPFL. Interestingly, after President Doe was captured and killed by Johnson's INPFL, the United States withdrew its support from the INPFL. Also, private individuals and groups played pivotal roles in helping to fund and arm the various militias.

Third, the chapter assessed the role of the peacemakers—both internal and external. At the internal level, the role of the RLL was discussed; and at the external level, the emphasis was on the ECOWAS.

Fourth, the civil war–state collapse nexus was probed. The findings show that the civil war accelerated the process of state collapse by introducing violence and anarchy, which the state and its institutions could not effectively counter. Accordingly, state institutions and processes disintegrated as the war advanced from one part of Liberia to another, with the state and its government incapable of containing and stopping the trend. The capture and killing of Doe in September 1990 marked the complete and total disintegration and collapse of the Liberian state.

Fifth, the war exacted enormous cost on Liberia in a variety of ways. At the core was the human cost as reflected in the deaths of between 150,000 and 200,000 people, mainly civilians. Also, thousands of Liberians were forced into exile as refugees, while scores of others were internally displaced Similarly, the infrastructure was decimated, and social services were destroyed. On the productive front, the economy was brought to a grinding halt. The war worsened the problem of environmental degradation.

Notes

1. General Thomas Quiwonkpa was one of the leaders of the military coup who brought Samuel Doe to power. Beginning in 1982, the relationship between him and Doe became strained, when Doe demoted him from his position as Commanding General of the Armed Forces of Liberia and the number four official on the ruling People's Redemption Council (PRC) to the ceremonial position of Secretary-General of the Council (the number six position in the restructured military council).
2. The conflict between the Gio and the Mano ethnic groups on the one hand, and the Krahn ethnic group on the other was manufactured by Head of State Doe, following the raid on Nimba County, after the 1985 Quiwonkpa-led abortive *coup d'etat*. It was designed to win support for the unpopular Doe regime from his Krahn ethnic group, in the midst of the regime's crisis of legitimacy.
3. During the April 6, 1996 round of the irregular war, ULIMO-J led by Roosevelt Johnson, defeated the combined forces of the Taylor-led NPFL and the Kromah-headed ULIMO-J.
4. Later, Tom Woweiyu defected from the NPFL-CRC, and rejoined Charles Taylor in the NPFL.
5. Several former officials of the Independent National Patriotic Front of Liberia (INPFL) indicated in interviews that the United States provided their militia with the intelligence regarding President Doe's visit to the Freeport of Monrovia, the temporary headquarters of the peacekeeping force of the ECOWAS. On the basis of the intelligence, the INPFL was able to storm the Freeport of Monrovia and capture President Doe. Subsequently, President Doe was taken to the Caldwell Base of the INPFL, where he was killed. Moreover, in a videotape on President Doe's cap-

ture by the INPFL, Prince Johnson, the leader of the INPFL was seen trying in vain to contact the U.S. Embassy in Liberia, after his group captured President Doe. Interestingly, he got no response, causing him to engage in a tirade against the United States.

PART IV: THE INSIGHTS

CHAPTER 9

Summary, Lessons, Prescriptions, and Conclusion

Introduction

The central premise of the book is that the first Liberian civil war was a by-product of the multifaceted crises of underdevelopment generated by the settler and neocolonial Liberian state. That is, the failure of the Liberian state to cater to and address the needs of the majority of the people created, inter alia, political, economic, social, and cultural crises. In turn, these crises provided the terra firma for the sowing, nurturing, and eventual germination of the conditions that occasioned the first civil war. In other words, the type of state that was established in Liberia, beginning in 1847, was of the "wrong type" (Samatar and Samatar, 2002). This was and continues to be reflected in the nature, mission, character, values, structures, and policies of the Liberian state and its attendant impact on the lives of Liberians. Hence, it was inevitable that the state was going to experience failure.

Against this background, the purpose of this chapter is threefold. First, the chapter summarizes the basic arguments of the book. Second, it deciphers the lessons that can be learned from the travails of the settler and then the neocolonial Liberian state. Third, it offers a prescription for the democratic reconstitution of the Liberian state. Fourth, the chapter recapitulates the major issues addressed in the book.

The Summary

The state architecture (settler and subsequently neocolonial construct) that was designed for Liberia was bound to fail and consequently produce crises. For more than eight decades, Liberia was a settler state. Essentially, this meant that the state was intrinsically the embodiment of the Weltanschauung and associated interests of the African-American repatriates or the Americo-

Liberians. To paraphrase Marx and Engels (1998: 1), the Liberian state became "the executive committee" for the management of the interests of the settler stock. In short, the settler state was an exclusionary construct that did not embody the hopes, aspirations, and interests of the indigenes who were resident in it. Clearly, this was vividly demonstrated by the fact that these indigenes were not considered citizens of the settler state. Instead, to paraphrase Mamdani (1996), they were "subjects." Although the settler state began to integrate the indigenes into the body politic by granting them citizenship in the early 1900s, this did not change the fundaments of the state: Settler values, customs, and interests remained dominant. This was reflected by the fact that they served as the "standards" for participation in the affairs of the polity. Hence, the indigenes were forced to adopt the "settler way" as the sine qua non for "meaningful" citizenship. Despite this development, the majority of the indigenes were still resistant to settler hegemony. Thus, there were continuing tensions and conflicts.

Another critical aspect of the settler state was its embryonic peripheral capitalist political economy. Under this rubric, the settler state was an emerging appendage of the international capitalist system as evidenced by, among other things, its serving as a plantation for the production of raw materials to supply the industrial and manufacturing machines of the metropolis; its vulnerability to the various shocks of the global capitalist order; and its reliance on the international capitalist to serve as the engine of its development by helping to provide remedies to its various economic problems. The dependent relationship between Liberia and the metropolitan-dominated global capitalist system was exacerbated by the failure of the Liberian ruling class to formulate and implement a national development plan that would, inter alia, develop the modalities for promoting domestic capital formation and the creation of wealth; diversify the economy to help minimize its vulnerability to the characteristic fluctuations in the global capitalist political economy; invest in human resource development so as to develop the requisite pool of skilled personnel; and develop the infrastructure.

Significantly, in 1926, the settler state was transformed into a neocolonial state with a full-blown peripheral capitalist political economy, as the consequence of the finalization of the process of fully integrating Liberia into the international capitalist order. This development was engineered by the establishment of the Firestone Plantations Company in Liberia. Subsequently, the state was reconstituted to conform to the imperatives of the new neocolonial realities. At the core of the reconstitution project was the ascendancy of class as the principal mode of identity. That is, an individual's relationship to the major means of production took priority over his or her ethnic stock. However, this did not mean that the perennial settler-indigene "ethnic divide" that had undergirded the state-building project disappeared. Instead, the divide became secondary. This is because the emergent neocolonial incarnation and its peripheral capitalist political economy made it exigent for the transformation of the state into a partisan construct in the service of the new pan-ethnic ruling class. This is because the centrality of ethnicity is antithetical to the logic of the capitalist mode of production— peripheral or otherwise. Accordingly, since the reconstitution project was not intended to rethink, deconstruct, and democratically reconstitute the settler Liberian state, its neocolonial permutation retained its basic nature, mission, character, and policies anchored on an antipeople, antidemocracy, and antidevelopment foundation. In essence, the change from the settler to the neocolonial phase of the Liberian state was analogous to, using the proverbial expression "putting new wine into old bottles." Thus, the underlying socioeconomic and political contradictions that the settler Liberian state had engendered were not resolved by the transition. Instead, these contradictions were sharpened and assumed new complexion under the neocolonial phase.

Importantly, the Liberian state both in its settler and peripheral capitalist form produced various crises—political, economic, social, and cultural. At the political level, the 1847 Constitution created several crises. Among them, for almost a century, it legalized segregation and discrimination by denying citizenship to the indigenes that were under its jurisdiction. Also, it privileged the propertied class by making economic holdings the bases for contesting for major public offices such as the presidency, the vice presidency, the senate, and the house of representatives. Similarly, only the propertied had the right to vote. Although the 1986 Constitution removed the property requirement as the major eligibility requirement for voting, it kept the requirement for candidates contesting the presidency and vice presidency. Another dimension of the political crisis was the state's violation of the political rights and civil liberties of its citizens.

Economically, there was abject poverty; spiraling unemployment, particularly after the fizzling of the so-called economic boom of the 1950s–1970s that was triggered by influx of foreign investment; low standard of living; and unbridled corruption. With the emergence of the state as the major employer since the end of the 1860s, the control of state power became a "life and death struggle" even among the various factions of the ruling class. Although the state served the general interests of the ruling class, the various compradors were responsible for amassing their own personal wealth. Hence, the control of state power provided the opportunity for the private accumulation of capital.

In the social sphere, the majority of the people did not have access to education, health care, safe drinking water, acceptable sanitation, and shelter. One of the major consequences was the mass vulnerability to diseases. Scores of Liberians died from various curable diseases. Similarly, the members of the ruling class and their relatives received medical care in the metropolis, even routine checkups. Clearly, these actions were admissions on the part of the members of the ruling class that the state, which they were "managing," was incapable of addressing even their own basic human needs; hence, they had to rely on the metropolis.

The cultural crisis was manifested in many ways. The core of the crisis was the perennial divide between the settlers or the African-American repatriates and the members of the various indigenous ethnic groups or the indigenes. The state generated this crisis from its inception and made it worse over time through the constitutional order and policies. Even the efforts such as the "unification policy," the creation of new political subdivisions, and positions in the public bureaucracy had the net effect of exacerbating the conflict. Another dimension of the crisis was the instrumental use of ethnicity by the Doe regime, in the midst of the government's crisis of legitimacy, to polarize the Krahn ethnic group (from which President Doe hailed) and the Mano and Gio ethnic groups.

However, for about three decades, a facade of stability and prosperity served as the bandage on the lesions created by the degenerative disease of state failure. Essentially, the façade was based on the notion that Liberia was peaceful, especially in the midst of the wave of political violence—military coups and civil wars—that enveloped the West African subregion and the African continent in general from the 1950s to 1970s. Also, Liberia was depicted as a model of economic prosperity because the majority of the eligible labor force had employment, and there was an appreciable amount of money in circulation that made it possible for people to minimally survive. The façade was maintained by a confluence of factors. At the base was a booming economy that was propelled by the infusion of foreign investments, especially as a consequence of the launching of the country's open door policy" in 1944. The influx of foreign investments was anchored by the mining sector: The discovery of high grade iron ore in the Bomi, Bong, and Nimba regions of the country spurred the establishment of the Liberian Mining Company (LMC) in Bomi, the Bong Mining Company (Bong County), and the Liberian American Swedish Mining Company. This development helped to create jobs and provide revenues for the Liberian state. Another factor was the establishment and maintenance of a patronage system, which provided "jobs" and largesse for an "army of unemployed." Also, the state developed a large security apparatus that was used to cow the populace into submission. In the same vein, the state recurrently used violence against individuals and groups, who were perceived as posing threats to the interests of the ruling class.

By the early 1970s, the core of the façade began to experience stress and strain due to several factors. One of the major factors was the deepening economic crisis occasioned by the vicissitudes of the international capitalist system. For example, the prices of iron ore and rubber, the two commodities that provided the "life blood" of the economy dropped. Consequently, the state's revenue base experienced a decline. One of the resultant effects was the state's inability to dispense largesse and to maintain the complex of patronage that had been pivotal to inhibiting the outbreak of violent conflict. In addition, two of the major foreign multinational corporations in the mining sector folded their operations. This left thousands of Liberians unemployed, which occasioned far-reaching economic and social consequences for them and their families. Another factor was the emergence of national reform movements such as the Movement for Justice in Africa, the Progressive Alliance of Liberia, and a transformational movement—the All People's Freedom Alliance. In addition, the labor and student movements emerged as major players in the polity as they joined ranks with the reform and transformational movements in politically raising the consciousness of the members of the subaltern classes, and simultaneously putting pressure on the state and its ruling class to reform and reconstitute the peripheral capitalist state.

On April 14, 1979, the prosperity and stability "bubble" burst, when a coalition of the social and transformational movements and the student and labor movements challenged the state and its ruling class by organizing a massive demonstration. Although, the proposed increase in the price of rice, the country's staple food, served as the catalyst, the demonstration was ostensibly designed to protest the decades of political repression and social and economic malaise that had been visited on the subaltern classes by the neocolonial state and its ruling class. Significantly, the demonstration shook the foundation of the state and exposed its vulnerability.

Capitalizing upon the state of mass disillusionment with the state and its custodians, the Liberian military used the legitimate grievances of the subaltern classes to stage a coup on April 12, 1980. But contrary to the conventional wisdom, the coup did not represent the end of Americo-Liberian or settler domination. This is because the transformation of Liberia into a neocolonial state in 1926 witnessed the ascendant of classes as the major actors in the Liberian political economy. Due to this, the coup then represented a change of the composition of the ruling class, especially its bureaucratic wing. In other words, the ruling class remained the dominant local force, but there was a reshuffling of its personnel. For example, President Samuel Doe replaced President William R. Tolbert as the new spokesperson of the local Liberian ruling class. Particularly, the fact that the post-coup era witnessed the retention of the basic features of the neocolonial Liberian state—including its pan-ethnic ruling class—was ample evidence that one faction of the ruling class simply replaced another.

Overburdened by the excesses of the settler and neocolonial phases of the Liberian state, and lacking the interest, orientation, and will to institute the systemic transformation of the construct, the Doe regime exacerbated and increased the political, economic, social, and cultural classes that the state had engendered since its formation. Accordingly, the horrendous performance of the regime and the attendant state failure provided the crucible for the eruption of a violent conflict. So, the Charles Taylor–led National Patriotic Front of Liberia took advantage of the propitious conditions to launch its insurgency, thereby triggering the first Liberian civil war. Overall, the first civil war represented the coup de grace that finally and completely shattered the facade of stability.

The Lessons and the Imperative of the Democratic Reconstitution of the Neocolonial Liberian State

The Lessons

The Liberian experience provides several lessons. First, settler and neocolonial state constructs are prone to violent conflicts because they are intrinsically conflictual. In the case of settler social formations, they are anchored on the fundamental tenets of discrimination and segregation. This is because the settler stock deposits a vision based on its purported ethnocultural superiority vis-à-vis the indigenous population into the shells of the state. On the basis of this, the features of the emergent state reflect and seek to promote the "superior-inferior divide." Consequently, conflicts ensue between the settler and the indigenous stocks. If the state is not restructured, these conflicts may then blossom into violence. In the case of the settler Liberian state, it engaged in a series of violent conflicts with several indigenous ethnic groups. Elsewhere in Africa, in South Africa and Zimbabwe, for examples, the indigenous Africans rose up against the settler Afrikaner state and the settler Euro-state respectively. Similarly, neocolonial state constructs are intrinsically based on the subordination of the citizens' interests to those of the metropolitan powers. Accordingly, the productive and other activities of the neocolonial state are tailored toward meeting and addressing the dictates of the metropolis. The patron-client relationship between the neocolonial construct and the metropolis is maintained by the collusion between the compradorial class in the neocolony and the bourgeois classes in the metropolis. As their material conditions continue to deteriorate and the prospects for the democratic reconstitution of the state seem impossible, the relationship between the compradorial and subaltern classes would become polarized; this would set the stage for the occurrence of violent conflict.

Second and related, peripheral capitalist economies cannot promote an agenda that caters toward the fulfillment of basic human needs—jobs, education, health care, food, and shelter. This is because, like its developed capitalist "parent," peripheral capitalism is fundamentally designed to cater to the needs of the ruling classes in the metropolis and the neocolonies. Accordingly, state resources are disproportionately used to address the material and protective needs of the ruling classes. Importantly, for the purpose of containing insurrection from the subaltern classes, the ruling classes in the neocolonies do minimally invest some state resources into areas of interests of the subaltern classes. But, these resources are usually woefully inadequate, and therefore are incapable of addressing the subaltern classes' basic human needs. In the Liberian case, even during the so-called economic boom of the 1950s–1970s, the phenomenal economic growth did not translate into improvement in the material conditions of the country's subaltern classes. Similarly, in various African neocolonies such as the Democratic Republic of the Congo, Rwanda, and Sierra Leone, the pantomimes of the peripheral capitalist economy eventually created the conditions for violent conflicts.

Third, state repression does not indefinitely provide an insurance policy against mass revolt. As the empirical evidence shows in Africa and in other parts of the third world, the neocolonial state might slow the pace for the occurrence of a violent conflict, but such action is temporary. This is because as the conditions worsen, the subaltern classes will find innovative ways of neutralizing the effects of state-sponsored violence. Eventually, the conditions would be created for various groups—some genuinely in the interests of the subaltern classes and others opportunistic—to launch insurgencies against the neocolonial state, thus engulfing the neocolony into the flames of violent conflict. As the Liberian case showed, the ruling class was able to stall the occurrence of violent conflict for a century and four decades through the use of what I called conflict inhibitors. But, over time, these "conflict inhibitors" became ineffectual; hence, the state became vulnerable to the violent conflict.

Fourth, a metropolitan patron cannot perpetually insulate a neocolony from the wrath of the subaltern classes. Again, several cases abound in

Africa to substantiate this. For example in Somalia, the United States could not protect the Barre-led Somali neocolony from implosion and subsequent disintegration, despite the infusion of money and weapons from its American patron. Similarly, in the Democratic Republic of the Congo, the neocolonial construct, despite receiving support from the United States and other metropolitan powers for more than three decades, eventually buckled under the weight of the violent crises. Ultimately, the Congolese neocolony was enveloped by a violent conflict. Clearly, the Liberian experience fits this continental pattern. Despite the fact that the United States played a pivotal role in the formation and maintenance of the settler and neocolonial Liberian state and propped up the various regimes, American patronage could not prevent Liberia's descent into the abyss of civil war. In fact, when it became clear to the United States that the Doe regime, which had received the "lion's share" of American aid to Liberia, was in danger of collapse, the Bush administration pulled the "proverbial rug." Thus, crippled by decades of illegitimacy and crises, the Liberian neocolony was eventually swallowed by the tidal waves of violent conflict. So, the critical lesson to be learned is that only holistically democratic states, especially in Africa and the rest of the third world—those that promote political, economic, social, cultural, religious, and environmental rights and freedoms based on a pro-people and pro-development agenda—can properly manage the conflicts that are inherent in every social formation (prevent violent conflicts).

Finally, the end of the first Liberian civil war in July 1996, and the subsequent holding of a multiparty presidential election were not the panacea for resolving the Liberian conflict. This was vividly demonstrated by the fact that barely two years after the cessation of the war and the inauguration of a democratically elected government, another civil war—the second—erupted and exacted death and destruction of the Liberian people. Significantly, the continuation of violent conflict was a clear demonstration that the post–first civil war peace-building project that ensued failed to undertake the critical and indispensable task of deconstructing, rethinking, and democratically reconstituting the neocolonial Liberian state. Against this background, I argue that the sine qua non for resolving the conflict that engendered the first civil war is the systematic transformation of the Liberian state and the establishment of a new social democratic construct. As Olorode (2000: 190–191) argues, "The reconstitution of the "state" is considered necessary because some wound is believed to have been inflicted on the state and its apparatus: some wounds that create crises and debilitate the state and how its effects sustain the observed crisis."

The Democratic Reconstitution of the Neocolonial Liberian State

In this section, I attempt to map out the trajectory of the state transformation project. This will include: the pathways, the deconstruction-rethinking-reconstitution dynamic and the elements of the democratic state reconstitution project.

The Pathways: The pathways that are used for the state reconstitution process are indispensable to the outcome. For example, if the pathways are anchored on substantive democracy, then the resultant state construct and its features would mirror the democratic orientation. Against this background, I suggest one major pathway and derivatives for undertaking the process of democratically reconstituting the neocolonial Liberian state. The process of democratic state reconstitution in Liberia should begin with the holding of a national conference—sovereign or otherwise. The conference should include representatives from all the major stakeholders—the counties, political parties, interests groups, religious groups, youth, women, and so on. Each stakeholder group should elect its representatives through a democratic process. This is absolutely critical to the success of the project, because only the democratically elected representatives of the various stakeholders can legitimately articulate these entities' views. Also, the agenda for the conference should focus on the creation of a new type of state construct and its associated features and systems. In this vein, the conference should map out the general framework of the new social formation and its associated constitutional order and systems—political, economic, social, and so on. The responsibility for the formulation of the specifics of the new state architecture should be assigned to a national commission, consisting of at least one representative from each of the stakeholders.

Importantly, the holding of the national conference should be followed by the setting into motion of a national dialogue. This discussion, which should be held on an ongoing basis, should take place at various levels of the Liberian society—homes, places of work, churches, mosques, the shrines of the various indigenous African religions, schools, and in the other sundry places and groups. The thrust of the national dialogue should be to participate in, and contribute to the designing of the new state architecture and the ongoing discussion about the welfare of the state, especially its people.

The Dynamic: To develop a new type of state, the old, exhausted, and failed neocolonial Liberian state, which has visited violence and its associated mayhem on the people, failed to address the basic human needs of the subaltern classes, benefited the compradors and their external patrons based in the metropolis, discriminated against and abused women, used ethnicity as an instrument of division, and committed myriad other crimes against the lower classes, must be deconstructed (gotten rid off), rethought, and democratically reconstituted. Specifically, the neocolonial construct must be replaced by a new type of pro-people, pro-democracy, and pro-development state. The democratic reconstitution dimension should endow the new construct with democratic nature, mission, character, values, institutions, rules, processes, and policies. Agbese and Kieh's (2007: xii) proposal about the democratic state reconstitution project in Africa is apropos to the Liberian context:

> Africa needs strong, democratic, and pro-people states that would provide the basic needs of the people, respect and defend their fundamental individual rights, promote gender equality, champion peaceful co-existence among various ethnic groups and religions, and defend the citizens from the exploitation and other vagaries of international finance capital.

Significantly, it is critical to note that reforming the neocolonial Liberian state will not result in the establishment of long-term peace and stability and will not usher in a democratic and people-centered social formation. This is because the neocolonial Liberian state and its peripheral capitalist mode of production are intrinsically antipeople, antidemocratic, and antidevelopment. In short, the Liberian neocolony, its base, and its superstructure are beyond redemption.

The Elements of Democratic State Reconstitution in Liberia: Despite the prevailing dominant view in the international system that the liberal democratic state and its so-called reformed peripheral capitalist economy are the best architectures for the establishment of stability and democracy and the promotion of democracy in Africa and the rest of the third world, I argue that a social democratic construct and a mixed economic system are the best arrangements for Liberia. My rejection of the liberal democratic state and its mode of production is based on several factors. First, liberal democracy, the ideological foundation, stresses the paramountcy of individual political rights and freedoms and the procedural aspects of democracy. While this is important, it is insufficient for constructing deep democracy, because it fails to accord similar importance to the economic, social, and cultural aspects. In effect, the liberal democratic state construct is not based on holistic democracy.

Second, capitalism, whether advanced or developed or peripheral, is a system that is intrinsically based on exploitation and inequalities. That is, under the capitalist political economy power and its attendant privileges are disproportionately skewed in favor of the bourgeois class and its compradorial collaborators. In short, the capitalist logic is based on a dialectical relationship between the ruling and subaltern classes: For the members of the ruling class to enjoy the disproportionate share of societal resources and power, the members of the subaltern classes must receive the crumbs and be relegated to a marginal and subservient role in the "division of power."

Third, the so-called reformed version of peripheral capitalism is not fundamentally different from the "old" version of the mode of production. Basically, both are based on the suzerainty of the market and its dominant force (the bourgeois class); privatization, which is designed to make super profits for corporations and other businesses at the expense of the welfare of the subaltern classes; and a weak and dependent neocolonial state that subordinates the interests of its citizens to those of international finance capital and the metropolitan states. So, the result is the same: The "old" version of peripheral capitalism exploited, marginalized, abused, and neglected the basic human needs of Liberia's subaltern classes. Equally, the "reformed" version of peripheral capitalism based on the neoliberal logic and driven by the new globalization will not fundamentally alter the material conditions of Liberia's subaltern classes.

Fourth, the capitalist mode of production is diametrically opposed to substantive democracy—holistic democracy that is anchored on individual and group political, economic, social, cultural, security, and ecological rights and freedoms with pro-people pillars. So, even a functional liberal democracy with its "reformed" peripheral capitalist mode of production will not build substantive democracy in Liberia.

Alternatively, the new type of state—social democratic—that I am proposing as the best construct for addressing and resolving the fundamental conflict that underpinned Liberia's first civil war would be based on several elements. The nature of the construct would reflect the objective cultural and historical experiences of Liberia. That is, lessons must be drawn from country's rich cultural mosaic comprising the experiences of the 16 indigenous ethnic groups, the Americo-Liberian stock, and the other immigrant groups. The focus should be to adopt useful lessons from these various historical and cultural experiences an blend them together as the composite of the nature of the state. As part of this process, the Liberian flag, motto, anthem, and other national symbols would need to be changed to reflect the new nature of the state. For example, the Liberian flag is a replica of the American one; the major exception is that the Liberian flag has one star, whereas the American one has 50. Alternatively, a new flag would have to be developed that reflects the country's "cultural melting pot." Also, the motto,

"The Love of Liberty Brought Us Here," would need to be changed to reflect the totality of the experiences of the constituent groups of the polity. In short, the nature of the new Liberian state would need to reflect the objective conditions of the country not those of the United States or any other country.

The mission of the state needs to be twofold. First, the state must be fundamentally committed to the pursuance of the collective interests of all of the Liberian people, irrespective of the class, ethnic, regional, religious, and gender differentiations. Operationally, this would mean, among other things, that the state's resources would be used for the advancement and well-being of the Liberian people. Second and related, in the sphere of international relations, the state must not subordinate the interests and well-being of the Liberian people to the narrow and particularistic national interest agenda of any state—metropolitan or otherwise. Third, the state must protect the Liberian people from exploitation and violence, both from internal and external sources.

In terms of its character, the state must be independent, democratic, developmental, strong, enabling, sensitive, and pan-Africanist. The independent dimension of the state's character must be reflected in the fact that the state should be freed from the control of any one particular class or group. As such, the state should be able to deal with various classes and groups in an even-handed way devoid of any preferential treatment. As a democratic construct, the new Liberian state must be rooted on the practice of constitutionalism and its associated respect for the contours of the constitutional compact, accountability, transparency, and consultation and collaboration with its citizens on the various matters affecting their well-being. The development aspect of the state's character must find expression in the state's active participation in the economy as an engine of development. For example, the state should invest in the development of the infrastructure—roads, bridges, and so on. Also, it should own and control the various natural resources—diamond, gold, and so on—and ensure that they are used for the benefit of the Liberian people. Similarly, it should own and control the ports and the airfields. Furthermore, the state should provide essential services to the Liberian people such as electricity and running water. It should work with business-minded Liberians to establish a nationalistic Liberian entrepreneurial group that would be committed to the welfare of the Liberian people. Subsequently, the state should establish a partnership with this group in the formulation and implementation of economic policies and programs for the advancement of the Liberian people. As a strong formation, the state must protect the Liberian people from exploitation and abuse. For example, the state must ensure that Liberian workers' labor is not exploited, by making sure that the workers are paid decent wages and provided excellent working conditions. This would include the establishment of a minimum wage that takes into account the meeting of the basic human needs of employees. Also, the state must protect the Liberian people from exploitation, abuse, and violence by both domestic and external actors. Central to the state's protective character should be to provide "society with an enabling environment for the creation of wealth to effectively confront poverty and deprivation" (Mbaku, 1999: 317). As an enabling construct, the state should provide conducive conditions for all Liberians—both individuals and groups—to pursue their interests legitimately and devoid of violating the rights of other individuals and groups. Similarly, as a sensitive formation, the state must be respectful of the views of all its citizens as individuals and groups, especially when they are critical of state policies. Also, the state should promote a culture of mutual respect and tolerance for divergent beliefs and views. Finally, as a pan-Africanist construct, the state must support continental, subregional, and basin cooperation and integration in all fields, as well as the building of strong bonds with diasporic Africans in the Americas and elsewhere. For example, the state must support and champion at the levels of Africa, West Africa, and the Mano River basin, the development of collective policies designed to promote the welfare of the African peoples in the areas of employment, education, health care, food, housing, and transportation. Similarly, the state should seek to help harness and mobilize the immense resources of African Americans and other peoples of African descent in the Americas, the Caribbean, Europe, and Asia in advancing the cause, interests, and well-being of African peoples everywhere.

Values are important because they serve as the major determinants of acceptable behavior in the society. Moreover, values must be designed to strengthen polity. Against this background, the proposed Liberian social democratic state must be based on several fundamental values. At the core must be a sense of positive nationalism. This is a genre of nationalism that develops in the individual and groups alike an overall sense of commitment to the state beyond their various ethnic, regional, religious, class, and gender identities. Also, Liberians must be sensitive to and understand and respect the subcultures of the various ethnic and religious groups that would constitute the polity within the context of peaceful coexistence. Another norm must be the development of a sense of selfless service to the polity, other communities, and family. In other words, Liberians must be socialized to develop the mind-set that service to others is the essence of life. Similarly, the development of honest, honorable, and dependable character must be a critical value. Families and the various secondary agents of socialization must be encouraged and empowered to stress this value in the development of children. In the case of adults, a public education program should be designed to help inculcate the value of an honorable character. Linked to the development of character must be the value of public service as an opportunity to serve the people, and to engage in the process of the personal accumulation of wealth. Also, a work ethos based on honest and hard labor must be cultivated.

Various public institutions should be designed to provide service and promote the welfare of the Liberian people. Specifically, the various institutions must have clearly delineated functions that are linked to particular objectives in the service matrix. Also, public servants must be socialized in the new culture of "service leaders," so that they can recognize the fact that the essence of their positions and agencies is the promotion of the well-being of the Liberian people.

Also, rules must be designed to regulate the interactions between the larger society and the custodians of state power; between and among the various sectors of the larger society; between and among the various segments of the public sector; between and among the custodians of state power and the private sector; between and among various segments of the larger society and the private sector; and between and among the various segments of the private sector. Certainly, it would not be possible to map out the specificities of these rules in this study. However, the various rules must meet certain criteria. First, they must be formulated based on broad-based consultations, debates, and discussion. Second, they must be designed to enhance and strengthen the principles of social democracy. Third, they must not seek to reward one group and punish another. As Mbaku (2001: 95) asserts, "The reconstituted state should provide mechanisms that do not place any individual or group at a competitive disadvantage or advantage in competition for resources." Fourth, the rules must be fairly applied to all individuals and groups, irrespective of their stations in the polity.

Several processes would constitute the operational bedrock of the polity. All individuals and groups, whether in the public or private sector, must be held responsible for their respective actions through a process of accountability. In other words, accountability at all levels of the society should be established as a permanent fixture. Another process should be transparency. Again, at the various levels of the society, the affairs of the state, the community, and other entities should be conducted in an open manner. This would help minimize corruption and other acts of impropriety. In the legal arena, due process should be the cardinal mechanism. This would help establish the sanctity of the rule of law.

Finally, the state should develop a set of pro-people cultural, economic, environmental, political, religious, security, and social policies. Briefly, the cultural policies should promote mutual respect for, and sensitivity to the cultures of all ethnic groups within a framework of pluralism, tolerance, and peaceful coexistence. Also, no one ethnic group should be privileged over the others, especially in terms of access to and the allocation of state resources (Mbaku, 2001).

In the economic domain, on the basis of a mixed mode of production, that state should design and implement policies that promote domestic capital formation and reduce the inequities in wealth and income. Also, the policies should subordinate the profit-seeking agenda of multinational corporations and other businesses to the national development agenda of Liberia.

As for the environmental sphere, the policies must stress, among other things, the reduction of pollution and arresting the riding tide of deforestation. Specifically, the policies must design modalities that would seek to reduce carbon dioxide emission, the indiscriminate felling of trees, and the use of various waterways as dump sites by individuals and businesses. Importantly, the environmental policies would have to be linked to the other policies to be effective. For example, the making of coal and the use of waterways as lavatories are linked to the broader issues of poverty, deprivation, and the lack of lavatory facilities in the various communities throughout Liberia.

Politically, the policies should seek to promote the respect for the political rights and civil liberties—including the freedoms of association, assembly, speech, the press, movement, and thought—of all individuals and groups; ensure effective checks and balances among the three branches—legislative, executive, and judicial—of the government; promote the centrality of the rule of law; hold regular, free, and competitive elections based on a multiparty system; and create an enabling environment for the thriving of a robust civil society. Also, the policies must seek to help the institutionalization of politics based on democratically established rules and processes that transcend the whims and caprices of individuals and groups.

In the religious sphere, a culture of tolerance and respect must be promoted between and among the country's Christian, Muslim, and indigenes African religious groups and sects. Moreover, state policies in this domain should not give preferential treatment to any one particular religious group. Simply, Liberians should be free to accept and practice the religion of their choice without the state's interference. In other words, state religious policies must not seek to force people to accept any particular religion or theological doctrine.

Fundamentally, security should revolve around the protection of the people and their properties from violence, robbery, and other crimes. This would mean, among other things, that state policies must seek to invest in the recruitment, training, compensation, and equipment of the police and other security personnel, so that they can perform their responsibility of protecting the Liberian people. As part of the process of creating the "new security," a new collaborative relationship must be established between the citizens, on the one hand, and state security agencies and personnel on the other. The focus of the partnership should be the development of mutual trust and respect and the orientation that all are working toward common cause.

Socially, the centerpiece of state policies should be the promotion of human development, so that Liberians can lead long and healthy lives, be educated, and enjoy a decent standard of living (United Nations Development Program, 1990: 2). This would mean the development and maintenance of a "social safety net." Specifically, in the health sector, state policies should seek to provide universal care for all Liberians at a nominal fee. Also, compulsory and free education should be provided from the elementary to the secondary level, and subsidized education at the tertiary level. Moreover, policies should be designed for the construction of decent public housing for low- and middle-income Liberians. Concomitantly, slums such as West Point, Clara Town, Slipway, and Soniewen should be demolished. The residents should either be compensated or be relocated to the new public housing communities that would be constructed.

Conclusion

The book has attempted to contribute to the development of the scholarly literature on peace and conflict studies, and to the praxis of democratic state building. The central thesis of the book is that Liberia's first civil war was caused by the multifaceted crises of underdevelopment engendered by the Liberian state over a long period of time. To provide the empirical basis for the thesis, the book began with the effort to formulate a theoretical framework. This involved the examination of the five major theories—ethnic, elite pathology, institutional pathology, spiritual anarchy, and political culture—that have been used to analyze the causes of the first Liberian civil war. Specifically, the major arguments of each theory were summarized and critiqued.

Next, the state-building project in Liberia—both settler and neocolonial—was discussed. The purpose was to identify the forces and factors that shaped the project and developed its portrait—nature, mission, character, values, institutions, rules, processes, and policies.

Having deciphered the travails of the state, the focus then shifted to the examination of the multifaceted crises—political, economic, social, and

Summary, Lessons, Prescriptions, and Conclusion

cultural—occasioned by the state. The dynamics of each dimension of the crises were discussed.

Importantly, the linkages between the state and its associated crises and the first Liberian civil war were drawn. This was followed by an analysis of the forces that shaped the war; the dynamics of war; its impact on the collapse of the Liberian state, and the costs of the war.

Also, the lessons from the Liberian experience were examined. They included the conflicting nature of settler and neocolonial state constructs and their proneness to violent conflicts and the fragility and vulnerability of peripheral capitalist economies to violence. When a civil war ensues, as it did in the case of Liberia, it is not enough to end the violence. Instead, to address and resolve the underlying conflict, the postwar peace-building project must be fundamentally based on the democratic reconstitution of the state.

Finally, since the settler-neocolonial Liberian state was the epicenter of the causes of the first civil war, I argued that the construct must be deconstructed, rethought, and democratically reconstituted. My proposal begins with an explicit rejection of reform as an alternative. This is because since the neocolonial Liberian state is beyond redemption, no amount of "reform" can correct its fundamental and intrinsic defects. Similarly, my proposal rejects the liberal democratic state as the panacea, because it will not occasion the building of deep or holistic democracy in Liberia—the confluence of the political, economic, cultural, social, security, and ecological dimensions. Instead, like in other states, including the metropolis, liberal democracy primarily focuses on political rights and freedoms and procedural democracy. Then, I map out the trajectory of the proposed social democratic state—its nature, mission, character, values, structures, rules, processes, and policies.

Bibliography

Adebajo, Adekeye (2002). *Liberia's Civil War: Nigeria, ECOMOG, and Regional Security in West Africa*. Boulder, CO: Lynne Rienner Publishers.

Adebajo, Adekeye (2002). *Building Peace in West Africa: Liberia, Sierra Leone and Guinea Bissau*. Boulder, CO: Lynne Rienner Publishers.

Adeleke, Tunde (1998). *UnAfrican Americans: Nineteenth Century Black Nationalists and the Civilizing Mission*. Lexington: University Press of Kentucky.

Agbese, Pita Ogaba (2007). "The State in Africa: A Political Economy." In George Klay Kieh, Jr. (ed.), *Beyond State Failure and Collapse: Making the State Relevant in Africa*. Lanham, MD: Lexington Books, 33–48.

Agbese, Pita Ogaba, and George Klay Kieh, Jr. (2007). "Introduction: Democratizing States in Africa." In Pita Ogaba Agbese and George Klay Kieh, Jr. (eds.), *Reconstituting the State in Africa*. New York: Palgrave-Macmillan, 3–32.

Akpan, M. B. (1973). "Black Imperialism: Americo-Liberian Rule over the African People of Liberia, 1841–1964." *Canadian Journal of African Studies*, 7 (2), 217–236.

Alao, Abiodun (1998). *The Burden of Collective Goodwill: The International Involvement in the Liberian Civil War*. Aldershot, England: Ashgate Publishing.

Alao, Abiodun (1999). *Peacekeepers, Politicians and Warlords: The Liberian Peace Process*. New York: United Nations University.

Alavi, Hamza (1972). "The State in Post-Colonial Societies: Pakistan and Bangladesh." *New Left Review*, 74, 59–81.

Amin, Samir (1974). *Accumulation on a World Scale: A Critique of the Theory of Underdevelopment*. New York: Monthly Review Press.

Armed Conflict Events Data(2006). www.onwar.com.

Azango, Bertha Baker (1968). *Education Laws of Liberia through the 1966–67 Session of the National Legislature*. Monrovia, Liberia: Department of Education.

Azikiwe, Nnamdi (1934). *Liberia in World Politics*. London: Stockwell.

Ballah, Heneryatta (2003). *Ethnicity, Politics and Social Conflict: The Quest for Peace in Liberia*. University Park, PA: McNair Scholar Program of the Pennsylvania State University.

Baran, Paul (1988). "On the Economy of Backwardness." In Charles Wilber (ed.), *The Political Economy of Development and Underdevelopment*. New York: Random House, 93–104.

Barrow, Clyde (1993). *Critical Theories of the State: Marxist, Neo-Marxist, Post-Marxist*. Madison: University of Wisconsin Press.

Beleky, Louis (1973). "The Development of Liberia." *The Journal of Modern African Studies*, 11 (1), 43–60.

Berkeley, Bill (1986). *Liberia: A Promise Betrayed: A Report on Human Rights*. New York: Lawyers Committee for Human Rights.

Best, Kenneth (1974). *Cultural Policy of Liberia*. Paris: UNESCO.

Beyan, Amos (1991). *The American Colonization and the Creation of the Liberian State*. Lanham, MD: University Press of America.

Binitie, Austin (1998). *Blood and Bones in Liberia*. Abidjan: Editions Souvenirs.

Boley, George (1983). *Liberia: The Rise and Fall of the First Republic*. London: Macmillan.

Braudel, Fernand (1982). *On History*. Chicago: University of Chicago Press.

Brehun, Leovard (1991). *Liberia: The War of Horror*. Accra, Ghana: Adwina.

British Foreign and Commonwealth Office (2005). *Liberia*. London: Government of the United Kingdom.

Brown, David (1982). "On the Categories 'Civilized' in Liberia and Elsewhere." *The Journal of Modern African Studies*, 20 (2), 287–303.

Brown, George (1941). *The Economic History of Liberia*. Washington DC: Associated Publishers.

Buell, Raymond (1965). *The Native Problem in Africa*. London: Frank Cass.

Burin, Eric (2005). *Slavery and the Peculiar Solution: A History of the American Colonization Society*. Gainesville: University Press of Florida.

Burrowes, Carl P. (1982) *The Settler Ruling Class Thesis in Liberia: A Reconsideration*. Occasional Paper. Chicago.

Burrowes, Carl P. (1989). *The Americo-Liberian Ruling Class and Other Myths: A Critique of Political Science in the Liberian Context*. African and African-American Studies Monograph Series. Philadelphia, PA: Institute of African and African-American Affairs, Temple University.

Burrowes, Carl P. (1998). "Textual Sources of the 1847 Liberian Constitution." *Liberian Studies Journal*, 23 (1), 1–41.

Cabral, Amilcar (1969). *Revolution in Guinea*. London: Stage 1

Canak, William (1984). "The Peripheral State Debate: State Capitalist and Bureaucratic Authoritarian Regimes in Latin America." *Latin American Research Review*, 19 (1), 3–36.

Carlsson, Jerker (1977). *Transnational Companies in Liberia*. Uppsala, Sweden: Scandinavian Institute of African Studies.
Cassell, C. Abayomi (1970). *History of the First African Republic*. New York: Fountainhead Publishers.
Catholic Justice and Peace Commission (1995). *The Liberian Crisis*. Monrovia, Liberia: National Catholic Secretariat.
Chalk, F. (1967). "The Anatomy of an Investment: Firestone's 1927 Loan to Liberia." *Canadian Journal of African Studies*, 1 (1), 12–32.
Clapham, Christopher (ed.) (1998). *African Guerillas*. Bloomington: Indiana University Press.
Clegg, Claude (2004). *The Price of Liberty: African Americans and the Making of Liberia*. Chapel Hill: University of North Carolina Press.
Clower, Robert, G. Dalton, M. Hawitz, and A. A. Walters (1966). *Growth without Development: An Economic Survey of Liberia*. Evanston, IL: Northwestern University Press.
Constitution of Liberia (1847). Monrovia, Liberia.
Constitution of Liberia (1986). Monrovia, Liberia.
Constitution of the American Colonization Society (1816). Washington DC.
Constitution of the Commonwealth of Liberia (1837). Monrovia, Liberia.
Constitutional Commission (1984). *Draft Constitution of the Republic of Liberia*. Monrovia, Liberia: Constitutional Commission.
Cordor, S. Henry (1979). *The April 14 Crisis in Liberia*. Occasional Paper. Monrovia, Liberia.
Cordor, S. Henry (1980). *Facing the Realities of the Liberian Nation*. Iowa City: School of Letters, University of Iowa.
Curry, R. L. (1972). "Liberia's External Debts and Their Servicing." *The Journal of Modern African Studies*, 10 (4), 621–626.
Daniels, Anthony (1992). *Monrovia Mon Amour: A Visit to Liberia*. London: John Murray.
David, Magdalene (1984). "The Love of Liberty Brought Us Here: An Analysis of the Development of the Settler State in 19th Century Liberia." *Review of African Political Economy*, 11 (31), 57–70.
Davis, D. F., Walter E. Stadler, and Gerald Rose (1997). *Liberian Elections Modeling*. Working Paper. Fairfax, VA: Program on Peacekeeping Policy and World Vision, George Mason University.
Discussions (1983–1984). *Chats Held by George Klay Kieh, Jr. with Four Leading Members of the People's Redemption Council*. Monrovia, Liberia.
Dolo, Emmanuel (1996). *Democracy versus Dictatorship: The Quest for Freedom and Justice in Africa's Oldest Republic*. Lanham, MD: University Press of America.

Dunn, D. Elwood (1979). *The Foreign Policy of Liberia during the Tubman Era, 1944–1971*. London: Hutchinson Benham.
Dunn, D. Elwood (1999). "The Liberian Civil War." In Taisier Ali and Robert Matthews (eds.), *Civil Wars in Africa: Roots and Resolution*. Montreal: McGills-Queen's University Press, 89–121.
Dunn, D. Elwood and Byron Tarr (1988). *Liberia: A Polity in Transition*. Methuen, NJ: Scarecrow Press.
Dunn, D. Elwood and Svend Holsoe (1985). *Historical Dictionary of Liberia*. Metuchen, NJ: Scarecrow Press.
Dunn, D. Elwood, Amos J. Beyan, and Carl Patrick Burrowes (2002). *Historical Dictionary of Liberia*. 2nd edition. Metuchen, NJ: Scarecrow Press.
Ellis, Stephen (1995). "Liberia, 1989–1994: A Study of Ethnic and Spiritual Violence." *African Affairs*, 94 (375), 165–197.
Ellis, Stephen (1999). *The Mask of Anarchy: The Destruction of Liberia and the Religious Dimension of an African Civil War*. New York: New York University Press.
Emmanuel, A. (1972). *Unequal Exchange: A Study of the Imperialism of Trade*. New York: Monthly Review Press.
Encyclopedia of Nations (2006). *Liberia*. Farmington Hills, MI: Thomson Gale.
Ero, Comfort (1995). "ECOWAS and Sub-Regional Peacekeeping in Liberia." *Journal of Humanitarian Assistance*, 1 (1), 1–15.
Executive Mansion, Republic of Liberia (1986). *Executive Order #2 Banning Student Political Activities*. Monrovia, Liberia: Government Printing Office.
Fahnbulleh, H. Boima (1985). *The Diplomacy of Prejudice: Liberia in International Politics, 1945–1970*. New York: Vantage Press.
Fanon, Frantz (1965). *The Wretched of the Earth*. New York: Grove Press.
Fatton, Robert (1988). "Bringing the Ruling Class Back In: Class, State and Hegemony in Africa." *Comparative Politics*, 20 (3), 253–264.
Flores, Margarita (2004). *Conflicts, Rural Development, and Food Security in West Africa. Food and Agricultural Organization*. Econpapers Working Paper No. 04–02. Rome: FAO.
Food and Agricultural Organization (1996). *Africa Report*. Rome: FAO.
Frank, Andre Gunder (1969). *Capitalism and Underdevelopment in Latin America*. New York: Penguin Books.
Frank, Andre Gunder (1978). *Dependent Accumulation and Underdevelopment*. London: Macmillan.
Gershoni, Yekutiel (1985). *Black Colonialism: The Americo-Liberian Scramble for the Hinterland*. Boulder, CO: Westview Press.

Ghoshal, Animesh (1974). "The Impact of Foreign Rubber Concessions on the Liberian Economy, 1966–1971." *The Journal of Modern African Studies*, 12 (4), 589–599.

Gifford, Paul (1993). *Christianity and Politics in Doe's Liberia*. Cambridge: Cambridge University Press.

Government of Liberia (2004). *Republic of Liberia: Millennium Development Goals Report, 2004*. Monrovia, Liberia: Government Printing Office.

Graff, William (1994). "The State in the Third World." Paper presented at the Conference of the British International Studies Association, York, December 1994.

Gramsci, Antonio (1994). *Antonio Gramsci: Pre-Prison Writings*. Cambridge: Cambridge University Press.

Green, Jack (1986). *The Intellectual Heritage of the Constitutional Era*. Philadelphia: The Library Co.

Gupta, Vijay (1996). *Africa: Post-Cold War Era*. New Delhi: Har-Aron and Publication.

Gurr, Ted Robert (1970). *Why Men Rebel*. Princeton: Princeton University Press.

Hacket, Rocalind I. J. (2003). "Discourses of Demonization in Africa and Beyond." *Diogenes*, 50 (3), 61–75.

Hibbard, Michael (2005). "Doing It for Themselves: Transformative Planning by Indigenous People." *Journal of Planning Education and Research*, 25 (2), 172–184.

Hlophe, Stephen (1973). "The Significance of Barth and Geertz's Model of Ethnicity in the Analysis of Nationalism in Liberia." *Canadian Journal of African Studies*, 7 (2), 237–256.

Hlophe, Stephen (1979). *Class, Ethnicity and Politics in Liberia*. Washington DC: University Press of America.

Hobbes, Thomas (1661). *The Leviathan*. London: Andrew Crooke.

Hobbes, Thomas. (1996). *The Leviathan*. Oxford: Oxford University Press.

Horton, S. Augustus (1994). *Liberia's Underdevelopment—In Spite of the Struggle: A Personal Analysis of the Underlying Reasons for Liberia's Underdevelopment*. Lanham: University Press of America.

Huband, Mark (1998). *The Liberian Civil War*. London: Frank Cass.

Huberich, Charles (1947). *The Political and Legislative History of Liberia*, Vol. 1. New York: Central Book Co.

Huberich, Charles (1947). *The Political and Legislative History of Liberia*, Vol. 2. New York: Central Book Co.

Human Rights Watch (1996). *Liberia: Human Rights Developments*. New York: Human Rights Watch.

Huntington, Samuel (1996). *The Clash of Civilization and the Remaking of World Order*. New York: Touchstone.
The Imperial Archives (2006). *Key Concepts in Post-Colonial Societies*. Working Papers. Belfast: Department of English, Queens University of Belfast.
Interviews (1998–1999). *Interviews Conducted by the Author with Some Members of the Doe Government and the Warlordist Militias Involved in the First Liberian Civil War*. Monrovia, Liberia.
Jaye, Thomas (2003). *Issues of Sovereignty, Strategy and Security in the Economic Community of West African States' (ECOWAS): Intervention in the Liberian Civil War*. Lewiston, NY: Edwin Mellen Press.
Jeffy Commission (1985). *Report on the Review and Revitalization of the Liberian Economy*. Monrovia, Liberia: Government Printing Office.
Jenkins, David (1975). *Black Zion: The Return of Afro-Americans and West Indians to Africa*. London: Wildwood House.
Jessop, Bob (1991). *State Theory: Putting States in their Places*. University Park: The Pennsylvania State University Press.
Johnson, Charles (1987). *Bitter Canaan: The Story of the Negro Republic*. New Brunswick, NJ: Transaction Books.
Kadallah, Khafre (1978). "Toward a Political Economy of Liberia." *Review of African Political Economy*, 5 (12), 105–113.
Kappel, Robert, Werner, Korte, and R. Friedegund Maschler (1986). *Liberia: Underdevelopment and Political Rule in a Peripheral Society*. Bremen, Germany: Institut fur Afrika-Kunde.
Kieh, George Klay (1988a). "Setting the Stage: Historical Antecedents to the April 12, 1980 Coup d'état in Liberia." *Liberia Studies Journal*, 13 (2), 203–219.
Kieh, George Klay (1988b). "Guru, Visionary and Superchief: An Analysis of the Impact of the Cult of the Presidency on the Development of Democracy in Liberia." *Liberia Forum*, 4 (6), 8–19.
Kieh, George Klay (1989a). "The Causes of the Liberian Coup." *TransAfrica Forum*, 6 (2), 37–47.
Kieh, George Klay (1989b). "Merchants of Repression: An Analysis of United States Military Assistance to Liberia." *Liberia Forum*, 5 (9), 50–66.
Kieh, George Klay (1990). *Civilians, Soldiers and Development: A Comparative Study of the Performance of the Tolbert and Doe Regimes*. Paper presented at the Annual Conference of the Liberian Studies Association, held March 29–31, Brattleboro, Vermont.

Kieh, George Klay (1991). "The Roots of Western Influence in Africa: An Analysis of the Conditioning Processes." *Social Science Journal*, 29 (1), 7–19.

Kieh, George Klay (1992a). "Combatants, Patrons, Peacemakers and the Liberian Civil War." *Studies in Conflict and Terrorism*, 15 (2), 125–143.

Kieh, George Klay (1992b). *Dependency and the Foreign Policy of a Small Power: The Liberian Case*. Lewiston, NY: Edwin Mellen Press.

Kieh, George Klay, and Doris H. Railey (1993). "Women, Sexual Harassment and Employment Opportunities in Liberia." *Liberian Studies Journal*, 18 (2), 192–202.

Kieh, George Klay (1993). "Resolving African Conflicts." *Peace Review*, 5 (4), 447–454.

Kieh, George Klay (1994). "The Obstacles to the Peaceful Resolution of the Liberian Civil Conflict." *Studies in Conflict and Terrorism*, 17 (1), 97–108.

Kieh, George Klay (1996a). "The Taproots of the Liberian Civil War." *Twenty-First Century Afro-Review*, 2 (3), 123–152.

Kieh, George Klay (1996b). *Ending the Liberian Civil War: Implications for United States Foreign Policy toward West Africa*. TransAfrica Forum Monograph Series No. 1. Washington DC: TransAfrica Forum.

Kieh, George Klay (1996c). "The Political and Economic Roots of Civil Conflicts in Africa: Implications for United States Foreign Policy." *Small Wars and Insurgency*, 7 (1), 41–54.

Kieh, George Klay (1996d). "Democratization and Peace in Africa." *Journal of Asian and African Studies*, 31 (1–2), 99–111.

Kieh, George Klay (1997). "The Crisis of Democracy in Liberia." *Liberian Studies Journal*, 22 (1), 23–29.

Kieh, George Klay (1998a). "State Collapse and Democratic Construction: Prospects for Liberia." In Julius Ihonvbere and John Mukum Mbaku (eds.), *Multiparty Democracy and Change: The Constraints to Democratization in Africa*. Aldershot, England: Ashgate Publishing, 151–170.

Kieh, George Klay (1998b). "International Organizations, Peacekeeping and Conflict Resolution in Africa." In Karl Magyar and Earl Conteh-Morgan (eds.), *Peacekeeping in Africa: ECOMOG in Liberia*. New York: Palgrave-Macmillan, 12–31.

Kieh, George Klay (1999a). "Beyond Authoritarianism: The Quest for Democracy in Liberia." *Liberian Journal of Democracy*, 1 (1), 5–14.

Kieh, George Klay (1999b). "The Economic Community of West African States, Conflict Management and the Liberian Civil War." *Low Intensity Conflict and Law Enforcement*, 8 (2), 129–150.

Kieh, George Klay (2000a). "Humanitarian Interventions in Civil Wars in Africa." In Andrew Valls (ed.), *Ethics and International Affairs: Theories and Cases*. Lanham, MD: Rowman and Littlefield, 135–150.

Kieh, George Klay (2000b). "Military Rule in Liberia." *Journal of Political and Military Sociology*, 29 (Winter), 327–340.

Kieh, George Klay (2001a). "Civil Wars in Africa." In S. C. Saxena (ed.), *Africa Beyond 2000*. New Delhi, India: Kalinga Publishers, 265–292.

Kieh, George Klay (2001b). "The Ethics of Military Humanitarianism: The Case of the North Atlantic Treaty Organization's Intervention in the Yugoslav Civil War." *Journal of Peace Studies*, 8 (2), 36–54.

Kieh, George Klay (2001c). "Reconstituting a Collapsed State: The Liberian Case." In Segun Jegede, Ayodele Ale and Eni Akinsola (eds.), *State Reconstruction in West Africa*. Lagos, Nigeria: Franked Press, 208–244.

Kieh, George Klay (2002a). "Civil Conflicts in Africa: Patterns and Trends." In George Klay Kieh, Jr. and Ida Rousseau Mukenge (eds.), *Zones of Conflict in Africa: Theories and Cases*. Westport, CT: Praeger, 35–52.

Kieh, George Klay (2002b). "Civil Wars in Africa: Now and Then." In Eghosa Osaghae (eds.), *The Aftermath of the Nigerian Civil War*. Ibadan, Nigeria: John Archers, 8–25.

Kieh, George Klay (2002c). "The Context of Civil Conflicts in Africa." In George Klay Kieh, Jr. and Ida Rousseau Mukenge (eds.), *Zones of Conflict in Africa: Theories and Cases*. Westport, CT: Praeger, 21–34.

Kieh, George Klay (2003a). "Africa, the New Partnership for Africa's Development and the International Capitalist Order." *Journal of Comparative Education and International Relations in Africa*, 8 (1–2), 111–127.

Kieh, George Klay (2003b). "Liberia: Leaders and Legacies." In Chandra Sriram and Karim Wermester (eds.), *From Practice to Promise: Strengthening United Nations Capacities for the Prevention of Violent Conflicts*. Boulder, CO: Lynne Rienner Publishers, 307–326.

Kieh, George Klay (2004a). *The Economic Community of West African States and the First Liberian Civil War*. Andrew Young Center for International Affairs Monograph Series No. 3. Atlanta, GA: Morehouse College.

Kieh, George Klay (2004b). "Irregular Warfare and Liberia's First Civil War." *Journal of International and Area Studies*, 11 (1), 163–184.

Kieh, George Klay (2004c). "Military Engagement in African Politics." In George Klay Kieh, Jr. and Pita Ogaba Agbese (eds.), *The Military and Politics in Africa: From Engagement to Democratic and Constitutional Control*. Aldershot, England: Ashgate Publishing, 37–56.

Kieh, George Klay (2004d). "Regional Security and Sustainable Development in Africa." In Okechuku Ukaga and Osita Afoaku (eds.), *Sustainable Development in Africa*. Trenton, NJ: Africa World Press, 169–189.

Kieh, George Klay (2005a). *Legislative Oversight of the Military: Lessons from Africa*. Yakubu Gowon Center Monograph Series No. 3. Abuja, Nigeria: Yakubu Gowon Center for International Cooperation and National Unity.

Kieh, George Klay (2005b). "Liberia: Government and Politics." In Neal Tate (ed.), *Governments of the World: Citizens' Rights and Responsibilities*. Farmington Hills, MI: Thomson, Gale, and Macmillan, 90–95.

Kieh, George Klay (2005c). "Post-Conflict State-Building in Sierra Leone." *African and Asian Studies*, 4 (1–2), 163–184.

Kieh, George Klay (2006a). "The Crisis of the Neo-Colonial State and the Sierra Leonean Civil War." *African Strategic Review*, 1 (1), 47–62.

Kieh, George Klay (2006b). "Elections and Voting Behavior: The Case of the 2005 Liberian Elections." *UMOJA: Bulletin of African and African American Studies*, 1 (2), 1–17.

Kieh, George Klay (2006c). "State Collapse and Democratic Construction: Prospects for Liberia." In John Mukum Mbaku and Julius O. Ihonvbere (eds.), *Multiparty Democracy and Political Change: Constraints to Democratization in Africa*. Trenton: Africa World Press, 157–178.

Kieh, George Klay (2007a). "Creating a Relevant State in Africa." In George Klay Kieh, Jr. (ed.), *Beyond State Failure and Collapse: Making the State Relevant in Africa*. Lanham, MD: Lexington Books, 255–267.

Kieh, George Klay (2007b). "The Hegemonic Presidency, the Constitution and Post-Conflict Peace-Building in Liberia." Paper Presented at the 39th Annual Conference of the Liberian Studies Association. March 23–25, Indiana University, Bloomington.

Kieh, George Klay (2007c). "Introduction: From the Old to the New Globalization." In George Klay Kieh, Jr. (ed.), *Africa and the New Globalization*. Aldershot, England: Ashgate Publishing.

Kieh, George Klay (2007d). "The Human Development Crises in Liberia." *Journal of Sustainable Development in Africa*, 9 (1), 78–94.

Kieh, George Klay (2007e). "The State and Basic Human Needs in Africa." In George Klay Kieh, Jr. and Pita Ogaba Agbese (eds.), *The State in Africa: Issues and Perspectives*. Ibadan, Nigeria: Program in Ethnic and Federal Studies, University of Ibadan.

Laremont, Ricardo Rene (2005). *Borders, Nationalism and the African State*. Boulder, CO: Lynne Rienner Publishers.

Levitt, Jeremy (2005). *The Evolution of Deadly Conflict in Liberia: From Paternalism to State Collapse*. Durham, NC: Carolina Academic Press.

Leys, Colin (1976). "The 'Overdeveloped' Post-Colonial State: A Re-Evaluation." *Review of African Political Economy*, 3 (5), 39–48.
Liberia: America's Step Child (2002). *A Video Documentary*.
Liberian Council of Churches (1990). *The Rebel Incursion and the Present Status of Chaos and Anarchy and the Lack of Objective Information in Liberia*. Monrovia: Liberian Council of Churches.
Liberian Market Women Group (1980). "*Country Woman Born Soldier, Congo Woman Born Rogue.*"
Liberty, Clarence E. Zamba (2002). *Growth of the Liberian State: An Analysis of Its Historiography*. Northridge, CA: New World African Press.
Liebenow, J. Gus (1969). *Liberia: The Evolution of Privilege*. Ithaca, NY: Cornell University Press.
Liebenow, J. Gus (1980). *Liberia: The Dissolution of Privilege*. Hanover, NH: American Universities Field Staff.
Liebenow, J. Gus (1987*). Liberia: The Quest for Democracy*. Bloomington: Indiana University Press.
Lincoln, Josh (1991). *Liberia*. Atlanta: International Negotiation Network.
Lowenkopf, Martin (1972). "Political Modernization in Liberia: A Conservative Model." *Western Political Quarterly*, 25 (1), 94–108.
Lowenkopf, Martin (1976). *Liberia: The Conservative Road to Development*. Stanford, CA: Hoover Institution of War.
Lowenkopf, Martin (1995). "Liberia: Putting the State Back Together." In I. William Zartman (ed.), *Collapsed State: The Disintegration and Restoration of Legitimate Authority*. Boulder, CO: Lynne Rienner Publishers, 91–108.
Mamdani, Mahmoud (1996). *Citizen and Subject: Contemporary Africa and the Legacy of Late Colonialism*. Cape Town, SA: David Philip Publishers.
Marinelli, Lawrence (1964). "Liberia's Open Door Policy." *The Journal of Modern African Studies*, 2 (1), 91–98.
Martinusson, J. (1997) *Society, State and Market: A Guide to Competing Theories of Development*. New York: Zed Books.
Marx, Karl (1984). Cited in Louis Althusser. *Essays on Ideology*. Thetford: The Thetford Press.
Marx, Karl, and Frederick Engels (1950). *Critique of Political Economy: Selected Works*, Vol. 1. Moscow: Progress Publishers.
Marx, Karl, and Frederick Engels (1998). *The Communist Manifesto*. Oxford: Oxford University Press.
Mattlehart, Armant (1980). *Mass Media, Ideologies and the Revolutionary Movement*. Sussex: Harvester Press.

Mayson, Dew Tuan-Wleh (1976). *Which Way Africa? Notes on the Current Neo-Colonial Situation in Africa and the Possibilities of Struggling Against It*. Syracuse, NY: Clearing House for Liberian Literature.

Mayson, Dew Tuan-Wleh, and Amos Sawyer (1979). "Labor in Liberia." *Review of African Political Economy*, 6 (14), 3–15.

Mbaku, John Mukum (1999). "Making the State Relevant to African Societies." In John Mukum Mbaku (ed.), *Preparing Africa for the Twenty-First Century*. Aldershot, England: Ashgate Publishing, 299–333.

Mbaku, John Mukum (2001). "Ethnicity, Constitutionalism and Governance in Africa." In John Mukum Mbaku, Pita Ogaba Agbese and Mwangi S. Kimenyi (eds.), *Ethnicity and Governance in the Third World*. Aldershot, England: Ashgate Publishing,

Mgbeoji, Ikechi (2003). *Collective Insecurity: The Liberian Crisis, Unilateralism, and Global Order*. Vancouver: University of British Columbia Press.

Miliband, Ralph (1969). *The State in Capitalist Society*. London: Weidenfield and Nicolson.

Miliband, Ralph (1973). "Poulantzas and the Capitalist State." *New Left Review*, 82 (1), 83–93.

Miller, Floyd (1975). *The Search for a Black Nationality: Black Emigration and Colonization, 1787–1863*. Urbana: University of Illinois Press.

Miller, Robert, and Peter Carter (1972). "The Modern Dual Economy: A Cost-Benefit Analysis of Liberia." *The Journal of Modern African Studies*, 10 (1), 113–121.

Ministry of Health and Social Welfare, Liberia (2005). *Liberia: Inter-Agency Health Evaluation Final Report*. Monrovia, Liberia: Government Printing Office.

Ministry of Planning and Economic Affairs, Liberia (1975). *1974 Census of Liberia*. Monrovia: Government Printing Office.

Ministry of Planning and Economic Affairs, Liberia (1970–1984). *Economic Surveys of Liberia*. Monrovia, Liberia: Government Printing office.

Ministry of Planning and Economic Affairs, Liberia (1985). *Economic Survey of Liberia*. Monrovia, Liberia: Government Printing Office.

Mitchell, Thomas (1993). "Review of Ronald Weitzer. Transforming Settler State: Communal Conflict and Internal Security in Northern Ireland and Zimbabwe." *The Journal of Modern African Studies*, 31 (4), 715–718.

Moran, Mary (1990). *Civilized Women: Gender and Prestige in Southeastern Liberia*. London: Cornell University Press.

Moran, Mary (2006). *Liberia: The Violence of Democracy*. Philadelphia: University of Pennsylvania Press.

Movement for Justice in Africa (1980). *The Situation in Liberia: MOJA's Proposals for Change*. Monrovia, Liberia: MOJA.

Mutua, Makau (2001). "Savages, Victims, and Saviors: The Metaphor of Human Rights." *Harvard International Law Journal*, 42 (1), 201–245.

Nanga, Jean (2003). "The Marginalization of Sub-Saharan Africa." *International ViewPoint*. December, pp. 1–6.

Nass, A. I. (2000). *A Study of Internal Conflicts*. Lagos, Nigeria: Fourth Dimension Press.

National Bank of Liberia (1981). *Annual Report*. Monrovia, Liberia: National Bank of Liberia.

National Legislature of Liberia (1978). *An Act Amending the Sedition Law*. Monrovia, Liberia: Government Printing Office.

Nimley, Anthony (1991). *Government and Politics in Liberia*. Nashville, TN: Academic Publishers International.

Nkrumah, Kwame (1965). *Neo-Colonialism: The Last Stage of Imperialism*. London: Thomas Nelson and Sons.

Nordenstreng, Kaarle (1982). Cited in Dallas Smythe. *Dependency Road: Communications, Capitalism, Consciousness and Canada*. Norwood, NJ: Ablex Publishing Corporation.

Olorode, Omotoye (2000). "Economic and Political Crises in Africa: Wrong Question, Wrong Answer." In Segun Jegede et al. (eds.). *State Reconstruction in West Africa*. Lagos, Nigeria: Franked Publishers, 190–207.

Omonijo, Mobolade (1990). *Doe: The Liberian Tragedy*. Lagos, Nigeria: Sahel Publishing and Printing.

Osaghae, Eghosa (1996). *Ethnicity, Class and the Struggle for State Power in Liberia*. CODESRIA's Monograph Series. Monograph #1. Dakar, Senegal, CODESRIA.

Osaghae, Eghosa (1998). "The Ethnic and Class Character of Political Conflict in Liberia." In Okwudiba Nnoli (ed.), *Ethnic Conflicts in Africa*. Dakar, Senegal: CODESRIA Books Series, 131–157.

Outram, Quentin (1997). "It's Terminal Either Way: An Analysis of Armed Conflict in Liberia, 1989–1996." *Review of African Political Economy*, 24 (73), 355–371.

Payer, Cheryl (1975). *The Debt Trap: The IMF and the Third World*. New York: Monthly Review Press.

People's Redemption Council (1981). *Republic of Liberia. Decree #12 Banning Labor Strikes*. Monrovia, Liberia: Government Printing Office.

People's Redemption Council (1984). *Republic of Liberia*. Decree #88A. Monrovia, Liberia: Government Printing Office.

Peters, May Mercado and Shahla Shapouri (1997). "Income Inequality and Food Security." *Economic Research Service*. November 9, pp. 44–47.

Pham, John Peter (2004). *Liberia: Portrait of a Failed State*. New York: Reed Press.
Porte, Albert (1974). *Liberianization or Gobbling Business?* Occasional Paper. Crozierville, Liberia.
Pottenbaum, David, and Ravi Kaubur (2001). *Civil Wars, Public Goods and the Social Wealth of Nations*. Working Paper WP 2001–23. Ithaca, NY: Department of Applied Economics and Management, Cornell University.
Poulantzas, Nicos (1973). *Political Power and Social Classes*. London: New Left Books.
Prado, Caio (1966). The Political Evolution of Brazil. *Sao Paulo, Brazil*: Editora Brasiliense.
Ramsay, Jeffress (1993). "Introduction." In Jeffress Ramsay (ed.), *Africa*. Guilford, CT: Dushkin Publishing Groups, Inc, 1–3.
Ranard, Donald, Robin Dunn-Marcos, Konia T. Kollehlon, Bernard Ngovo and Emily Russ (2005). *Liberians: An Introduction to Their History and Culture*. Washington DC: Center for Applied Linguistics.
Reno, William (1996). "The Business of War in Liberia." *Current History*, 95 (601), 211–215.
Reno, William (1998). *Warlord Politics*. Boulder, CO: Lynne Rienner Publishers.
Richardson, Nathanie. (1959). *Liberia's Past and Present*. London: Diplomatic Press and Publishing Co.
Riley, Stephen (1996). *Liberia and Sierra Leone: Anarchy or Peace in West Africa?* London: Research Institute for the Study of Conflict and Terrorism.
Ruiz, Hiram (1992). *Uprooted Liberians: Casualties of a Brutal War*. Washington DC: U.S. Committee for Refugees.
Samatar, Abdi, and Ahmed Samatar (2002). "Introduction." In Abdi Samatar and Ahmed Samatar (eds.), *The African State: Reconsiderations*. Portsmouth, NH: Heinemann, 1–16.
Sarup, Madan(1978). Marxism and Education. London: Routledge and Kegan Paul.
Saul, John (1974). "The State in Post-Colonial Societies: Tanzania." *The Socialist Register*, 11 (1), 349–372.
Sawyer, Amos (1973). *Social Stratification and Orientation toward National Development in Liberia*. Doctoral Dissertation. Northwestern University.
Sawyer, Amos (1987). "Effective Immediately: Dictatorship in Liberia, 1980–1986: A Personal Perspective." Working Paper. Bremen, Germany: Liberia Working Group.

Sawyer, Amos (1987). "The Making of the 1984 Liberian Constitution: Major Issues and Dynamic Forces." *Liberian Studies Journal*, 12 (1), 1–15.
Sawyer, Amos (1992). *The Emergence of Autocracy in Liberia: Tragedy and Challenge*. San Francisco, CA: Institute for Cultural Studies Press.
Sawyer, Amos (2005a). *Beyond Plunder: Toward Democratic Governance in Liberia*. Boulder, CO: Lynne Rienner Publishers.
Sawyer, Amos (2005b). "Transcending the Cycle of Violence through Governance Reform: A Lesson for Liberia." Seminar Presentation for the Workshop on Political Theory and Public Policy. Indiana University. May 2005.
Sawyer, Amos (2005c). "Liberating Liberia: Understanding the Nature and Needs of Governance." *Harvard Journal of International Affairs*, 27 (3), 1–6.
Seyon, Patrick L. N. (1988). "The Results of the 1985 Liberian Elections." *Liberian Studies Journal*, 13 (2), 220–239.
Seyon, Patrick L. N. (1998). "Quick-Fixing the State in Africa: The Liberian Case." African Studies Center Working Paper No. 217. Boston: African Studies Center, Boston University.
Singler, John Victor (1977). "Language in Liberia in the Nineteenth Century: The Settlers' Perspective." *Liberian Studies Journal*, 7 (2), 73–85.
Smith, Mark (2000). *Rethinking State Theory*. London: Routledge.
Smith, Robert (1972). *The American Foreign Policy in Liberia, 1822–1971*. Monrovia, Liberia: Providence Publications.
So, A.Y. (1990). *Social Change and Development: Modernization, Dependency and World System Theories*. London: Sage Publications.
Sundiata, Ibrahim (1974). "Prelude to Scandal: Liberia and Fernando Po, 1880–1930." *Journal of African History*, 15 (1), 97–112.
Sundiata, Ibrahim (1980). *Black Scandal: America and the Liberian Labor Crisis*. Philadelphia: Institute for the Study of Human Issues.
Therborn, Goran (1978). *What Does the Ruling Class Do When It Rules?* London/New York: Verso Publishers.
Tipoteh, Togaba Nah (1986). "Crisis in the Liberian Economy, 1980–1985." *Liberian Studies Journal*, 11 (2), 125–143.
Townsend, E. Reginald (1969). Cited in J. Gus Liebenow. *Liberia: The Evolution of Privilege*. Ithaca, NY: Cornell University Press.
United Nations Children Fund (2006). *At a Glance: Liberia*. New York: UNICEF.
United Nations Development Program (1990). *Human Development Report, 1990*. New York: Oxford University Press.

United Nations Development Program (1990). *Promoting Good Governance in Liberia: Towards the Formulation of a National Framework.* New York: UNDP.
United Nations Development Program (1999). *The Common Country Assessment.* New York: UNDP.
United Nations Development Program (2004). *Liberia: Contribution to Needs Assessment-Education.* New York: UNDP.
United Nations Development Program (2006). *Liberia: National Human Development Report, 2006.* New York: Oxford University Press.
United Nations Human Settlements Program (2006). *Liberia: Urban Sector Profile.* Nairobi: UN HABITAT.
United Nations Mission in Liberia (2006). *Newsletter.* Monrovia: UNMIL.
United States Agency for International Development. (2006). *Liberia.* Washington, DC: USAID.
United States Government (1964). *The Civil Rights Act, 1964.* Washington, DC: Government Printing Office.
United States State Department (2006). *Background Note on Liberia.* Washington, DC: Bureau of African Affairs.
vander Kraaij, Fred (1983). *The Open Door Policy of Liberia: An Economic History of Modern Liberia.* Bremer, The Netherlands: Museum.
Villalon, Leonardo, and Phillip Huxtable (eds.) (1997). *The African State at a Critical Juncture: Between Disintegration and Reintegration.* Boulder, CO: Lynne Rienner Publishers.
Vogt, Maragaret (ed.) (1992). *The Liberian Crisis and ECOMOG: A Bold Attempt at Regional Peacekeeping.* Lagos, Nigeria: Gabumo Publishing.
Wallerstein, Immanuel (1979). *The Capitalist World Economy.* Cambridge: Cambridge University Press.
Weitzer, Ronald (1990). *Transforming Settler States: Communal Conflict and Internal Security in Northern Ireland and Zimbabwe.* Berkeley: University of California Press.
Weller, M (ed.) (1994). *Regional Peacekeeping and International Enforcement: The Liberian Crisis.* Cambridge: Cambridge University Press.
West, R. (1970). *Back to Africa: A History of Sierra Leone and Liberia.* London: Holt, Rinehart and Winston.
West Africa. (1990). "America Involved." August 20–26, 2330.
Whiteman, Kaye (1991). "Taylor's Ambition." *West Africa.* March 18–24, 401.
Wilson, Charles M. (1947). *Liberia.* New York: William Sloane Associates.
Wonkeryor, Edward Lama (1982). *The Military Coup as a Fiasco Revolution.* Chicago: Struggler's Press.

World Bank (2006). *Liberia: Country Brief*. Washington, DC: The World Bank.
World Health Organization (2003). *Liberia: Health/Nutrition Sector Report*. Brazzaville, Congo: WHO.
World Health Organization (2005). *WHO Country Strategy: Republic of Liberia, 2005–2010*. Brazzaville, Congo: WHO.
Wreh, Tuan (1976). *The Love of Liberty Brought Us Here*. New York: C. Hurst.
Yoder, John (2003). *Popular Political Culture, Civil Society and State Crisis in Liberia*. Lewiston, NY: Edwin Mellen Press.
Zartman, I. William (1989). *Ripe for Resolution: Conflict and Intervention in Africa*. New York: Oxford University Press.
Zartman, I. William (ed.) (1995). *Collapsed States: The Disintegration and Restoration of Legitimate Authority*. Boulder, CO: Lynne Rienner Publishers.
Zartman, I. William (2005). *Cowardly Lions: Missed Opportunities to Prevent Deadly Conflict and State Collapse*. Boulder, CO: Lynne Rienner Publishers.
Ziemann, W., and M. Lanzendorfer. (1977). *The State in Peripheral Societies. Socialist Register*, 14 (3), 145–177.

Index

('n' indicates a note; 't' indicates a table)

A
"Absentee farmers," 12
Adams, Samuel, 37
Africa
 civil wars, 3
 coups d'état, 3
 underdevelopment crisis, 3
African American repatriation, 36-37
"Age of consent," 120
Agricultural sector
 apparent prosperity of, 5
 colonial state, 40
 Commonwealth Epoch, 43
 civil war's impact, 158
All People's Freedom Alliance (APFA)
 emergence of, 10, 54
 mass demonstrations, 11-12
"American Christianity," 128
American Colonization Society (ACS)
 colonial state, 38-39
 Commonwealth Epoch, 42-43
 establishment of, 37
 ethnic conflict, 127
 Liberian independence, 46
 skin pigmentation, 132
"Americo-Liberian imperialism," 124
Americo-Liberians
 constitutional convention, 46
 cultural crisis, 15
 economic system, 89
 ethnic claims, 124
 ethnic conflict, 127-128, 129
 ethnic model, 18-19
 ethnocultural composition, 126t
 political culture model, 21
 skin pigmentation, 131-133
 state intervention, 137
 state role, 65
 underdevelopment crisis, 123
Angola
 civil war, 3-4
 resistance struggles, 9-10
Antisystem values, 58
Appointments, 77-78
April 14 coalition members, 59
"April 14 episode," 12, 83, 169
Armed Forces of Liberia
 and civil war, 148-149
 establishment of, 54, 61n.3. *See also*
 Military
 and INPFL, 146

B
B. F. Goodrich, 90
Bacon, Samuel, 39t
Balance of power system, 34, 35
Banjul Meeting
 civil war dynamics, 155
 peace making, 154
Barclay, Arthur, 50-51
Barclay Plan
 elements of, 50-51, 61n.4, 67
 "hegemonic" presidency, 77
Bassa, Commonwealth Epoch, 42-43
Bassa group
 colonial resistance, 41
 ethnocultural composition, 126t, 127t
 Kwa cluster, 34
 Liberian state, 46
Belle group
 ethnocultural composition, 126t, 127t
 Kwa cluster, 34
 LDF, 148
Benedict, Samuel, 46, 47t
Blyden, Edwin Wilson, 60n.1
Boley, George, LPC, 147
Bong Mining Company
 establishment, 168
 neocolonial state, 90
 resource exploitation, 53
 state strike-breaking, 57, 91
"Brainwashing," 110, 111
Brander, Nathaniel, 39t
Bright, W. O., 73

Britain, Liberian debt crisis, 94, 95, 100
British imperialism
  constitutional crisis, 66-67
  persistence of, 48, 51
Buchanan, Thomas, 43t
Buffet service, 100
"Bula Mutarian state," 52, 61n.4, 70
Bureaucracy
  criminalization of the state, 100
  expansion of, 103-104
  gender relations, 119-120
  patronage system, 7
  peripheral capitalist state model, 27
"Bureaucratic bourgeoisie," 27
Burkina Faso, Liberian civil war, 150-151

C
Camp Schefflin Military Barracks, 136
Campaore, Blaise, Liberian civil war, 150-151
Camwood, 89
Cannibalism, 21
Cape Mesurado, 38
Cape Verde, 9-10
Capitalism, rejection of, 174
"Capitalist theology," 111-112
Carey, Lott, 39t
Carribean origin, 126t
Carter, Jimmy, 83
Cassell, C. Abayomi, 75
Caste. *See* Class relationships
Catholic Justice and Peace Commission, 18
"Caudillo of civil war," 3-4
Chiefdoms, 137
"Child-soldiers," 146
"Christian rhetoric," 128
Christianity, 41
"Christie Commission, 82
Church, socialization agent, 5, 6
Citizenship
  Constitution of 1847, 66
  ethnic conflict, 129, 130
Civil society, 14-15

Civil war
  in African, 3-4
  conflict inhibitors' failure, 143
  cost of, 143, 157-159, 160
  emergence of, 4, 12-13
  forces/dynamics, 144-145, 154-156
  international support, 149-151
  model critiques, 22-24
  neocolonial state, 13-14
  peripheral capitalist state model, 25, 26-29
  pretexts for, 143, 144
  settler state model, 25-26, 29
  Taylor-led, 55
  theoretical models, 14, 17-22
  and the underdevelopment crisis, 13
"Civilizing mission," 25
Clash of Civilizations, The, 60n.1
Class relationships
  colonial state, 40-41
  Commonwealth Epoch, 44-45
  conflict inhibitor, 6-7
  Constitution of 1847, 67
  economic crisis, 15
  economy, 88-89, 90-92
  ethnic conflict, 129, 130, 131
  Liberian state, 49-50, 56-57
  peripheral capitalist state model, 26-29
  underdevelopment crisis, 124
"Club of subordinate players," 93
Cohen, Herman, 151-152
Colonial Agent, 38-39, 39t
Colonial state, cultural system, 41
Colonial state
  economic system, 40-41
  establishment of, 38
  expansion of, 41-42
  legal system 39-40
  structure, 38-39, 39t
Color. *See* Skin pigmentation
Commonwealth Epoch
  cultural policy, 45
  economic system, 43-45
  establishment, 42

Index

government structure, 42-43
independence movement, 45-46
Communalism, 35
Competition, 58
Compradors
　in the colonial state, 40-41
　and indigenous culture, 35
　in the neocolonial state, 91
"Compulsory education policy," 109
Conflict inhibitors
　facade maintenance, 5-9
　failure, 143
　term, 4
Congos
　class structure, 88-89
　colonial class divide, 41
Constitution of 1847
　"hegemonic" presidency, 77-78
　political crisis, 66-67, 167
　political parties, 75-76
Constitution of 1986
　changes in, 67-68
　flaws of, 68, 167
　"hegemonic" presidency, 77-78, 85nn.1, 2, 86n.3
Constitutional convention, 46, 47t
Constitutional issues, 14-15
Constitutional rights, 9
Co-optation, 7
Corruption
　conflict inhibitor, 7
　economic crisis, 15
Côte d'Ivoire, NPFL base, 145, 150, 154
Council of elders, 34
"Coup virus," 3
Coups d'état
　Africa, 3
　attempted coup, 70-71
　Krahn domination, 18
　Liberia, 4, 12, 54, 76, 134, 143, 169-170
　neocolonial state, 13-14
Crawford, William, 37
Criminal Investigation Department, 54
Criminal state, 58

Crozer, Samuel, 39t
Cultural imperialism ethnic conflict, 128
Culture, underdevelopment crisis, 15, 123-141, 168
"Culture of peaceful coexistence," 14
Curricula, 112
Cuttington University, 8

D

Dapper, Olfert, 34
Day, John, 47t
Debt, 94-96, 95t
Decree #12, 83, 91
Decree #88A, 83
Dei group
　colonial resistance, 41
　ethnocultural composition, 126t, 127t
　Kwa cluster, 34
"Deification of the president," 80
Democracy
　political culture model, 21
　state reconstitution, 174
"Desperate struggle for survival," 3
"Dissolution of privilege," 134
"Divine rule," 38
"Doctrine of Judicial Review," 80
Doe, Jackson, 73-74, 156
Doe, Samuel,
　and Armed Forces of Liberia, 148-149, 160n.1
　and civil war, 143, 144
　coup d'état, 54, 70, 76
　death of, 147, 157
　draft constitution, 86n.3
　ethnic conflict, 131, 134-136
　fraudulent elections, 73-74, 76-77, 156
　human rights violations, 83
　Krahn domination, 18
　looting the state, 100
　mediation talks, 152
　military regime, 12-13, 55, 70-71, 170
　mismanagement of, 101
　one-party system, 79-80
　overthrow of regime, 154-156

pretext for civil war, 144
and RLL, 153
andstate collapse, 156
state intervention, 137-138, 140-141
and United States, 150, 151-152
Dokie, Samuel, NPFL-CRC, 148
Dozoa Island, 37
Dress
  colonial state, 41
  cultural imperialism, 128
  Tolbert regime, 130
Dubar, Henry, 148

E

Economic Community of West African States (ECOWAS)
  civil war dynamics, 155, 156
  Liberian civil war, 150, 152
  peacemakers, 153-154
Economic Community of West African States Monitoring Group (ECOMOG)
  civil war dynamics, 155, 156
  INPFL, 146-147
Economic inequality
  economic crisis, 15
  impact of, 4
  neocolonial state, 104t, 104-105
Economy
  class structure, 6-7, 15, 87, 88-89, 167
  colonial state, 40-41
  Commonwealth Epoch, 43-45
  and corruption, 15
  debt bondage, 94-96, 95t
  foreign investments, 15, 92, 97-99, 98t, 167
  income decline, 101-102
  mismanagement of state resources, 101
  neocolonial state, 90–94
  standard of living, 15
  state reconstitution, 179
  state structure, 88-94
  underdevelopment crisis, 87-88
Education
  colonial state, 41

as mass socialization agent, 5-6
social crisis, 15
social underdevelopment crisis, 107, 108-113
Egypt, 3
Elections
  fraudulent, 72-74
  Liberian conflicts, 172
  political crisis, 14-15
"Electoral games," 74
Elite model
  civil war, 17, 19
  critique of, 22, 24
Elizabeth, repatriation, 37
"Emergency Powers Act," 79
"Engines of community development," 133-134
English language, 128
"Enlightened members," 75
Environment, 179
Ethnic claims, 124-125
Ethnic conflict, 15, 127-136, 166-167
Ethnic instrumentalism, 125
Ethnic model
  civil war, 17, 18-19
  critique of, 22, 24
Ethnic relations
  forces/dynamics, 125
  underdevelopment crisis, 125-131, 126t-127t
European trade, 35
Executive Action Bureau, 54
Executive Order #2, 82
Extractive industries, neocolonial state, 92-93

F

Fahnbulleh, Henry B., 83-84
"Fahnbulleh Trial," 83
Faulkner, Thomas J. R., 72-73
Fernando Po Crisis, 81-82
Financial contributions, 7
Finley, Robert, 37
Firestone Concession Agreement, 95-96

Index

Firestone Plantations Company
  anti-union activities, 91
  civil war, 158
  concession agreement, 95-96
  conflict of interest, 71
  establishment of, 52
  human rights violations, 81
  neocolonial state, 90
  peripheral capitalist state, 166
  predatory foreign investments, 97
  profiteering, 98
  state repression, 8, 57
First All Liberia Conference
  civil war dynamics, 155
  peace making, 154
"Flag independence," 4
Flamboyance, 58
Foreign investment
  apparent stability, 4, 5
  economic crisis, 15, 92, 97-99, 98t, 168
"Free education policy," 109
Freedom House, 84t, 84-85
French imperialism
  constitutional crisis, 66-67
  persistence of, 48, 51
"Fusion of powers," 38

G

Gardner, Anthony W., 47t
Gbandi group
  ethnocultural composition, 126t, 127t
  LDF, 148
  Mande cluster, 34
Gender relations
  Constitution of 1847, 67
  educational access, 110-111
  social underdevelopment crisis, 107, 118-120
Gio group
  cultural crisis, 15
  ethnic conflict, 131, 134-136, 160n.2
  ethnic forces/dynamics, 125
  ethnic instrumentalism, 125
  ethnocultural composition, 126t, 127t
  Mande cluster, 34
  NPFL, 145-146
  state intervention, 137, 140-141
Global capitalism
  neocolonial state, 93
  settler economy, 89-90
"Godliness," 5
Gola group
  colonial resistance, 41
  ethnocultural composition, 126t, 127t
  Mel cluster, 34
"Gordian Knot," 6
Grain Coast
  ethnic conflict, 127
  history of, 34-35
  repatriated settlers, 37-38
  underdevelopment crisis, 123
Grebo group
  ethnocultural composition, 126t, 127t
  Kwa cluster, 34
Greenleaf, Samuel, 60n.2
"Greenleaf Constitution," 42
"Greenleaf Draft," 42, 60n.2
Gripon, John B., 47t
"Growth without development," 97
Guinea-Bissau, 9-10
Guinness Book of World Records, The,
  fraudulent elections, 73
Gurr, Ted, 17

H

Habre, Hisan, 150
Harmon, Emmett, 73
Health professionals, 114
Health system
  civil war, 159
  social crisis, 15
  social underdevelopment crisis, 107, 113-116, 116t
"Health trips," 116
"Hegemonic filters," 6
"Hegemonic masculinity," 111, 118-119
"Hegemonic practices," 18-19
"Hegemonic" presidency, 77-80

Henries, Richard, 71
Herring, Amos, 47t
"Home town associations," 133-134
Hospitals/clinics, 113-114
Houphouet-Boigny, Felix, 150
Housing, social crisis, 15, 107, 117-118
Human rights, LFF abuse of, 51-52
Human rights
  political crisis, 14-15
  state abuse of, 80-81
  warlord militias, 158
Human Rights Index, 84t, 84-85
Humiliation tactic, 53
Hut tax, 8

I

Illiteracy rate, 110, 111t
Immorality, 19
"Impartial mediator," 124
"Imperial mentality," 123
Impunity, 58
Independence movement, 45-46, 47
Independent National Patriotic Front of Liberia (INPFL)
  civil war dynamics, 155, 156, 160-161n.5
  United States support, 152
  warlord militia, 146-147
Indigenes
  cultural crisis, 15
  ethnic claims, 124-125
  ethnic conflict, 127-131
  intra-indigenous schisms, 133-134
  skin pigmentation, 132-133
Infant mortality rates, 116t
Institutional model,
  civil war, 17, 20
  critique of, 22-23, 24
Institutions, 27
Instruction, 112
International Monetary Fund (IMF)
  debt crisis, 96
  income reduction, 101-102
Iron ore
  neocolonial state, 92, 93, 99
  price decline, 11
Ivory, 89

J

Jackson, Andrew, 37
James, Frederick, 39t
Johnson, Edmond, 155
Johnson, Elijah
  ACS Colonial Agent, 39t
  constitutional convention, 47t
Johnson, Gladys, PAL, 76
Johnson, Prince
  civil war dynamics, 155
  INPFL, 146-147
  state collapse, 157, 160-161n.5
Johnson, Roosevelt, ULIMO, 147, 160n.3

K

Karpeh, Albert, ULIMO, 147
Kesselly, Edward B., 73
King, Charles D. B.
  fraudulent elections, 72-73
  human rights violations, 81-82
King Peter, 38
Kissi group
  ethnocultural composition, 126t, 127t
  LDF, 148
  Mel cluster, 34
Kpelle group
  ethnocultural composition, 126t, 127t
  Mande cluster, 34
  Tolbert regime, 130-131
Kpolleh, William Gabriel, 73
Krahn group
  cultural crisis, 15
  ethnic conflict, 131, 134-136, 160n.2
  ethnic forces/dynamics, 125
  ethnic instrumentalism, 125
  ethnocultural composition, 126t, 127t
  Kwa cluster, 34
  LPC, 147
  state control, 18-19
  state intervention, 137, 140, 141

Index

ULIMO, 147
"Krahn nationalism," 147
Kromah, Alhaji, ULIMO, 147
Kru group
  ethnocultural composition, 126t, 127t
  Kwa cluster, 34
Kwa cluster
  ethnocultural composition, 127t
  Grain coast ethnic groups, 34, 59
  ethnic conflict, 127

L

Labor
  ethnic conflict, 129
  human rights violations, 81
Land
  ethnic conflict, 129
  settler state model, 26
Language
  colonial state, 41
  cultural imperialism, 128
  Tolbert regime, 130-131
Latex, 71
"Law and order" functions, 28
Legal system
  colonial state, 39-40
  Commonwealth Epoch, 44
  gender relationships, 119-120
  Liberian state, 51
  political crisis, 14-15
  state intervention, 138
Legislature
  ethnic representation, 139
  "hegemonic" presidency, 78-79
Lewis, John N., 47t
Liberal democracy, 174
Liberia
  apparent stability of, 3, 4, 5-9
  brief history of, 14, 36-55
  civil war, 4, 12-13, 14, 33. *See also*
  Civil war
  collapse of state, 143
  Commonwealth Epoch, 42
  Constitution of 1847, 66-67

Constitution of 1986, 67-68
constitutional structure, 46-47, 51, 66-68
coups d'état, 4, 12, 54, 134, 169
democratic reconstitution of, 173-180
ethnocultural composition, 126t
foreign investment in, 4, 92, 97-99, 98t, 168
governance of, 69-71
lessons learned, 170-172
mass demonstrations, 4
neocolonial state, 56-58
political subdivisions, 137, 138-139
postconsolidation state, 33, 53-55
pre-state history, 34-35
social struggles, 58-59
social underdevelopment, 107-108
stability shattered, 9-13
state collapse, 156-157, 159-160
state consolidation, 33, 50-53
state expansion, 33, 4, 48-50
state formation, 33, 46-48, 58, 69
state values, 57
underdevelopment crisis, 123
Liberia College, 132
Liberian Action Party (LAP)
  Doe regime, 76
  fraudulent elections, 73-74
Liberian American Swedish Mining Company (LAMCO)
  anti-union activities, 91
  closure of, 11
  establishment, 168
  excess profits, 97-98
  neocolonial state, 90
  resource exploitation, 53
  state strike-breaking, 57
Liberian Council of Churches (LCC), 153
"Liberian exceptionalism," 5
Liberian Frontier Force (LFF), 51-52
Liberian, Human Rights Index, 84t, 84-85, 107
Liberian Mining Company (LMC)
  closure of, 11, 98
  establishment, 168

neocolonial state, 90
resource exploitation, 53
Liberian Peace Council (LPC)
  civil war dynamics, 155-156
  warlord militia, 147-148
Liberian People's Party (LPP)
  fraudulent elections, 73
  leader murdered, 70
  political debarment, 82
Liberian Unification Party (LUP)
  Doe regime, 76
  fraudulent elections, 73
"Liberian Way," 57
Libya, Liberian civil war, 149-150
Life expectancy, 15, 115, 116t
"Life was good," 5
"Live and let's live," 7
Lofa Defense Force (LDF), 148
Longue durée," 13
Lorma group
  ethnocultural composition, 126t, 127t
  LDF, 148
  Mande cluster, 34
"Lucrative sector," 100
Lumpen class, 90 92

M

Mande cluster
  ethnic conflict, 127
  ethnocultural composition, 127t
  Grain coast ethnic groups, 34, 59
Mandingo group
  ethnocultural composition, 126t, 127t
  Mande cluster, 34
  and ULIMO, 147
"Manifest destiny," 37
Mano group
  cultural crisis, 15
  ethnic conflict, 131, 134-136, 160n.2
  ethnic forces/dynamics, 125
  ethnic instrumentalism, 125
  ethnocultural composition, 126t, 127t
  Mande cluster, 34
  NPFL, 145-146

state intervention, 137, 140-141
Masochism, 58
Mass demonstrations, 4, 11-12
Mass socialization, 5
Massaquoi, François, LDF, 148
Materialism, 27
Meclin, Joseph, 39t
Media, 5, 6
Mel cluster
  ethnic conflict, 127
  ethnocultural composition, 127t
  Grain coast ethnic groups, 34, 59
"Men on horseback," 3
Mende group
  ethnocultural composition, 126t, 127t
  Mande cluster, 34
"Merchant sector," 40
Mesurado Group of Companies, 72
Military
  conflict inhibitor, 4, 8
  coup, 4, 54
  establishment of, 54, 61n.3
  and Guinean military, 12
"Minimalist state," 87
"Monopoly peripheral capitalism," 72
Monrovia
  Commonwealth Epoch, 42-43
  Liberian state, 46
  repatriated settlers, 38
"Monrovia Draft," 42
Mortality rate, 15
"Mother country," 26
Movement for Justice in Africa (MOJA)
  closure of mines, 11
  emergence of, 9-10, 54, 169
  mass demonstrations, 11-12
  military regime, 54-55
Mozambique
  civil war, 3-4
  resistance struggles, 9-10
Mulattos
  colonial state, 40-41
  Commonwealth Epoch, 44
Murray, R. E., 47t

Index

Mythology
  conflict inhibitor, 4, 6
  settler state model, 25

N

National Bureau of Investigation, 54
National conference, state reconstitution, 173
National Democratic Party of Liberia (NDPL)
  Doe regime, 76, 77
  ethnic model, 19
  fraudulent elections, 73, 156
  one-party system, 79
National Intelligence Security Service, 54
National Patriotic Front of Liberia (NPFL)
  civil war, 55
  spiritual anarchy model, 20-21
  state control, 157
National Patriotic Front of Liberia - Central Revolutionary Council (NPFL-CRC), warlord militia, 148
National Patriotic Party, 156
National Redemption Council, Doe regime, 55. *See also* People's Redemption Council (PRC)
National symbols
  ethnic conflict, 129-130
  state intervention, 138
  state reconstitution, 175-176
Natural resource exploitation, 53
Neocolonial state
  ethnic claims, 125
  formation of, 14
  peripheral capitalist state, 166-167
  state intervention, 137-140
  underdevelopment crisis, 123
  underdevelopment impact, 13-14
Nepotism, 58
Nigeria
  civil war, 3
  ECOWAS role, 153-154
  Liberian civil war, 150

Nimba County, 70-71
"Nokos," 4

O

"Octopus," 146, 156
Old Whigs Party, 48
One-party system
  fraudulent elections, 75-77
  "hegemonic" presidency, 79
"Open door policy," 92, 96
Organization of African Unity (OAU)
  meeting, 96, 101
Overcrowding, 112-113

P

Patrilineages, 34
Patriotic Front of Liberia (NPFL)
  Burkina Faso support, 150-151
  civil war, 144-145
  civil war dynamics, 154-156
  Libyan support, 149-150
  pretext for war, 144
  and RUF, 151
  state collapse, 157
  True Whig Party support, 152
  warlord militia, 145-146
Patron-client relationship, 35
Patronage system
  conflict inhibitor, 4
  operation of, 7
Patrons
  civil war, 143, 149-152
  failure to insulate, 171-172
Peacemakers, 143, 153-154
Peasants, 90, 92
People's Party, 72-73
People's Redemption Council (PRC). *See also* National Redemption Council
  Decree #12, 83, 91
  Decree #88A, 83
  Doe regime, 70
  Quiwonkpa role, 135
  salaries, 96
Peripheral capitalist state model

civil war, 14, 25, 26-29
ethnic conflict, 130
lessons learned, 171
Liberian economy, 88, 93-94, 96
Liberian state, 57
reproduction of, 111
settler state, 166
Petit bourgeois, 90, 91
Phillips, Robert, 70
Pierre, James A. A., 54
Pinney, Joseph, 39t
Plan for Civil Government of 1824, 38-42, 39t
"Plan for Training Freed Negroes in the American Colonies as Colonizers and Missionaries, A," 37
Political culture model
civil war, 17, 21-22
critique of, 23-24
Political liberalization, 9
Political parties
emergence of, 48
skin pigmentation, 132
"Political reform agenda," 75
Political repression, conflict inhibitor, 4. See also Repression
Political system, state reconstitution, 179
Poro institution, indigenous culture, 34
Porte, Albert
critic of conflict of interest, 72
democracy advocate, 22
imprisonment of, 83
Poverty
food insecurity, 114-115
rise of, 101-102, 167
Power, 19
"Presidential imperialism," 67
Progressive Alliance of Liberia (PAL)
emergence of, 10-11, 54, 75-76, 169
mass demonstrations, 11-12
military regime, 54-55
Progressive People's Party (PPP), 76
Prosperity's facade, 5
Prout, Jacob W., 47t

Providence Island, 38
Public education
inadequate access, 108, 112-113
inadequate support, 113
Public nuisance law, 39-40
Public relations officers
dissolution of, 9
patronage system, 7
Public sector, 71-72

Q
Quiwonkpa, Thomas
attempted coup of, 70-71
Doe regime, 160n.1
ethnic conflict, 134-135
NPFL, 145
Thomas, state intervention, 140, 141

R
Randall, Richard, 39t
Reformation Party
human rights violations, 82
Tubman treatment of, 53
"Relative autonomy," 88
Religion
civil war influence, 20-21
colonial state, 41
state reconstitution, 179
Religious Council of Liberia (IRCL), 153
Religious Leaders of Liberia (RLL), 153
"Renegade members," 53
Rent-seeking, 7
Repression
Doe regime, 55
failure of, 171
impact of, 4
major weapon, 8
state action, 80-81
Tubman regime, 53-54
Republican Party
establishment of, 48
state politics, 50
Revolutionary United Front (RUF), 151
"Rice issue," 12

Index

Ritualistic killing, 21
Roberts, Joseph Jenkins, 43t
Ross, Samuel, 81-82
Rubber, neocolonial state, 92, 93, 99
"Rubber farmers," 71
"Rubber stamp body," 79
Ruling class
  conflict inhibitor, 4
  criminalization of the state, 99-100
  ethnic model, 19
  and health system, 115-116
  income inequality, 104t, 104-105
  myth of invincibility, 6
  neocolonial state, 90-91
  stability of, 169-170

S

Sabbath law, 39
Sande institution, 34
Sanitation crisis, 15
Schools, 5-6
Security agencies
  conflict inhibitor, 7-8
  dismantling of, 9
  Tubman regime, 54
Sedition Law, 83
Seekie, Raleigh, and ULIMO, 147
Senegal, 3
Settler state
  civil war, 25-26, 29
  economic system, 89
  ethnic claims, 124
  inevitable failure of, 165-166
  inherent conflicts, 170-171
  mission of, 56
  model of, 25-26, 29
  state intervention, 136-137
"Settler stock," ethnic theory, 18
Settlers
  cultural crisis, 15
  ethnic conflict, 127-131, 136
"Shock therapy," 96
Sierra Leone, 151
Sinoe

Commonwealth Epoch, 42-43
  Liberian state, 46
Skin pigmentation
  colonial state, 40-41
  Constitution of 1847, 66
  ethnic conflict, 131-133
  state intervention, 136-137
Skinner, Ezekiel, 39t
"Slave psychology," 36
Social, underdevelopment crisis, 15, 107, 108-120, 168
Social democratic state, 174, 175-177
Social malaise, 4
"Social safety net," 96, 180
South Africa, 9-10
Special Security Service, 54
Speech rights, 82-83
Spiritual anarchy model
  civil war, 17, 20-21
  critique of, 23, 24
"Spiritual imagination," 21
Stability facade, 3, 4, 5,
Standard of living, 15
State
  neocolonial, 55-57
  peripheral capitalist state model, 27, 28
  role of, 179-180
Stockton, Robert, 38
"Storm of civil war," 13
"Strategy of regime survival," 135
Structural Adjustment Program (SAP), 96
Student Unification Party
  mass demonstrations, 11-12
  pro-reform movement, 9
Subsistence agriculture, 35
Substantive democracy, 175
Sudan, 3
"Superior people," 127
"Superior-inferior divide," 170
"Superior-inferior myth," 25, 125, 128
Supuwood, J. Lavela, NPFL-CRC, 148
Sycophancy, 58
Syen, Thomas Weh
  arrest of, 55

execution of, 135

T
"Tammy boss," 78
Taxation
  ethnic conflict, 130
  human rights violations, 81
  neocolonial state, 91, 92
Taylor, Charles
  Burkina Faso support, 150-151
  civil war dynamics, 154-156
  civil war leader, 55, 170
  Côte d'Ivoire support, 150, 154
  and INPFL, 146
  Libyan support, 149-150
  mediation talks, 152
  NPFL, 145-146
  pretext for war, 144, 160n.4
  and RLL, 153
  state collapse, 157
Teage, Hilary, 46, 47t
Teah, Cooper, 155
Timber, 92
Titler, Emphraim, 47t
Tolbert, Adolphous Benedict, 150
Tolbert, Stephen, 72
Tolbert, William R.
  authoritarian regime, 10, 54
  conflict of interest, 71
  fraudulent elections, 74
  indigenes policy, 139
  Kpelle language, 130-131
  liberalization program, 9-10, 54, 70, 75-76
  mismanagement of, 101
  overthrow of, 12, 54, 76, 150
  rice price increase, 11-12
  ruling class, 170
Touré, Ahmed Sékou, 12
Trade
  colonial state, 40
  Commonwealth Epoch, 43-44
  export mainstays, 99
  neocolonial state, 92-93

"Troublemakers," 110, 112
True Black Man Party, 48
True Liberian Party, 48
True Whig Party
  ethnic model, 19
  ethnic representation, 139
  execution of leadership, 76
  fraudulent elections, 72-73, 74
  NPFL support, 152
  one-party state, 75-76, 79
  opposition to, 10
  patronage avenue, 53
  state politics, 50
Tubman, William V. S.
  conflict of interest, 71
  death of, 54
  ethnic integration, 18
  fraudulent elections, 73
  gender relations, 119
  intra-ruling class factionalization, 53-54
  legal reform, 138
  mass fatigue with, 9
  on military's function, 51
  mismanagement of, 101
  one-party state, 82
  patronage system, 7
  repression of, 69-70
  security systems, 8, 54
  "Unification and Integration Policy," 52
Tubman, William V. S., Jr., conflict of interest, 71
Twe, Didhwo, 53

U
Underdevelopment crisis
  African state, 3
  peripheral capitalist state model, 29, 88
Unemployment, 15, 98, 102-104, 103t, 167, 168-169
"Unification and Integration Policy," 52, 138
Unions, 91
United Liberation Movement for

Democracy in Liberia (ULIMO)
  civil war dynamics, 155-156
  Sierra Leone support, 151
  warlord militia, 147
United Liberation Movement for
Democracy in Liberia (ULIMO-J)
  civil war dynamics, 155-156
  warlord militia, 147, 160n.3
United Liberation Movement for
Democracy in Liberia (ULIMO-K)
  civil war dynamics, 155-156
  warlord militia, 147
United Nation, 107
United Nations Human Settlements
Program, 117
United People's Party (UPP)
  debarment of, 82
  fraudulent elections, 73
United States
  "black problem," 36
  Doe regime, 150, 151-152
  influence of, 23
  and INPFL, 146
  and Liberian civil war, 151-152
  Liberian debt crisis, 95-96
Unity Party (UP)
  Doe regime, 76
  fraudulent elections, 73
University of Liberia
  education system, 108, 113
  pro-reform movement, 9
  and security organizations, 8
  skin pigmentation, 132
University of Liberia Student Union
  arrest of leaders, 83
  mass demonstrations, 11-12

V
Vai group
  ethnocultural composition, 126t, 127t
  Mande cluster, 34
Values, state reconstitution, 177-179

W
"Warlord logic," 144-145
Warlord militias
  civil war, 143, 144
  human rights violations, 158
  INPFL, 146-147
  LDF, 148
  LPC, 147-148
  NPFL, 145-146
  NPFL-CRC, 148
  ULIMO, 147
Washington, Bushrod, 37
Water
  lack of safe, 115
  social crisis, 15
"Wave of repression," 77
West Africa, 3
"Western civilization," 124
Why Men Rebel, 17
William V. S. Tubman College of
Science and Technology, 109
Williams, Anthony, 39t
Williams, Anthony D., 39t
Wilson, Beverly, 47t
Workers
  Firestone exploitation, 97
  multinational corporations, 98-99
  neocolonial state, 90, 91
World Health Organization (WHO), 115
Woweiyou, Tom, NPFL-CRC, 148, 160n.4

Y
Yancy, Allen, 81-82

Z
Zimbabwe, 9-10

SOCIETY AND POLITICS IN AFRICA

Yakubu Saaka, General Editor

This multidisciplinary series publishes monographs and edited volumes that provide innovative approaches to the study and appreciation of contemporary African society. Although we focus mainly on subjects in the social sciences, we will consider manuscripts in the humanities that treat context as a significant aspect of discourse. Within the social sciences, we are looking for not only analytically outstanding studies but, what is more important, ones that may also have significant implications for the formulation and implementation of public policy in Africa. We are especially interested in works that challenge pre-existing hierarchies and paradigms.

For additional information about this series or for the submission of manuscripts, please contact:

>   Peter Lang Publishing
>   Acquisitions Department
>   29 Broadway
>   New York, New York 10006

To order other books in this series, please contact our Customer Service Department:

>   800-770-LANG (within the U.S.)
>   (212) 647-7706 (outside the U.S.)
>   (212) 647-7707 FAX

Or browse online by series at:

>   www.peterlang.com